WOMAN'S HOUR: A THIRD SELECTION

WOMAN'S HOUR

a third selection, edited by Mollie Lee

British Broadcasting Corporation

Published by the British Broadcasting Corporation,
35 Marylebone High Street, London W1M 4AA

ISBN 0 563 12000 2

First published 1971

Printed in England by Jolly & Barber Ltd, Rugby

Contents

The Backward Glance

These Islands Now

Foreword

This is the third *Woman's Hour* anthology to be issued over the past six years and this one is timed to coincide with the programme's twenty-fifth birthday – an anniversary which makes it about the longest-running magazine programme on the BBC. Started in 1946 it began by being a somewhat cosy chat show designed to help women through the slough of rationing and shortages that followed the war. Today it could not, I hope and believe, be described as 'cosy'. Its listeners range in age from school children to those who happily claim to have listened to us without a break from the very first edition; from titled women with imposing addresses to those who are struggling their way through the mazes of social security regulations in order to keep themselves and their children going; from JP's and Oxbridge degrees to those whose writing betrays the fact that their formal education almost doesn't exist but who display as much intelligence and character as their more lettered co-listeners. And the programme has a surprisingly large number of male devotees; even more male droppers-in. To me as Editor, this is a reassurance; if men never listened to us I would be forced to the conclusion that we weren't catering for women as people; that we were, in fact, still treating them as beings shut off in an airtight corner of so-called 'feminine' experience.

A particularly satisfying development over the years has been the evident growth and widening of the listeners' horizons. Nowadays there is an infinitely more vital response to items on national and world problems than to queries as to what to do with cold porridge. The Common Market, pollution, over-population, artificial methods of food production, sex instruction in schools, conservation – subjects such as these are sure-fire winners with today's *Woman's Hour* listeners. Very rare is that letter which says: 'We aren't interested in politics: give us tips on keeping the house clean.' One of the reasons being, I suppose, that we do that too.

Woman's Hour appears to have a peculiarly close and personal relationship with its listeners – much of it probably due to the unlimited affection which its compère, Marjorie Anderson, is able to inspire; much of it to the sincere involvement of the programme's producers with the listeners' interests. We may sit over our luncheon after the morning's rehearsal congratulating one another on what we think to be a good programme; but by ten o'clock next morning, when the mail reaches us, we can be well and truly cut down to size. Many we have irritated, many we have shocked, many we have angered and many we have pleased! To the listeners whose swift and lively reactions are so important a part of our daily operation, this book is dedicated. May the ones we please ever be in the majority, may the ones we annoy ever feel free to tell us so. And may the twenty-five-year partnership between producers and listeners flourish for another quarter century!

Sadly for me, this is my farewell to the programme to which I have given fifteen years of my professional life. I leave it in the knowledge that the quality of its staff and its new editor will maintain and strengthen the standards set by such earlier editors as Janet Quigley, Joanna Scott-Moncrieff and Monica Sims, and to which, throughout my years with the programme as producer, deputy editor and editor, I felt myself indebted.

A word about the contents of the anthology – as usual they can only indicate the range of the programme. So much of the spoken word – especially in these days of tape recording – cannot survive translation to print. So I hope readers will forgive the omission of those interviews and exchanges which may well remain in their minds as worthy of perpetuation, but which – without the voice – die.

Mollie Lee

Abroad

HOLLYWOOD HOUSEWIFE *Rachel Billington*

Lady Rachel Billington is one of the 'writing Pakenhams' – daughter of Lady Longford, who wrote the much praised books on Queen Victoria and on Wellington; and sister of Lady Antonia Fraser who wrote the best-selling life of Mary Queen of Scots.

After four days I realised we had been placed in a society which was stark staring mad and that in order to preserve our own delicate balance we must have our Englishman's castle. We found it at a rate of £150 a week – paid for by the film company. It was in the style recognised by Hollywood as French eighteenth century. Although it was only two blocks up from Sunset Strip the noise of police sirens was drowned by the twittering of birds and the smell of gasoline was replaced by mint hedges and verbena. The drawing room was golden with sunlight and filled with beaded lamps, shell flowers, velvet couches and even a leather-bound book or two – the Californian Social Register was, I noticed, prominent. French windows opened out to the garden where there was a blue expanse of water surrounded by flowering camellias, spotted orchids, and a whole grove of lemons and lime trees.

The first morning as we breakfasted on the balcony leading off our enormous bedroom, I looked down at the steaming city glittering below and said: 'It's impossible to believe that Los Angeles is such a violent place.'

Later that day the son of the Producer whose film my husband was to direct was shot dead by an addict looking for heroin. So I began to look at Hollywood more closely.

I heard about the murder on the radio first at nine o'clock, then at nine-thirty, then at ten and ten-thirty. By the afternoon I knew the flash by heart. I hoped his father had managed to escape the assault.

'Oh, no,' said my husband when he'd returned home. 'He watched his son's body on the television news.'

The murder of the young hippy son blew a cold wind into my paradise at an unfortunate moment. My husband was off to look for locations in Canada and I would be left alone.

'But you've got everything,' he said. 'A sunken bath with wall-to-wall lights and a dozen chandelier-style make-up lights, a bedroom complete with six cherubs (antique) and an eau-de-nil silk-lined dining room; plus a housekeeper, a pool man and a gardener.'

Indeed it was true. I had a coloured housekeeper. She had arrived through an agency which had charged ninety dollars (about forty pounds) for supplying her name. She cost over seven pounds for a nine-to-four day. The first morning she had not only ordered about twenty pounds' worth of cleaning equipment including special fleece-lined plastic gloves and an enormous assortment of spray-on polishes, but also an extensive menu for her luncheon. A special chocolate cake, a Diet Grape Soda, the best hamburger meat, onion rolls, Monterey Jack Cheese (sliced), pickle relish for the meat and a kind of expensive synthetic cream for her coffee. After lunch she revealed with a well-fed grin: 'I'm on a diet, see, Mrs Bill.'

Later I grew more sympathetic. One morning I called her out to the garden to take her photograph. 'Jus' a moment, Mrs Bill!' She fled away. When she reappeared her black hair was covered with a luxuriant Jane Russell type red wig, curling smoothly over her shoulders.

She posed, hand on hip, beaming self-satisfaction.

So when my husband went to Canada, he left me surrounded by all the comforts of Hollywood. Unfortunately, my confidence in this paradise, already shaken by the murder, was further upset as I started to read regularly the *Los Angeles Times*. It came, like everything, by remote control, thrown outside our house from a car that didn't stop.

Hollywood itself tried not to read these general newspapers. They have daily trade papers which tell them the only news that really matters: box office news.

I was looking for world news. 'Boy eight, rapes three women,' read one particularly gay headline. The others were almost as bad.

Aside from the crime and violence my sense of isolation was increased by the realisation that in Hollywood you must approach a car and driving as you do your socks and shoes. No one walks in Hollywood.

I had, however, learnt to order my food by telephone, which produced extraordinary misunderstandings from my English approach – a gallon jar of peanut butter when I'd wanted a tin of cocktail nuts, twelve cartons of sour cream instead of six bottles of bitter lemon. So, I was a rather bruised English rose on that first evening alone, when it became dark and started to rain. I found myself suddenly very frightened. Now all the horror stories surged up. I sat down quavering to a solitary dinner. Then there was a loud noise in the hall. I crept towards it terrified. A vast man stood there in a flapping mackintosh with a huge holster bulging on his thigh. I gaped pathetically.

'Foothill Patrol!' he shouted. 'You left your key in the lock, ma'am.'

He told me three cars patrolled our area from nine at night to seven-thirty the next morning. It was a private police force paid for by the local house owners. So I was reassured. At first. But later it seemed an even more sinister fact that in Hollywood and Beverley Hills this sort of protection should be necessary.

So when my husband at last returned from Canada, he got a particularly warm welcome. In the days that followed I found out more about the Hollywood code of living. Going out to dinner, for example. First of all the restaurants are so noisy that conversation is out of the question. And when you reach your table husbands and wives sit implacably together. This doesn't help conversation, but it demonstrates publicly – or rather to the select restaurant public – how delightedly happy they are in each other's company. Personally, I still find it trying to be at dinner with a childhood hero like Gregory Peck and see him solidly flanked by his wife and mother-in-law.

Incidentally, I never saw a woman who looked over thirty except by daylight – but the older man, hippy, Hollywood-style, was a sad sight with his long grey Rip Van Winkle side-burns and turquoise trousers flaring over his ageing knees. And now their wives won't even let them go chocolate brown . . . I complimented a dashing young man on his glowing sun tan and he apologised for its vulgarity. 'No one sits in the sun! No one swims in the pool!' he said. 'Except Katherine Hepburn and me,' I learnt to reply.

Of course it would be unfair to deny Hollywood a glamour as precarious as a star's waistline and as solid as Wall Street. And in the evenings when the lights lit up – cinemas, garages, motels, restaurants – they turned the city into a fairyland below us.

Yes, I'm afraid I have to admit it, I was sorry when my husband found that the film he wanted to make was not the one Hollywood wanted him to make. 'Billington Walks Out,' said the *Daily Variety*.

'Don't worry,' said our friends, 'it happens all the time here. You'll be back. Everyone in films comes back to Hollywood.'

NIGHT TRAIN *Madge Tildesley*

My husband says that the coffee in the breakfast car on the Simplon Orient Express tastes like nectar. I point out to him that, according to the menu, it's a proprietary brand of instant coffee and what gives it its divine taste is the night of torture which has preceded it, plus the journey to the breakfast car which involves being smashed from side to side of the corridor whilst traversing about seventeen coach lengths in a train travelling over ninety miles an hour. Which brings me to my subject – Night Travel.

Up to four years ago we had each successive year joined this celebrated express train at Venice. The time was always in the evening, the temperature invariably in the high nineties, and inevitably one found all six couchettes in the compartment occupied by itinerant pedlars who had joined the train at Trieste and were ruthlessly determined not to budge for the lawful ticket holders. Only by laying about with one's luggage and screaming for the police would they finally reluctantly vacate the couchettes. During these hostilities, the sleeping berth attendant, stricken blind and deaf, immediately recovers in order to check one's tickets when he can be certain no effort is called for on his part.

On one such occasion, each of these aforesaid pedlars appeard to be carrying about five life-size dolls strung round his person and, on being dispossessed, they proceeded to lie along the corridor and also take possession of each loo which they thereupon locked and wherein they remained firmly entrenched.

As the miles sped by, I began to feel the call of nature and after some searching, I found the attendant with his master key and I insisted, with some inspired mime, that it was imperative that I should wash my hands. He accepted this English euphemism literally and unlocked a door and forcibly evicted about ten sweating peasants – just like a Marx Brothers film really – and I found myself in a compartment expressly designed for the washing of hands and not a loo to be seen. I did, however, discover a tiny grille in the floor and I later emerged feeling, as you might say, 'relieved'.

On yet another occasion, my husband found an ancient crone stretched out on his berth with long grizzled hair like mattress stuffing festooning his pillow. Her husband explained that she had a fever and the two children huddled up with her were her grandchildren. We begged the attendant for alternative accommodation, but that worthy indicated that we could, if we preferred, sleep on the floor as everywhere else was fully occupied. We returned to the compartment and by now there was an added horror, the floor was awash. Fixing the children with a glare, I declared that it was 'revolting,' 'disgusting,' and so on. The attendant said it was obvious that the rain had come. My voice rose to a scream. 'Rain ?' I queried, pointing at a sky which was positively molten with late evening heat. 'Nonsense, rubbish,' and other disclaimers. By this time the feverish old lady realised where my suspicions lay and pointed a gnarled finger at my mineral water which had evidently blown its cool and its cork in the heat and drenched the floor. It was physically impossible for me to blush, my face was already puce coloured. I did the only thing I could and opened a very expensive box of Italian chocolates and handed them round to try to improve a very wilting entente cordiale.

The night that followed could only be viewed calmly in retrospect; the small boy whined, 'Grandpère' at intervals, and we never did learn what he wanted, as each time Grandpa roused himself, shouted 'Tais toi Patrice' and dealt him a savage slap across the face which echoed like a pistol shot. The small girl would then, in her turn, address her grandmother in a penetrating whisper thus: 'Grandmère, Grandmère, I wish to pi pi.' Grandmère would then piously call on Jesus and the Holy Virgin to witness her trials and totter down the corridor with her leaking grandchild. I timorously demanded of my husband in the top berth whether he was comfortable and back came the bitter answer: 'I'd be better off in my bloody coffin.'

Once we decided to travel to Athens together with friends and do the journey in style by Wagon Lit. We had a marvellous journey, time passed quickly as we played cards and threw dice and brewed endless cups of tea on our portable stoves. However, due to our depredations, the drinkable water supply on the train soon ran out and at Belgrade, deaf to my entreaties not to leave the train, my husband alighted and crossed a maze of lines to a water tap to fill all available containers. Quite oblivious to my cries of 'Dick, Dick,' he took his time and soon the evening rang with cries as my fellow passengers joined in 'Deek,

Deek, please come back.' When my husband rejoined the train with his brimming containers, he informed me, in savage tones, that if I wished to travel with him in future, I must avoid making violent and unnecessary scenes. He had, he informed me, his own unfailing methods for knowing when a train was about to depart – I should respect his judgement and shut up.

Travelling by myself between Johannesburg and Cape Town, I congratulated the steward in the breakfast car on the smooth running of the train. 'Never,' I declared, 'have I spent such a tranquil and restful night on a train, so smooth, quite delightful.' 'Mevwrow,' he replied, 'due to a derailment, the train hasn't moved for the past eight hours.' In fact, the journey took so long that I felt the story told about a South African train wasn't entirely unbelievable. It seems that a woman on the train was about to give birth and when a doctor had been found among the passengers, and had safely delivered her, he said, 'You know, you really shouldn't travel in this condition.' 'Doctor,' she replied, 'when I got on this train I wasn't in this condition.'

In my experience, the nicest way to travel is by British Rail sleepers. In the morning a uniformed father figure gently wakens you with tea, Marie biscuits and the morning paper, and when you moan quite untruthfully that you haven't slept a wink, the soothing reply is 'There, there, Madam, drink your tea and you'll feel better.'

Finally, we do have plans to go by Trans-Siberian Railway to Vladivostock, and no doubt my husband and I will either end the journey bound closer by the bonds of suffering, or will have decided to get a quick Russian divorce.

MACHINES *Mary Hampson*

Mary Hampson is a journalist and traveller and spends much time in her caravan.

I have a fairly open, unsuspicious nature, I think – except I don't trust a single machine. To anything with works, I am the original spanner. I once put a whole room of sewing machines out of action, at a demonstration designed to prove that any fool could do embroidery and buttonholing. What I got was a blinding flash. All the machines stopped chattering, and all the demonstrators said that I should stick to hand sewing and preferably stay at home.

It's the same with washing machines. Mild, well-mannered twin tubs take a funny turn when I approach. They start pouring water *out* when I want it *in*, and switching themselves off when I expect them to be on. I just don't have what it takes with a washing machine, but give me a stream and a stone and I can beat it out with the best of them.

Show me an icy stream tumbling along beside a mountain road in Algeria and I can have it foaming like a detergent ad in two seconds flat.

As soon as I get in a caravan I become a compulsive washer. I travel everywhere with one eye open for a pump or a scenic well; I've done the washing in some marvellous places. I think of them on Monday mornings.

There was that lake in Northern Greece – I never knew its name. The mountains drifted away in the background in a blue grey haze and the sun was a misty concentration of light in a cloudy sky. And the lake – smoke grey water shot with silver and reeds, and in the distance a shepherd playing a pipe; the sound of sheep bells faint and far away and no other noise.

It was *the* lake for Morte d'Arthur. It lacked only the arm clothed in white samite, and the sword. And what it had was me, blissfully washing my smalls. Then there was the time I did the washing down by the river of Jordan. After the oily, salty bitterness of the Dead Sea, the Jordan *is* the river of life. It flows through that desolate, damned wilderness like a blessing. The other thing about doing your washing in the open air is that you never know who you will meet by the well. It's better than joining a club. You can't always get on with your washing, but then you don't always want to.

I've met some very interesting people when I've been scrubbing away on a stone. Take that morning in the Lebanon in the mountains behind Beirut. I saw the well from the road. It was really a spring which had been controlled by a bit of old pipe, and somebody had made a tiny reservoir.

I clambered down and washed everything I'd got, and thought how excessively pleasant it was to sit on a stone all by yourself on a sunny, gorse-scented morning, messing about in soapy water surrounded by marigolds and poppies, serenaded by fourteen honking frogs.

I didn't think anyone could see me from the road. They must have had radar. First, a little boy came and gave me a fire salamander. It was steely grey, splashed with orange, and I didn't like it as much as its name.

Then came the little boy's mother and father. They gave me orange blossom, mint, and a bunch of spring onions – and his mother inspected my washing and gave me good advice. At least, I think it was advice. It sounded like water in the petrol, but when she had finished exploding, she washed my jeans again. She made a good job of them, too.

By this time, two cars had stopped on the road above. Out of the first came a plump, important man in a dark and dusty city suit. He slithered down the stony path, making the pebbles skid, and even while he was travelling on the seat of his shiny pants, he was talking.

He told me he was an economist and a Druze. He did a breakdown on the economic situation in Europe and the Middle East, and told me that as a Druze, he believed in God, and the five poles of his religion were wisdom, logic, power, will and love.

While he was broadening my mind, the occupants of the second car arrived and shot down the path which was fast turning into a shute, polished with stones and mud and traffic and soap.

They were three middle-aged Syrian ladies who shook hands all round and then leapt off to collect wood and fir cones to make a fire. One of them produced a coffee-pot and began to get breakfast under way. The eldest lady climbed a little tree nearby, and roosted like some strange black bird with spiky legs in a cleft in the branches. Don't ask me why . . .

Finally, the milkman came with the milk – it was still in the goat. He sat down placidly and milked away on the edge of the lunatic fringe.

I don't know who they were, where they were going, or why. I don't even care. But you do see why I like doing my washing in the open air.

KOSTENA, THE ALL-BEAUTIFUL   *Antonia Ridge*

Antonia Ridge is one of the most popular Woman's Hour broadcasters. Of French, Dutch and British background, several of her books have been serialised for the programme, including the story of Papa Meilland and the Peace rose, which was recently repeated in response to many requests.

It's 150 years since the Greeks rose in rebellion against the Turks who'd ruled over them for four hundred years.

There's still many a story told of that savage struggle for freedom, but to my mind, none equals the one I heard from the gentle old priest of a village high in the mountains of Crete. (He once spent some years in America so he speaks English). It's the story of a Greek fisherman's daughter who had been christened Panoraya: and never was a poor child so ineptly named, for Panoraya means 'all-beautiful'. And this Panoraya grew up to be the plainest, the homeliest of girls, and to add to the cruel irony, she had bandy legs.

But bandy-legged Panoraya was no fool: moreover, she was quick, deft, cheerful and very hard-working. So a fisherman, called Kostas, had the good sense to marry her. And from that day on Panoraya saw to it that she was called Kostena, which means 'the wife of Kostas'.

So there was Kostena now, wife of Kostas, the fisherman. They were poor, heaven knew, but they were happy and contented. They had four fine, healthy children and the proudest moment of Kostena's day was supper-time when she served up a great steaming pot of soup made from all kinds of fish, onions, tomatoes and plenty of good olive oil. And hunks of black bread to mop up the soup.

Then it came – the terrible day when all Kostena's humble little world suddenly shattered. In one of the savage surprise attacks of that war, the whole village was set ablaze and Kostena lost her husband, her four children and all her neighbours. She, too, had been left for dead and when she managed to struggle to her feet, there they lay in the heartless sunshine – dead, all dead.

Blind with grief, reeling with shock and misery, Kostena was suddenly swept along by a surge of refugees and presently found herself in a crowded boat making for the north coast of Greece.

In that desolate boatload of human misery were six terrified children who, like Kostena, now hadn't a friend or a relative left in the world. Kostena saw their faces and gathered them around her, and when they landed, she found an abandoned hut on a hillside near the little port, and moved in with the six children. The next day she spent her last few coins on a bar of soap and a length of rope. And she strung a clothes-line between two trees, and began to take in washing.

On the days when the washing ran out, Kostena would pocket her pride – no easy thing for any Greek – and go from door to door begging. A little olive oil here; some black bread there; some beans, a few figs; and Kostena could, as the Greek saying goes, 'get juice from a stone'. So somehow, some way, she managed to feed those six children.

When the nights grew cold and the wind came whistling through the cracks in their hut, they would huddle close to Kostena and she would tell them stories and sing songs about the daring young heroes who, all down the years, had fled to the mountains, lived in bands of partisans, and defied and harassed the Turks. As for the mules that carried these heroes along the steep mountain tracks, they were prodigious, no other word for it, prodigious! And Kostena would sing:

> Kosta's mule eats iron bars!
> Alexis's mule devours stones!
> The mule of John, the shepherd-boy,
> Uproots and eats up trees!

And often the children would fall asleep as Kostena softly sang a song with a melody that sounded like the waves breaking on the sea-shore:

> My dearest bird
> I'm weary, weary
> Of looking at the sea.
> Of asking the postman
> Day after day,
> And never, never,
> A letter comes my way.

Oh, yes, Kostena did far more than feed those six children, she mothered them.

When the fighting at last came to an end, the Government of liberated Greece began to build homes for the many hundreds of children orphaned in the struggle for freedom. And one day, someone came to take Kostena's six children to one of these new orphanages.

'Oh, you'll see,' said Kostena, 'it will be like a palace, no cracks in the walls, no holes in the roof. And you'll each have a bed of your own.' But still they wept and clung to Kostena.

'Now, now,' she said, 'do you think I'd ever leave you ? No, no! I'm coming too, of course.'

And she picked up her bar of soap and her clothes-line; and followed her six children. And promptly became the washerwoman, the unpaid washerwoman, of that orphanage. Day in, day out (except on Sundays) Kostena washed and ironed; just washed and ironed and asked nothing better of life, for every orphan there soon learned to love and trust Kostena. It was to *her* they ran if they fell down. Kostena knew just how to comfort them and send them back to play again.

As for clothes . . . well, the Greeks have a custom of offering gifts or money on New Year's Day, 'the good hand' they call it. And kind souls would offer Kostena 'the good hand', maybe some material to make a black frock, or a warm black shawl. And some offered money with which she always bought sweets for the children. Kostena, too, liked to have the dignity of offering 'the good hand'.

In this way, year in, year out, Kostena washed and ironed, till one day she quietly died.

And no more moving sight was ever seen than the long line of orphans who wept to see Kostena laid to rest – among them those six children now grown up and married with children of their own.

To them she was surely Panoraya, the All-Beautiful; and no woman more deserved the name.

HERE'S WOOL OVER YOUR EYES   *Don White*

It was ten to five on a Friday when I arrived in Perth, Western Australia. So the staff of the Youth Employment Bureau weren't too happy to see me . . . they were already washing their hands ready for a quick getaway.

'Well, what can you do ?' I was asked. I was wearing shorts, a curry-stained shirt, and sandals.

'We can hardly get you into a bank or insurance office like that,' they told me. And offered me a job in the Bush.

I said I wouldn't mind a job in a pub. But no, the Bush isn't a pub in Perth, it's the Australian outback, and I had a choice of wheat, sheep or forestry.

I plumped for sheep. I'd heard that shearers got enormous salaries, just for running an electric razor over a ram's back, so they gave me a form to present to the Station Overseer at Kellerberrin.

'Thanks. What number bus do I catch ?' But no, no bus. Kellerberrin was four-and-a-half hours away by train. They weren't too happy about that, either – they had to loan me the fare to get there.

I arrived at five in the morning and there was a station wagon – a 'ute' they called it – to pick me up and drive me out to the sheep station about thirty-five miles away. They even let me sleep in . . . till nine-thirty before I started work.

That's when I discovered that you need years of experience to become a shearer. I was starting at the bottom–in more ways than one!

The shearing season is twice a year, every six months. However, half-way between each season comes the dagging period.

Sheep stations over there are pretty big – some are larger than a whole English county. Kellerberrin was a big one. And because of the dry climate and sparse vegetation – sometimes each sheep has a whole acre or two to itself for grazing – the flocks are spread out over a vast distance. With so little rain, too, the sheep tend toget rather messy, particularly, well, you know what I mean. This is bad for the fleece, and the smell will attract packs of wild dingoes who could ravage an entire flock. So half-way through the season, all the sheep are brought in and dagged.

The sheep go through a dip, dry off, then as they come into the shearing sheds, the shearer lifts them by their back legs and shears off the dirty wool at the back. Then he takes the dirty wool and throws it onto a big table. That's where I was.

I was on the table. I was a dag sorter. It was my job to sort the dags into three grades. There were the dags from the relatively house-trained sheep. These, I was told, would be scoured several times, and the wool would be used to make something like . . . don't tell your husbands . . . army blankets! Then there were dirty dags. These, after scouring, still could not be used to manufacture clothing. But as they retained a great deal of natural oil, I was told they were made into pads for cleaning things like the inside of gun barrels.

And then there were the absolutely unmentionable dags. These, at the end of each day, would be shovelled onto the back of a truck, driven miles out into the bush and burned or buried.

It was a short job. Only two weeks. And after the first day you don't notice the smell any more. At least I didn't. But I was the only one actually up to my elbows in the back ends of sheep every day – and everybody else noticed. I had to eat my meals on my own, so I didn't put everybody else off their food, and slept in a corner of the bunk-house yards away from anyone else.

At the end of the two weeks I got a fabulous amount of pay, even after board and lodging and my rail fare had been deducted. I don't remember how long the money lasted. But I do remember that I had the aroma of the back ends of sheep with me till I reached Sydney two weeks later.

A BALCONY IN THE MIDI   *Pearl Binder*

Pearl Binder, artist and writer, is married to the Rt Hon. Sir Frederick Elwyn Jones, QC, MP, Attorney-General in the last Labour Government.

On a blistering August morning we found ourselves in a ramshackle village bus climbing up into the gold hills of Provence. I won't tell you just where it is. It's like a village in a dream. There let it remain. It's high up amongst terraced rocks, all of the same dry warm colour, which is sometimes yellow and sometimes the colour of a ripe apricot.

The village is built into the rock and out of rock; from a little way off you can't be sure it is there at all, so closely is it married with its background. Its narrow streets and zigzag houses are cobbled and paved and everything is stone, stone, stone; dry crumbling old stone, for this village was there before the Romans came to Provence and most of the buildings go back at least to the sixteenth century. Arched walls suddenly open onto unexpected vistas of vineyards and the harsh dry maquis. Fig trees push through cracks in gateways. The sun is baking hot. It almost never rains, and your washing dries before you have time to carry it home from the fountain. It's too dry for the peasants to scratch much of a living from the hard soil.

Once there was a silk factory here, but now that nylon has triumphed, the factory and mulberry trees are abandoned. The peasants who cling on to the hillside in their rocky houses are crinkled and baked like the soil. They are friendly, generous; desperately poor; wedded to a life of work, garlic and endless games of *boule*.

My friend's house, a beautiful ruin, is a series of rooms with broken stone steps leading up and down inside and outside to nowhere. It has a broad verandah facing the valley and the hillside beyond, and I decided to sleep out there. But I couldn't bear to sleep. It was too strange; too beautiful an experience to waste in unconsciousness.

Twilight is brief in the Midi. The hot apricot-coloured village rapidly fades to pink, fawn, grey, and seems to hesitate for a moment till one pale star emerges. Then the sky is a heartbreaking blue. Swallows wheel and skim below the terraces and the village lights pop up like so many more stars. And suddenly the village takes on most dramatic effects. Every archway, every street-corner becomes the second act of an Italian opera – with a theatrical crescent moon, dangling just above the rooftops. As the night darkens the winding stone terraces, pale beneath their thatches of dark tiles and lit curiously from below, stand out like the concentric circles of some unearthly planet – a crater in a moonscape.

I ought to get into my bed and go to sleep. But I can't. I switch on the electric light for the pleasure of watching the myriads of lovely and extraordinary winged insects dance slowly round the light, and bask against the whitewashed wall; bronze and silver-grey creatures; straw and stone coloured; insects the colour of ashes; and a glow-worm burns with a steady green-yellow light.

I lean over the railing and watch my elongated shadow project itself waveringly for two miles across the silent valley. The air is cold and pure and extremely still. Now I can switch off the light and enjoy the noises of the night. The big church clock strikes the hour; ten slow liquid bongs; the only moist sounds in this desert-dry village.

Now the crickets begin their steady dry rasping. Big owls sigh in their nests in the crannied walls, ruffle their feathers and utter their melancholy double hoot, B Flat, A. A male frog calls unceasingly to his mate – a plaintive B natural – all night long he calls, and after each sad little call, like an echo, comes the muted female reply.

The hours slip away. Before dawn the whole universe is hushed. I imagine a spectacular sunrise is going to flood the dark sky, like those unlikely chalk drawings, all pink and ochre, rubbed into the London sidewalks by pavement artists. But this dawn isn't at all like that. By imperceptible graduations the darkness slowly drains away, until at last a faint ray of cold sunlight, pale and silver as moonshine, touches the topmost crag of rock and dim colours begin to separate themselves.

The surrounding hills emerge from the sky: crumpled hills – the faraway lonely blue of love-in-the-mist – and it is morning. And then my family came bounding noisily onto the verandah ravenous for their breakfast.

CHRISTMAS PARTY *Muriel Lucie-Smith*

Muriel Lucie-Smith was for some time Governess to the Princesses of the Royal House of Iraq. Here she describes what happened when she attempted to translate the traditional English Christmas Party to the Middle East.

I realised how much the princesses loved parties. I'd given one or two little ones and I thought I'd give a real Christmas party at Christmas for them, so I asked Azza and Racha, my two princesses, if they would like it and I told them about the tree and they were thrilled at the idea. I had to get things for the tree so I quickly wrote to England to my family and they played up wonderfully and sent me all the tinsel and the balls and the candles. Then I had to get the tree. There are no trees in Iraq except date palms, so in the end I had to have a date palm. That doesn't lend itself very readily to decoration, still it was the best I could get.

I should think it must have been about six feet tall. The room was very high, so I was able to get it in and I said to the princesses, 'Christmas is the children's festival so ask your twelve best friends that have children, but no more.' They said yes, and gave me the list of names, and I bought in the bazaar little presents for all of the palace people, and children. I managed to get two tinned Christmas puddings and I thought if I put one on top of the other that would be enough and I bought all the little things you put in a pudding, sixpences, the ring, a thimble, etc. The party was organised for 22nd December and the night before we had a wonderful time. I had never seen the princesses so happy tying up the parcels, and on the morning of the 22nd we started decorating the tree.

I put the parcels round the bottom and the ornaments and the candles I managed to tie on to the palm arms. And when we had decorated it all I locked the door and took the key. Then we had lunch and I went to have a little lie-down. The party was due to start at six o'clock. I had a small sleep and I woke up hearing a milling noise in the passage. I opened the door and looked out and I saw at least forty women and children, babies at the breast, all ages of children, grandmothers, cousins, aunts, milling about the passage. I went to the princesses, and said: 'What are all these people doing here and why have they come?' They cast down guilty eyes and said, 'Each friend we asked to bring a friend and each friend bring a friend and what can we do?' I was appalled. I said: 'There are only twelve presents and there are at least forty people outside.'

Well, what could we do? Nothing. I couldn't go down then and buy more presents. The tree was planned for six o'clock because the king said he wanted to come and see it and I didn't want to light the candles till he came but by three o'clock there was such a crying of children and the palace was getting in such disorder that the queen sent for me and said, 'Please start the party.' It was a very dark afternoon and I drew the curtains, lit the candles and with a beating heart threw open the double doors. The mob poured in and there was a gasp of astonishment. For a moment I had great gratification, but the moment was very short-lived. It didn't take long to give out the twelve presents to the twelve children whose names I had and then there was a deathly hush when all these women realised there was nothing more coming. They crowded round me, they almost pulled my hair out, they almost pulled my clothes off, they caught me by the arm, they beat their breasts, they cried, they said, 'I get nothing, my child get nothing, I a poor miserable woman!' They tore everything off the tree, candleholders and burnt out candles, and the tree was a shambles in a minute.

A lot of them stayed on for dinner and when that happened the table was pushed to one side and we all sat on the floor. We had dinner and then the pudding came. Unfortunately my princesses had mentioned something was in the pudding. It was served to the queen, who refused, the princesses took a minute portion, I refused, knowing it couldn't go round the table, and the two women next to me took the lot. They never ate a crumb. They smashed it up on their plates and held up the little things. 'Look what I've got, look what I've got.' The others immediately burst out crying, beat their breasts again and said, 'I get nothing, I a poor unhappy woman!'

My party was not a success, but I learnt a valuable lesson: the law of Arab hospitality allows 'a friend to bring a friend', so never give presents.

THE TWENTY-FOUR-HOUR SUIT *Bruce Angrave*

The temperature in Japan had been below freezing and I was on my way to Rangoon where it was over 100. So I stopped off at Hongkong to get acclimatised because the temperature there was about half-way between the two.

I had met someone on the plane who had wanted to have a pearl set in a ring, so, ever curious and ever anxious to learn, I went with her to a jeweller's in an arcade near the waterfront.

Inside were intense Indian shopkeepers. The one who specialised in setting pearls in rings engaged in a long and technical discussion with my friend, occasionally breaking off to try and sell her one of the innumerable brooches and trinkets that kept catching her eye. 'Velly cheap,' he would say, holding up a glittering and bejewelled earring. 'For you, twenty-five dollar.' 'Really no,' she would reply. 'Why not ?' said the Indian. 'You not afford twenty-five dollar ? How much it worth to you ?' 'Really and truly no,' repeated my friend. 'Twenty dollar,' said the Indian. 'I really mustn't.' 'Eighteen dollar for you special.' 'Please don't press me,' said my friend. 'Fifteen dollar,' said the Indian. I watched fascinated.

Just then I became conscious of heavy breathing in my ear.

'You like a suit ?' a voice whispered.

I looked around. Elvis Presley, or possibly his double, was looking soulfully at me. 'If only I could,' I smiled comfortingly at him, 'but no time I'm afraid.'

'How much time you got ?' said Elvis Presley.

'Twenty-four hours.'

'Lissen mister, I make you suit in twenty-four hours,' confided Mr Presley.

'No, no,' I smiled uneasily. 'How can anyone expect a tailor to make a suit in twenty-four hours ? It wouldn't be fair to his craft.'

'Lissen,' said the soulful one relentlessly. 'I make suit, with fitting, in twenty-four hours. I take your measurements.'

'Really no.'

'Lissen mister, we got lot of materials from England. Velly good.'

I looked appealingly at my friend. She didn't look back.

'Cost you nussing to look,' said Elvis.

That was true. I comforted myself with the thought that I could dither over materials long enough for my friend to finish her negotiations with the jeweller. And then I could escape. The maddening thing was that the first bale of material was the exact colour I intended my next suit to be.

Elvis perceived my hesitation and leapt at the chink in my defences. 'Velly best English silk and worsted mixture. I make you suit in twenty-four hours. With fitting.'

'How much ?' I said hopelessly.

'To you velly cheap,' he said. 'Nineteen pounds. Velly cheap.'

It did seem cheap. I had expected to pay forty or fifty in London. Anyway, he was already measuring me.

I spent a sleepless night. 'Fool,' I kept telling myself. 'At least if your're going to have a suit chucked together in twenty-four hours, in a far country where you can't come back if you're not satisfied, at least go to a *tailor*, not a *jeweller*.'

The time came for my fitting. And suddenly I knew it would be all right, for Elvis was only the front man. The real tailor was a stringy little Chinese who knew his stuff. You could tell by the way he handled his chalks and pins. 'Tloo flull hlere ?' he shouted. 'Yes.' 'Tlouser length OK ?' 'Yes,' I said. 'Tlwo slide vlents ?' 'Yes.' 'Nlo tlurn-ups, yes ?' he shouted.

And it *was* all right. I collected the suit exactly twenty-four hours after ordering it. A marvellous fit and lovely silky material.

But I'd forgotten just one thing. To haggle. I could have got it for fifteen pounds. 'Nit,' I said to myself.

LATE DEVELOPER *Gillian Martin*

I was quite bright at school. I mean I could gather facts and remember dates, and even with a bit of effort got the message about long division of pounds, shillings and pence. But I was nevertheless a late developer. Until I was in my twenties I couldn't open my mouth without uttering some monumental inanity. I was so afraid of admitting to an opinion of my own I tried to be polite by agreeing with everyone. It always ended in confusion and embarrassment. I still go cold just remembering.

When I was twenty, I went to France as a student, solo for the first time in my life, and with my head spinning at the thought of the lovely freedom before me.

I took up residence at a small hotel recommended by my tutor as suitable for an unchaperoned young lady. The whole aspect of the place suggested that it was unsuitable for any young lady. It had a long dark staircase leading up from the street to a main hall with tasselled lampshades. There were tasselled plush covers on every surface and a great number of yellowed notices. The two I remember in particular read, 'Travellers without luggage are requested to pay in advance' and one which graced the wc and said 'Do not introduce daily newspapers into the waters.'

Two days later I returned from a lecture to find that a couple of travellers without luggage were still occupying my room. The proprietress, implying that I was very inconsiderate, required me to go away till she had time to replace my sheets on the bed. I paid my bill, sneaked into the WC to introduce a weekly newspaper into the waters as a tiny defiance and took my leave. Then I moved into a bed-sitter.

It was on the ground floor of a two-storey house and separated from another rented room by a bathroom. The bath didn't work, neither did the hot tap on the basin and there were no locks. As the other room, facing the street, was shared by two girls, I didn't worry about that, particularly as the WC wasn't there but in a corner of the garden. I hadn't reckoned with the French girls' habit of tossing their key through their window to their boy-friends who would then pass through my room and the bathroom. Although these young men surprised me whilst engaged in almost every imaginable activity, every situation seemed to be covered, for them at least, by a polite bow and smile.

My landladies lived next door . . . a charming pair of elderly maiden sisters. They were small and gentle – talked in a duet, or sometimes in canon, but usually managing to finish together. The day after I arrived, they called on me, twittering in chorus that they had something of a delicate nature to impart about the lady who lived in the room above mine. I couldn't make it out at first. 'You see, Mademoiselle, our father was wise and kind, but not a worldly man, you understand. And the poor lady has a good heart. For thirty years she has lived here and by long usage we have grown to have an affection for her. Not that we condone, dear Mademoiselle, please understand. But it would be wise if you did not become intimate with her. Politeness, of course, but as an unmarried young lady, not a close connection.'

I sat on the edge of my seat, bewildered. But as the days, or rather the nights, went by, I began to suspect. The doorbell rang at odd hours, there were footsteps on the stairs late at night, there were male voices murmuring.

She can't be one of Those, I told myself a dozen times after I at last saw the upstairs lady. She was, as the French put it, of a certain age, even past it. Her hair was a frizzed mop of an intense matt black and her usual dress a flowing kimono. Her flat had a tiny balcony and there she would sit most afternoons taking the sun and singing, memorably, a song called 'Forget me, my love'. On the balcony she kept bantam chickens and her cat nested in the tangle of roses atop

the garden wall. With her lived a poodle, an ancient man, reputedly
her father-in-law, and an Algerian with very thin legs. I knew about
the legs because of his habit of taking the poodle to the front porch
clad only in a short dressing-gown.

In due time, I decided to give a party and felt I should ask the
upstairs lady if she minded as it might be noisy. Giggling nervously,
I went for the first time up the stairs.

Madame greeted me with rapture. She was delighted to meet me,
enchanted to have young people in the house, utterly charmed at the
prospect of a party. 'My dear,' she shrilled, 'make as much noise as
you like. Live your youth, alas it does not last. And perhaps, too, my
clients have occasionally disturbed you, though I beseech them to
enter and leave quietly. Ah! You are too polite to complain. I will tell
them to try harder. I have only a very few clients now and all gentlemen no longer young. I would like to retire but they beg me not to.
They feel too old to move their custom elsewhere and it is so con-
venient for them here near the station.'

For the rest of my stay I was on the most comfortable terms with
with my landladies and Madame upstairs. When I left, all three were
on the doorstep to wave me off, the Demoiselles fluttering lacy handkerchiefs and Madame, the cat under her arm, flapping some nameless garment she happened to have in her hand at the moment.

The point of this is that I was, as I said, a late developer. It was a
long time before I realised that I'd learned something from the three
ladies . . . that you can be tolerant without sinking your own principles.

Now how do I teach *that* to my children, especially my daughter ?
I would like to have the strength not to shelter her as I was sheltered,
so that she can do her growing up a bit earlier than I did. After all, if
I can't do that much, who's to benefit from it all in the end ?

VENICE IN THE RAIN   *Verily Anderson*

My goodness, how wet a wet day in Venice is! It's not just the
ordinary rain pouring down and the sopping pavements and the
slippery alleys and the streaming windows and roofs, but water comes
bubbling up from underneath the pavements to join the rain coming
pouring down from the sky. If the tide's high, too, the sea overlaps
the quayside and the gondolas and boats seem to be floating about

into the squares. The lagoon looks like melted mother-of-pearl and
the light seems to be filtered through crystals.

There's plenty of cover in Venice so holiday-makers don't need to
get wet unless they want to. You can go gaping round the fish market
with its colourful crowds and intriguing mediterranean seafood –
squids and soft-shelled crabs, giant lobsters and mussels and fish of
every hue. The fruit market's covered too, or you can walk up the
steps of the Rialto bridge and keep dry under the sun blinds of the
little shops selling glass beads and paper-weights and musical gondola-
lamps. Inside every church there are pictures with scenes that surpass
any colour television and then when the sun comes out there are
rainbows everywhere. When the rain stops and the sky clears the
Dolomites seem to come right down to the sea and you can sometimes
even see snow on their peaks.

But the Venetians themselves, who have one of the worst winter
climates in those parts with months of rain, damp and cold, are not so
keen on wet days.

'I agree that Venice is the most beautiful and cultured city in the
world,' one told me, 'but the most cultured thoughts I ever have
when I'm trying to get from one place to another, is which landing
stage is that man going to get out at so that I can grab his seat on the
water-bus ?'

Yes, it's one thing to go about in boats instead of buses and cars on
a bright summery day with a little breeze blowing and water gently
lapping against the bows – and quite another to wait in winter on a
tossing landing stage for a boat that may not even come at all if the
fog's really thick – 'What we need here is a fast, dry, regular service,
like you have with your London Underground.' I laughed it off at the
time, and then found that plans have actually been drawn up for an
underground railway in Venice, to rumble deep down under the
lagoon and the canals, with its passengers surfacing inside ancient
buildings whose ground floors are at present too damp to use for
anything else.

For the Venetians realise that something really drastic must be
done if their beautiful city is to survive. Overflowing canals and deep
puddles in St Mark's Square on rainy days remind them all too clearly
that the level of the lagoon, which has been flooding their alleys and
ground floors since the eleventh century, has in the last twenty years
risen very much faster. The serious 1966 flooding brought it home that

industrial drilling of a new oil refinery on the mainland causes subsidence in the islands themselves and that artificial islands made in the lagoon can't help but displace water and deepen it at high tide.

The visionaries of Venice want laws passed against this, as well as against industrial pollution of the water – and of the air, for it's smogs that are hurrying the deterioration of the lovely buildings.

The industrialists want to see the city work for its living. To live on tourists and cultural grants is not healthy, they say. Modern industry and modern housing should replace some of the crumbling ancient buildings on the islands. Roads should augment the canals, and causeways link the islands.

The visionaries would rather let Venice sink into her own lagoon than see her beauty marred by motorways and fly-overs and this is why it is the poets and artists and professors and lovers of culture and history who are pressing for an underground railway. Of course, that's only part of the possible cure. The tides that twice daily flush the canals – which in some cases are the only drains – need to be controlled in some cunning way so that the water level is lowered without the delicate tidal flow being upset.

To make Venice a living city, as against a museum, would entail encouraging the small clean industries for which Venice has always been famous – glass blowing, lace making and repairing antiques. And there are plans for expanding the students' centres and making use of some of those beautiful but tumbling down palaces as homes for them and places where they can meet.

Unless all these great changes come quickly, one of these wet days the city and the canals and the lagoon all round really will become all one again as they were before Venice rose from the mud 1,200 years ago.

ANCIENT BRITONS *Noel Clark*

Noel Clark was formerly BBC Correspondent in Latin America, is now BBC Correspondent in Vienna.

I have to report the recent discovery by my family and myself of a long-extinct meal – the traditional old-English farmhouse tea – in an excellent state of preservation, deep in central Argentina. The tea, consisting of huge platefuls of hot buttered toast, several varieties of cake, including walnut and chocolate – all, like the various jams and preserves, home-made – hove into sight every afternoon on the stroke of four in the firelit dining-room of a country hotel perched in the hills southwest of Cordoba. The tea seemed to symbolise an almost forgotten way of life which flourishes still in that remote, airy outcrop of the Andes – a Shangri-La simulacrum of the way things used to be before – before what ? Before Britain began swinging, one might say. For the British who live in this secluded place – mostly retired folk, some of whom worked on the railways long ago when these were British, while others were in business or managing *estancias* – Britain remains essentially her old, unswinging self. One lady said, 'We call ourselves the ancient Britons, you know.' She chuckled demurely. A demure chuckle, come to that, is pretty rare these days. The elderly gentleman in tweeds who advanced upon me with a twinkle in his eye said, 'We hear you have a lot of children.' Somehow, in the almost eerie silence of the hills, word – no, rather a genteel whisper – had gone round, from Tanglewood to Dunroamin, from Rottingdean to Rawson Court – 'there's a new family visiting from the old country.'

The old gentleman explained that he was collecting and delivering card tables in preparation for the monthly British Community Bridge Drive and Tea. 'Are you coming ? You'll meet us all there – I should think we'll run to ten tables this month.' He added: 'Of course, we're all getting on, you know – average age about seventy up here.' But how well they all looked, how youthful still these charming people and how gracefully their precise, outdated English rang in the rarefied air amid the conifers, the tumbledown stone walls and the wrought-iron gates.

Hundreds of miles away, down on the plains, their children's children these days speak Spanish first and English with an accent. But the old people – if they weren't actually born in Britain themselves, certainly went home – as they say – to school and their Spanish is even now not always as good as it might be. One old gentleman to whom I was introduced was asked if he'd met me. 'No,' he said thoughtfully, abandoning the car-engine with which he'd been tinkering, 'I don't think I've met anyone today.'

They're great listeners to London, these hill-folk and the chimes of Big Ben boom out nostalgically from many an old-fashioned but still serviceable wireless set. Occasionally, a villager goes by on horseback in black sombrero and a poncho, a touch of local colour in this still-life of good works, golf, gardens and gossip. A local tradesman, I was told in a fascinated sotto voice, was once involved in a murder. 'He found somebody with his wife, if I recall correctly,' said the elderly lady. 'Nothing was ever done about it; they passed it off as a *crime passionel*, rather like Italy, don't you know?'

WHERE FRANKNESS IS ALL *Jane Gregor*

Agony columns are nothing new – but the ones we have in Ghana make all the others seem tame. The majority of the letter writers seeking help with their emotional problems are men. They seem to have no fear of airing their wrongdoings and whilst they don't exactly brag about getting two girls pregnant at the same time or pinching their brother's fiancée, there's no mealy-mouthed beating about the bush.

There's a frank acceptance of man's nature as it is, not as it ought to be, and an almost joyous relish in the description of the physical details of love-making and physique generally.

That money is the root of all evil is a constantly recurring theme: so is the belief that true love conquers all. In fact, 'love', usually in the sexual sense, is strongly upheld as the reason for all lawbreaking, society-flouting behaviour and if, to use a favourite phrase, 'the heart be strong', then all barriers should give way before its passion.

Not that right and wrong aren't clearly marked. They certainly are. The young man who, for instance, complained: 'I'm married to an old, rich lady, but she is always so serious . . . shall I sack her?' was smartly told by the 'Aunty' conducting that particular column of advice, 'Old ladies are always serious but that is good for your livelihood; still, ask her to smile and not keep a face as a woman suffering toothache; if this fails, charm her with stories.' He'd made his bed and on it he would lie!

The perennial student, too, who always seems to be anxious to ditch his teacher once she's got him through his exams gets short shrift in our 'answers to the lovelorn'. 'Do your duty where you have promised' is the uncompromising and never varying advice.

On an even more practical level are the letters, most frequent in Lagos magazines, asking for specific advice on how to increase one's amorous prowess; how actually to improve one's physical attributes, whether by means of exercise, oils, pills, potions or magic, is a very popular theme, too. To make love well seems to be every young man's desire and no prim fobbing off with 'I suggest you consult your doctor' sidesteps the issue in Africa's papers.

Nor are the answers as deadly earnest as those we're used to reading in our similar columns. The bubbling African sense of fun comes through all the time and never more so than in a piece of correspondence I'll never forget.

A young Nigerian wrote that he had been in the habit for years of eating a huge number of groundnuts . . . peanuts, that is. Recently falling in love with a beautiful girl, he was dismayed to find that his amatory skill fell far short of what he'd like it to be. 'Friends tell me,' the letter continued, 'this may be due to over-indulgence in groundnuts. What shall I do, please, Aunty ?'

The answer to his plea, which, I should tell you, was much more plainly worded than I've dared to repeat, was:

'Since you cannot make love satisfactorily, find another girl-friend . . . one who'd rather eat groundnuts with you, this time. That way you'll both be happy! As two groundnut addicts you could spend your time chewing instead of trying to make love unsuccessfully.'

Not that it's always the men who write.

One lady of startling outspokenness wrote recently:

'I know I ought to give up my boy-friend and stick to my husband alone, but I can't. Please help me with your suggestions. You see, although I know it's wrong, I simply can't do without my boy-friend, for, quite honestly, he's the only one who really gives me the works.'

Shocking ? No, I don't think so. Just honest, open acceptance that happy sex is one of the facts of life – in Ghana anyway.

THE WORRYING SOCIETY   *Ruth Adam*

Ruth Adam, writer and journalist, is co-author of a Life of Beatrice Webb, published in 1968. She has recently made regular visits to the US where her husband, Kenneth Adam, is Visiting Professor of Communications at Temple University, Philadelphia.

Usually, there's nothing more satisfying than to discover that the rich are not happy. But I don't feel that way about the Americans at all. I should like them to be happy as well as having all the good things they take for granted. They are so lovable, so generous, so eager to share

their riches, so conscience-stricken about their way of life and its
shortcomings. I wish they wouldn't worry so much.

Sooner or later, at any party, some young-looking, well-groomed,
middle-aged matron will say hopelessly, 'Well, we live in a sick society
and that's for sure.' The great overhanging anxieties are Vietnam, the
racial hostility, the angry rebellion of the young and violent crime.
These large worries seep down into everyday life and become individual family problems. Trying to avoid the draft, for instance, affects
everyone with a young man in the family circle. 'He's got deferment
by doing welfare work at the moment; but we never know how long
it will last; he could be called and sent to Vietnam any day,' says the
father who has a new car every year and a holiday home in the West
Indies. 'I lie awake at night wondering how soon my daughter's hippie
friends will get her started on hard drugs,' says the woman who seems
so happily occupied in moving into a purpose-built retirement house
with her husband. Race tension and violent crime boil down to
remembering a lot of tedious precautions; such as connecting and dis-
connecting the burglar alarm as needed, putting up the chain on the
apartment-door again every time anyone comes in or goes out;
arranging to go to a neighbour's for an evening coffee without walking
the streets alone. Most days, in the local paper there is a cautionary
tale of how someone who scamped a bit of the regular routine was
taken off to hospital in a battered condition.

And as if this wasn't enough, they feel obliged to worry about
health all the time as well. Supermarket shopping isn't just making a
selection from all those splendid goodies on the shelves. It's a grim
reminder that man is mortal and that fat men have a higher mortality
rate than thin men. Or, as a recent investigation of overweight Americans pointed out: 'The longer the belt line, the shorter the life-line.'
Practically every kind of food will predispose you to a particular
ailment and all of them carry the risk of making you dangerously fat.
So the conscientious housewife must look for substitutes – low-
caloric margarine instead of butter, fat-free milk (or skim milk as we
say in England) and sugar replacement which 'contains natural and
non-nutritive artificial sweeteners' and dietetic candy with 'no salt
added'. But she can't win, because the doctors have recently discovered that some of the substitute foods are just as dangerous as the
real thing; for instance one dietetic cookie substitute is equal to
approximately half a slice of bread and as everyone knows (everyone

over here, anyway) you have to walk twenty minutes to walk off one
slice of bread. Also instant substitute chocolate bars make up for having less sugar by having more fat and fat is a greater peril than sugar.
And as she waits at the cash-desk there are a lot of notices accusing her
of not really caring about her family's health because she hasn't yet
bought them vitamin pills, which they will need to make up for being
on a diet. And has she ever considered the fact that: 'You yourself
may be short of iron in your body without knowing it' ?

The anti-cigarette campaign is really more nerve-racking than the
anti-eating one. There's all the government propaganda (like having a
notice that smoking is a health hazard on the side of the packet) and
a lot of social pressure as well. It is only right to nag your neighbours for their own sake about smoking and it is socially acceptable
for a hostess to say to a guest who has just taken out a cigarette,
'Haven't you managed to kick that habit yet ?' A smoker who stays for
the week-end in a home where the host family *has* kicked it is reduced
to sneaking away and having a drag in private, like a visitor staying at
Windsor in the days of Queen Victoria.

To add to it all, Ralph Nader, the self-appointed defender of the
consumer, has pointed out that the average expectancy of life has
declined since 1962 (after rising steadily since 1900). He puts it down
to artificial fertilisers used on the land, liable to poison the public
without their realising it. And now the Environmental Science
Services Administration has issued a warning to the public about
tornadoes, which, they point out, are most likely to strike the country
on summer afternoons between four and six p.m. The warning starts,
'Someday soon you may have to protect your family from a tornado.
Will you know what to do ?' Now *I'm* getting worried.

The Diversities of People

A PASSION FOR TIMETABLES *Marghanita Laski*

Miss Laski is a true broadcaster in the sense that she does not write scripts – she talks her pieces. This eulogy of timetables is taken from an off-the-cuff recording and to get its real flavour you should imagine the voice speaking it – as with all the pieces in this book.

I get the impression that a passion for railway timetables is peculiarly British; I certainly never met an American or any other European who shares it. But Britain is full of people who, at the drop of a hat, will tell you how to get to Birmingham by way of Beachy Head or if not will spend a happy few hours looking it up.

But one of the troubles about Britain is we haven't had the right railway timetables for playing this game. The ABC doesn't pretend to, it tells you how to get from here to there but not how to go from there. And, of course, a lot of people were devoted to Bradshaw which died a few years ago, but I always thought it was unnecessarily complicated. So I, who adore this game, never played it in Britain but always played it with an abroad timetable, with Cook's Continental Timetable which had the single disadvantage that it didn't include the British Isles. But what else didn't it include? It included railways in the whole of Europe and in all the countries bordering the Mediterranean; it took its railways right across Russia, right to China; it gave you every little steamship line that scanned the coasts of the Mediterranean and the Baltic and the North Sea and even some that went to the China Seas. And if you would just give one hour to learning its signs and symbols – which, after all, you've got to do with any instructional book – you knew exactly what every train provided.

Let me give you an example. We were once taking a train from Syracuse in Sicily to Rome, a rather swish train and it was even the train that had the new special sleepers – the ones where you sleep in a top storey and live down below – and we were going on these for the first time. It was leaving Syracuse at six in the evening, it didn't occur to me for a minute that it wouldn't have a proper restaurant car. Just for pleasure I was looking it up as we sat in the gardens at Syracuse and I saw it wasn't marked as having one. There was no time to go and inquire, no time to do anything but to trust Cook's Continental Timetable and go off and buy a cold roast chicken. And, of course, we were right. Cook's said it hadn't a diner – it hadn't a diner.

But an even better occasion I had with it, I remember, was when my husband and I decided to go to Constantinople just for the fun of going on a train. This was just after the war. Judge of our horror and amazement when the Bulgarians didn't give us a visa in time. It was essential to go through Bulgaria we thought. But we read Cook's Continental Timetable and it seemed to us that if we got off at Salonika in Greece and if we took a little train to Alexandroupolis and if we changed from Alexandroupolis town to Alexandroupolis maritime we could get a little train with a revolving restaurant – you know, a little boy who came round with biscuits – which would take us to the Turkish frontier just half an hour before the great express from Edirne thundered through to Istanbul. That worked and since then I'd trust Cook's anywhere.

But the reason I'm talking about it now is because this year for the very first time the British Isles are included. This is a great day for anyone who loves railway timetables and if any of you don't love railway timetables it wouldn't do you any harm to start doing so because to be able to read a timetable, to have one with you when you travel, makes you free. Supposing you have suddenly got to come home from goodness knows where and perhaps with a car, you don't know the language, but you've got a timetable and you're free.

This beautiful, this exquisite timetable comes out every month but there's no need for us ordinary people to buy it then; what we need is to buy it in October when everybody goes over to winter schedules; and buy it at the beginning of June by which time everybody has gone over to summer schedules. (We, of course, in our insular way go over to summer schedules at quite a different time from everybody else.) But believe me, if just one per cent of those of you who are listening to me buy Cook's Continental Timetable, whether to read for sheer delight at home or to take on your travels, your life will be enriched; or as they say nowadays, the quality of life will be improved.

LACE BOBBIN KING *John Body*

I'm snowed under with lace-bobbins – my whole house is coming down with lace bobbins.

A few weeks ago I was visiting in South Dorset and there I met a W.I. member who was lamenting her inability to get hold of any lace-bobbins. She was thinking of starting classes, she told me, and what she wanted were sets of a hundred.

I, mad fool that I was, offered to get some for her.

The bobbins are about the thickness of a slender pencil, three or four inches long with a narrow neck at one end. The thinking behind my offer was logical enough. In these days most men have a small electric drill for use around the house and a good many of these drills are adapted to run a small lathe.

Surely, I thought, any number of men would be only too glad to turn (literally) an honest penny at the kitchen table of an evening.

Home I came and without delay dispatched advertisements to two monthly magazines – the kind which are read in their tens of thousands by do-it-yourselfers.

'Wanted,' I wrote, 'quantity of lace-bobbins. Send for drawing and then submit quotation.'

From the first magazine I heard nothing – magazine number two wrote a very nice friendly letter, thanked me for the money, and regretted that I had just missed the next edition so that the advertisement wouldn't appear for another month. Well, that didn't matter because there sure enough within a few days was advert number one. Almost at once in came the replies. Six by the first post, six by the second post and, heavens, nearly thirty by the third post. And I had promised to send a drawing to each one.

I bet you I'm the best lace-bobbin drawer in the whole of England . . . in the world. Every day more and more. The postage stamps! Ruinous! At first I wrote things like, 'When sending your quotation will you also kindly submit a specimen bobbin ?' After a few days this became 'send sample'!

And on the drawing. At first it was a little arrow pointing to a tiny hole, with the legend, 'hole for thin wire to add glass beads for additional weight.' Soon I was writing savagely, 'hole for wire.' And at the end of ten bewildering days I suddenly remembered the advert in magazine number two.

'Urgent,' I wrote. 'Please cancel advertisement about lace-bobbins. Do not require refund of money, just cancel advertisement.'

Hysteria threatened as I opened their reply. 'Too late! Advert already in print – here is a cutting for you to see.' And letters from the first one were still arriving.

And now the samples started coming in. In envelopes, in cheroot packets, in wadding, in cardboard, in soap wrappers. And the prices! At first I wondered if the senders were mad, or if I was. £35 for a hundred was the first I got, then £32 and another £37 10s. How much each was that? Let's see, £35 – that's 700 shillings – 7 shillings each – impossible. I'd thought about sixpence each. Oddly enough, as time went on the prices seemed to get lower and the true values were revealed when I got letters from craftsmen who are already well familiar with these dainty little bobbins. A gentleman from Harrogate writes, 'I have eight dozen in stock, and I make them for craft centres in the Pately Bridge, Ripon, Leeds areas. I make them in Walnut, Beech, Oak and Sycamore.' His price – half a crown each and the workmanship – superb. From County Durham a lady writes,' What I thought was a sprain turns out to be a fracture, so my wood turning activities are suspended and I am unable to quote after all. Bone and ivory,' she adds, 'are more satisfactory than wood.' I bet they are, and what about the cost?

A sweet letter and a beautiful bobbin from someone near Buntingford in Herts: 'This one,' he writes, 'I turned over thirty-five years ago and it has been in regular use ever since. I have been making them for forty years, often in Beech and Lime, but Walnut, and Lignum Vitae last the longest. My wife and myself would be pleased to help the lady who wants them – we like to keep alive the rural crafts.'

I can't leave out what is perhaps the oddest incident in the whole affair. Just a week ago I was busy in my own workshop when knock knock and in came my housekeeper.

'There's a man to see you, about bobbins.'

A few minutes later I went cursing to the front door. Now, I thought, it's invading my very home – it's like a sort of Bobbin Quatermass. There stood a bright smartly-dressed little countryman of, I'd guess, eighty years or so.

'Well?' I said.

'It's about them bobbins.'

'Come in,' I said reluctantly.

There, spread out on chairs, on the table, on the hearth-rug, lay rows and rows of letters, each with its appropriate bobbin on top. I pointed to them, they told their own tale.

'My God,' said the little man, making for the door, 'I'm off – you're up to your arse in bobbins!'

And so I am!

WHO WANTS TO BE SEXUALLY EQUAL ? *Dorothy Gharbaoui*

It's flattering for an old married woman like me to receive a bit of masculine admiration. But, when the compliments develop, as they so often do nowadays, into the preliminary skirmishing before a projected affair, it becomes awkward.

There must be millions of women who prefer their husband's company and find the thought of adultery highly distasteful. Equally, there must be many, many young girls who have no desire for a trial marriage with their boy-friends.

A great myth of permissiveness is prevalent today. Along with it goes the myth of sexual equality for women. 'If men can sin, so can we!' is the fashionable cry. 'If men enjoy sex, so must we.'

Where exactly, I wonder, does the permissive society benefit women ? Living in sin may sound better when the sinful tag is removed, but a woman without wedding lines will still find herself doing the chores. Unmarried husbands are no more likely than the married ones to iron their own shirts or scrub the kitchen floor. They are, however, more likely to disappear when their lady-love's attractions become dulled by familiarity.

And what is so marvellous about being sexually equal ? Women today are bullied by popular psychologists into believing they have to respond to their husbands with equal ardour. For instance they mustn't, while amorously engaged, do shopping-lists in their heads. Why ever not ? Shopping-lists are such a weight on *my* conscience that I used to find myself dictating them to my GCE class instead of notes on Milton. If shopping-lists can get mixed up with 'Paradise Lost', why not with what is supposed to be paradise on earth ?

If female society were really composed of all those passionate birds getting carried away by their desires, life would be chaos. Women, on the whole, are just too busy. A man can sink into an armchair when he comes home from work. Nothing impedes him, when so moved, from rushing hot-bloodedly to bed. But his partner has to wash the supper dishes. If not, she is aware of them, stacked in greasy horror in the kitchen, waiting for her to get up again. If that doesn't chill her ardour, I don't know what will.

I am something of a feminist in my principles. I hate men to get away with unfair privileges, such as the right to commit adultery. But in my heart I feel a bit like my mother. When she heard that a woman of our acquantainance was seen drunk at a dance, she exclaimed in shocked disbelief, 'But she's got four children!'

No one ever remembers that about an intoxicated father. Unfair, I know, but it's a fact of life that motherhood often stands in the way of indiscretion or downright immorality. Does that last word exist nowadays, or should I say 'liberal attitudes'?

Anyway, how does a mother entertain her illicit lover at home when she knows that, at any moment, a little voice may cry, 'Mummy, come and wipe my bottom'? If she tries to conduct her liaison away from home, who will baby-sit? And, to crown it all, how often, after tending and grooming her husband and her brood, has she had time to groom herself? With unset hair and laddered stockings, it's not that easy to inspire an illicit affair.

The permissive age, in theory, is permissive for everyone. But who can really take advantage of it except all those well-groomed men and young unmarried girls? And even the latter must find it a bit of a strain. It's a vicious circle. Or, to put it another way, a self-perpetuating myth. Set in motion, I can't help feeling, by men, in the first place, for their own convenience.

When, I wonder, are women, young and old, going to have the courage to shriek, 'We don't want it. The permissive society is no fun for us'?

NO SCENT PLEASE *Clement Freud*

I like the smell of clean women; I am prepared to accept a tinge of peppermint on the breath, even a suspicion of baby soap emanating from the hair, but I hate perfume.

In the nineteenth century and before – when people slept in the clothes in which they worked, when dentistry consisted of extracting black teeth or painting them white – a woman rubbed with garlic or rose petals might have been a more acceptable product than one emanating the *à la maison* fragrance.

This is no longer the case. We now have unlimited water supplies, a National Health Service and an educational system that stresses the importance of cleanliness. So why must every woman dab herself with pungent emulsions that bear no relationship to the sort of smells women might naturally exude ?

What I mind most about perfumes is their synthetic quality. Goodness, if someone wanted to baste herself with the juices of crushed watercress, rub her face with lemon or cucumber, or dab a little coffee liqueur behind her ears, I might find that mildly fetching.

But perfume! Overpowering scents fixed by the excretions or whatever of a tom-cat and then blended to come across as Spirit of Gladioli at twelve-and-six a go.

What is it that women are frightened of ? They go around without bras, without knickers, without clothes, if all that one hears is true. They go to parties swearing like shop stewards (who swear much more fluently than troopers), drinking like men of the Royal Pay Corps – but just before leaving home they make for the perfume bottle.

Why is it that women, who are, one has to admit, the best other sex we have, feel that in order to woo successfully they must smell of something unnatural from a bottle ? It doesn't seem to do very much for men; it does absolutely nothing for me.

If it is self-therapy couldn't they use perfume when they are alone and have a decent bath before they go out ? Possibly a herb bath or a yoghurt bath, or if they have me in mind, just a bath – though a touch of raspberry brandy in the water might be quite nice.

LET'S TAKE THE MOTOR   *Sarah Graham*

When I offered to take Mrs Warren for some drives into the country,
I was given a brisk briefing by the old lady's niece: 'Let's hope the
change of scene will distract her for a time, but don't you listen to a
word she says. Her conversation's quite absurd. She's just not with us.'

Mrs Warren and I hadn't met before, and I'd no idea that she
would become my most memorable passenger. I'd driven the glum,
the critical, the apprehensive, and the enthusiastic 'oh-do-look-ers',
but having Mrs Warren beside me was like driving with a benign
Duchess of Wonderland. Far from being 'absurd' as her niece had
said, I found the old lady's conversation fascinating. By some twist in
her mind it was as though she'd fallen asleep in the days of her real
world, the world of green lanes, cobbled streets and the horse-drawn
carriage, and had woken up into unreality, our world, through whose
forest of signs and mad hordes of traffic she was now being driven by
a stranger. What was she doing, a passenger in this plebeian little car ?
More puzzling still, what were all these crowds of people doing, dart-
ing hither and thither at the direction of so many rude and ridiculous
signs ?

From our very first encounter, I realised that I should have to keep
my wits about me, or else I'd find myself caught up in Mrs Warren's
wayward mood, and then the rules of road safety would scatter to the
winds. I could see that my bucket-seated old car was a most improb-
able setting for this tall black-clad old lady, who carried herself with
such melancholy dignity. She must have sensed my unspoken feelings
of apology for the car, and with a quick turn of courtesy and a startling
unexpectedness of phrase (a combination that I soon came to know as
entirely characteristic) she endeared herself for ever to its owner by
saying, 'I'm sure your motor is very good for the liver, but is it any
good at climbing trees ?'

I was never to know which of the oddities of Mrs Warren's speech
were slips of the tongue and which were slips of the mind, but I
decided there and then that for the sake of the flow of talk and general
amity I'd always assume that she'd made a perfectly commonplace,
sensible remark, and we'd see where that took us. So I answered her
question, 'Is it any good at climbing trees ?' with 'Yes, remarkably
good,' and we set off, in holiday spirits, for the first of our many
drives into the bare winter landscape.

Like most drivers, I find the proliferation and clutter of signs, warnings and directions a great nuisance, but accept them as a necessity. These, to me, quite commonplace signs and signals made Mrs Warren exclaim with astonished amusement and plain incredulity. " 40 ". Forty what ? I can't see forty of anything, can you ? How absurd! "Lay by." Laid by ? Lullaby ? What do they think they mean ? "Children Crossing." How delightful, dear! I always like to see a lot of children. "Give way." Give away, I suppose. Quite so. I've often read that in the Bible – but it doesn't mean give everything, of course – they ought to explain that or people will be wondering what to do. "Stop." Why should we, if they can't take the trouble to say please ?' And the last word on lollipop men, 'I say, do look at that old chap in a pinafore, holding up a banner, I think he rather likes himself, don't you ?'

Traffic lights seemed to her ornamental but pointless. At red we waited, and a string of lorries passed in front of us. Mrs Warren saw this as an act of outstanding politeness on my part, 'How good of you to let those fellows through!' Another time, I paused while a young man crossed the road on a zebra crossing. 'That was very pretty of you,' said Mrs Warren. 'Do you know him intimately ?'

This very old lady, with her deeply lined face and sad grey eyes, looked on the humdrum scenes we passed with an extraordinary freshness. The Midland countryside through which we drove was far from spectacular, in fact it was noticeably drab, but Mrs Warren saw a succession of beauties in it.

'Those four trees on the hill-top, how erect and brave! Oh look . . . those birds on wind-back!'

In her approach to people she had something of the same quality, transformed into a sort of hopefulness for the possibilities of every chance encounter. There was an ingrained courtesy in her manner which was extended to everyone she met. I remember how once she beckoned an unsuspecting mechanic across the forecourt of the garage where we'd just filled up, and to his astonishment she laid her hand on his sleeve and said confidingly, 'We've so much enjoyed our visit here. I do hope you'll call on me soon with your wife.' Her sincerity shone through the oddness of the little speech, and how thankful I was to the young man when he replied, with only the slightest flicker of surprise, 'Thank you, madam, that'll be a pleasure.'

Mrs Warren's enthusiasm for drives grew and grew, and we began to go further afield. She proposed all manner of things, a jaunt to Newmarket, a visit to her old home in Stamford, even a show in town. We had great fun mulling over these plans, but nothing was to come of them. One day I called for her as usual, and was met by the prim-faced niece.

'I'm sorry we couldn't let you know, but we've had to send my aunt away. She was getting altogether too troublesome, and obviously didn't appreciate what any of us were doing for her. I'm afraid those drives were just a waste of your time. She hadn't a clue where you'd been together, and, of course, couldn't take anything in. But don't worry, we've found an excellent nursing home for her, in Devon, and she'll be very well looked after.'

I'm sure she was beautifully looked after, and perhaps, as friends and relations say, she was in the right place, but how I missed her company! Driving became a routine business again, and my reactions to road-signs returned to normal. I never saw Mrs Warren again, but she comes often to my mind as the roads all round us become daily more crowded and the traffic more impatient. 'All these motor-cars! What can people be doing?' For the answer, one could always refer to traffic surveys or the findings of some recent commission, or the earnest investigations of the local Civic Society. But I still prefer Mrs Warren's explanation: 'Ah yes, of course, they'll all be coming in for their luncheon parties!'

THE UNSETTLED   *C. Gordon Glover*

'Then,' proclaims mother, 'there's our Peter – he's the odd one. He's a great worry. He just doesn't seem to want to settle to anything.'

In any place where parents of young people are gathered together we hear these laments. We are told of Tom steadily studying medicine, of Jack doing well as a budding quantity surveyor and of Bob just crazy about his job in catering. Then up pops Peter. And what, we ask, is Peter doing at the moment, then? The parents aren't really quite sure, but the last they heard of him was when he wrote from Sheffield where he was beating the drums in a back-street pub.

'We're terribly worried about Peter.'

I wonder if they need be. We, too, have the near-relative who is the 'odd one,' a big handsome fellow in the second half of his twenties, a conversationalist of great charm, well-read, left wing, a devotee of Wagner, Schoenberg and the Beatles. He does not smoke cannabis resin – though tried it once and said he'd rather have a pint. His clothes vary, according to his current occupation, from sweat-shirt, pullover and jeans to suits of an almost daunting conformity. His hair is trendy, but a good three inches short of shoulder-length.

The near-relative is not a drop-out or layabout. He works with breath-taking ferocity and for relatively brief periods at whatever may be offered to his liking – and sometimes not – at the 'Labour'. He has maintained himself with dignity and in all manner of ways since the age of eighteen, and it is always a pleasure when the telephone rings and the near-relative proposes himself for a short visit.

We never quite know what to expect when we meet the train – the jeans or the twenty-five-guinea suit. Only one thing is certain – a paper carrier-bag containing a change of underwear, toothbrush, razor, egg-head weekly and a couple of paperbacks. The near-relative travels light in the clothes he stands up in.

On one occasion he was in transit to a brickfield in Bedfordshire where, in a spell of labouring and overtime, he hoped to save enough money for his fare to Cuba where he would cut sugar-cane to the glory of Fidel Castro and the memory of Che Guevara.

He laboured for eight weeks, saved the money and turned up, not with a one-way ticket to Cuba, but with an eighty-pound tape-recorder. He had noticed that for the next five days there was to be a feast of Wagnerian roaring on the Music Programme, and, if we didn't mind, he'd like to get the whole lot taped.

We asked – how about Cuba ? He'd not gone *off* Castro, he said, but Cuba remained a high-minded idea, whereas a tape-recorder was a hard fact, a lifetime of spiritual feasting.

His sky is filled with pie, and every so often he gets a taste of it. We were interested when the pie assumed the image of toughness, and he decided to seek acceptance as a Marine Commando. A real man's life, he said. His name was duly taken and he was bidden to report for a Medical in a week's time. He felt he'd better toughen himself up for the Medical, so for five days hurled himself against Snowdonia to the point of almost total debility. Wreck though he was, he impressed a girl whom he met on a night Manchester-London coach. He would forsake the brawny masculinity of life as a Marine Commando, get a well-paid job in London, work for this wonderful girl, marry her and settle down. The money, he assured us, was enormous for strong men young at heart and willing to undergo the ardours of working on the Victoria Line. To his absolute dismay and affronted physical pride he was turned down flat with a 'Sorry, son, but we just don't think you've got what it takes.'

But was he down-hearted for long? Oh, dear me, no. He became in quick succession a petrol-pump attendant, an assistant hall porter in a Manx hotel and for six months, which seemed settlement at last, a reporter on a provincial weekly. The money was less than he received at the petrol pumps, the Municipal Baths and as a waiter in a small Austrian restaurant.

I dare say you may feel this to be the account of a most unsatisfactory and inadequate character, shallow and shifting, unable to settle and do something worthwhile. This is only partly true, since the near-relative knows a great deal more about sundry aspects of life than we do. He is devastatingly witty about them, and has only to enter the saloon bar of our little country pub of a Sunday morning to be greeted with delighted cries of affection by all assembled.

Well-rooted persons, they drink up the spicy nectar of the rootless, and admire the gaiety with which the way of life is lived.

The near-relative is generous in his judgements and with whatever money he may happen to have. He never *asks* for money and owes not a penny to any man. His younger brother, who is thrifty, diligent and charged with worries, isn't really much fun to have about the place. One of this young fellow's principal worries is the person he refers to as 'my poor benighted fool of a brother'. He pities him, and the pity is mutual.

Once upon a time we, too, were worried about the near-relative, but no longer. Rather feckless and infinitely reckless, he proceeds through life not as a tram but as the next bus to anywhere, cheerful, open-minded and game for anything.

EMANATIONS *Muriel Waddington*

My sense of taste had never returned to me after an attack of flu. I found that savoury dishes, in fact anything with salt in it, tasted like brine, and sweet things pretty sickly. Everything I ate had the nightmare quality of some kind of revolting mush. It was bad enough to be deprived of the joy of eating, but as a housewife, although I could remain 'a good plain cook', anything subtle or adventurous was now quite beyond me. I had no idea how any new sauce or dish was progressing, nor finally what peculiar concoctions I had produced.

The G.P. whom I had seen had said to me, 'How old are you? Ah, well, we have to learn to live with these things, don't we?' Which, of course drove me to fringe medicine.

What a variety there is at the periphery of the profession! I tried all sorts, I was desperate; I would gladly have consulted a witch-doctor if I had known of one in the vicinity. Eventually, I found myself sitting in the consulting-room of a charming and unusual man who was instructing me to acquire some jewellery. 'You must wear topaz,' he said suddenly. 'That's it,' he repeated, 'you must get your husband to buy you a topaz.'

This strange little man had been peering into one of the books that littered his desk and this was the instruction that he gave me.

'I don't quite understand,' I said.

'Emanations, my dear,' he replied. 'Emanations.'

'Of course,' I said. I respected this man's advice – he had cured me of other ailments.

My husband, who was waiting for me in the car, listened attentively, and then gave me what is known as an old-fashioned look; he thought it was a devious method to remind him that my birthday was imminent.

A week or so later, however, he was in London and, remembering the topaz affair, he wandered into a jeweller's.

'May I see something in topaz?' he asked.

'Certainly,' replied the assistant, producing a delightful ring with a beautiful stone.

'How much would that be?' asked my husband.

'Two hundred and fifteen pounds,' was the reply.

We are on a modest pension and this amount would keep us for months. My husband thought that a pendant might be cheaper and that any emanations would be much nearer my mouth, so he inquired again.

'A pendant, sir? Certainly. A very fine one here; beautiful stone, fine gold chain, only three hundred and fifty pounds.' As Robin started to move towards the door, the assistant continued, 'We have other stones, you know, but you may be wanting a particular birthstone.'

'No,' answered Robin, 'for medical reasons, emanations, you know.'

The young man in the shop looked rather scared and my husband moved out. But the hunt was on.

One day, as we were passing an antique shop, a delightful little topaz necklet caught our eye, a Victorian trinket for a mere thirty pounds. After the shock of Regent Street, to my husband, this was almost a gift; in fact he was feeling for his cheque-book when I remembered all those sheets, sides to middles, that I wanted replacing. I had to kick him on the ankle to divert his attention from the extravagance, and from my rather speculative cure.

Another day we found a charming little art shop with pictures, cards and pottery, and also stones of all descriptions. We went in and described exactly what we wanted, 'for the emanations, you know.'

'Of course,' said the shopkeeper, not even raising an eyebrow. 'But unfortunately I haven't any topaz at the moment, but if you go down to the left, you will find a little jeweller's who may be able to help you.'

We followed the directions and discovered a tiny shop down three steps. When the door was opened, and we had eased ourselves in, the locks were thrown again behind us and we found ourselves in what seemed to be a treasure house. Once again the owner of the shop heard our request without registering the slightest surprise, saying only, 'Of course, but it must be pure topaz,' and thereafter he turned out box after box of rare and magnificent stones, some just beautiful, some very valuable as well.

We tried to dissuade him, we were taking so much of his time, but we were locked in and he refused to be diverted from the search. Eventually he found it, a small lump of transparent stone, hardly worthy of the name of topaz.

He held it out. 'There we are,' he said, 'the pure stone.' And he proceeded to show us its particular properties.

In fear and trepidation we asked, 'How much would that cost?'

'Oh, say thirty shillings,' he answered.

We bought it, and when he had unlocked the door, we left the shop clutching our newly acquired treasure.

Which is why, if you meet me, you'll see a small piece of rather grubby, browny-yellowish rock hanging about my neck.

And my sense of taste? Oh, the topaz never touched it, made no difference at all in my case. No, I cured that with a few shillings' worth of herbs; I read a recipe in a magazine for a tisane of verbena – which did the trick!

HOW WELL YOU'RE LOOKING   *Peter Bull*

Peter Bull is an actor, writer, and amateur on teddy bears, which were the subject of his recent book.

It's curious what a devastating effect an innocent remark can have on one, if it is badly timed. How often have you been furious when some-one has said, 'How well you are looking!' when you are in fact feeling ghastly or recovering from a hangover? The reverse is also true. 'You look a bit pale. Are you sure you're all right?' when, for once, you're on top of the world and in the pink of condition. Then there is the direct attack. 'You have put on weight,' or 'How thin you've got,' are pronunciamentos which come to other people's lips far too readily, not that the second phrase has ever been, or indeed is likely to be, addressed to me, alas!

Then there is the identity gambit which always seems to me extremely hazardous. 'You're exactly like someone I used to know in the army,' tends to make me dislike the speaker at sight or rather sound. He usually delivers the line with a condescending smile and intonation as if he were conferring a great honour on one. He very rarely elaborates on the likeness or submits an Identi-Kit of his friend's character but I don't think there is anyone in the world who wants to be told that he or she has a double lurking around. There is something spooky about the idea and the phrase 'spitting image' has never endeared itself to me. Another hopeless and unanswerable opener is, 'It is you, isn't it?' usually spoken by a face one has never seen in one's life and hopes never to see again.

Being an actor one is frequently accosted by total strangers who are convinced that they know you personally, having met you on their midget screens in lounges, bedrooms, or mother-in-laws' houses. Usually the encounter starts with a penetrating stare which makes one think one has not adjusted one's dress properly. Then the braver specimens advance for a verbal attack. 'I know you, don't I?' is the customary approach. I tend to remain impassive and totally unhelpful, favouring them with a wry but quizzical smile.

After several floundering sentences they give up and say 'I know the face . . .' and retire defeated. Sometimes I come to the rescue and volunteer my name but this step is usually disastrous for both parties. They look even more puzzled and are, I think, convinced that I've given them an alias and the whole operation isn't very good for my morale. So I usually look sadly at them and slink away, hoping that they may imagine that I'm one of those lovely wrestlers who bite each other on Saturday afternoons while one is waiting to check one's pools.

Sometimes the assailant is certain that he or she knows more about you and your career than you do yourself and it's rather depressing to be assured over and over again that one was in *Oliver* and *A Man for All Seasons* when one hadn't in fact even been offered a role in either of these splendid entertainments on stage or screen. 'Oh, but you were in it,' the idiots insist, even after I have assured them that they are mistaking me for some other ample character artiste.

But in our profession we are really up against it when it comes to the layman and his comments and questions. 'Do you have to do it every night ?' (if one happens to be in a West End play), 'Does the make-up hurt ?' and 'How do you know when it's your turn to speak ?' are typical examples.

And heaven help you if you are in a television programme which has displeased the majority of the viewers. In the days when there were still greengrocers, butchers, florists and fishmongers in my part of the King's Road, Chelsea, I had to be very careful what engagements I accepted, or I'd be greeted the following day by cries of 'The things you do for money, nowadays, Mr Bull!' or 'Hello, Strangler.' On these occasions one was often forced back indoors to face possible starvation.

But I think my most unfavourable form of address was used the other day as I was coming out of the laundry, minding my own business and doing nobody any harm. ''Ello,' a voice said just behind me and I turned to face a cheerful man waiting at the bus stop. I said 'Hello' politely because I was at a school where the motto was 'Manners Makyth Man'.

'You 'aven't been very busy lately,' the voice continued.

I was absolutely livid. I explained that there were other media in which I could find employment. I told him of the films I'd made recently in Hollywood, the plays in which I'd starred on Broadway and Shaftesbury Avenue and of the best-sellers and film scripts I had written. When I came to the end of my mythical achievements, he smiled pityingly, 'Yes, but you 'aven't been on telly,' as if I'd committed some frightful crime.

If I'd known what bus he was catching, I would have pushed him under it.

ON APPROACHING FORTY *Claire Rayner*

Last week I achieved – with the best will in the world I can't pretend I celebrated – the age of thirty-nine, the start of my fortieth year. A sobering thought, because all my life so far I've been young. But from here on I've got to accept the fact that I belong in the ranks of the middle-aged. No longer can I feel secure in the knowledge that people half my age are mere children. They aren't. They're parents themselves, a lot of them, with a new generation crowding their heels.

So, a time for taking stock. A time for putting away into moth-balls the hopes and joys that have filled my life so far, a time for finding replacements for them.

I suppose the first thing that I must wrap in tissue paper is anticipation. I used to look forward so much, wondering, planning, dreaming. Would I have a career? Would I marry? Have children? In the intoxicating young years the road ahead was a marvellously mysterious one, twisting, shadowed, with who knew what splendid excitement lurking round each corner.

But now I know what lay round those corners. I've got my career. No more struggles to make the grade now. I have my husband – a splendid one in every way – so no new men to meet and judge as potential husband material. I have my children, three of them, so no more hopeful pregnancies for me. The road ahead now runs straight into the horizon, shadowed only by the possibility of something nasty happening. The exciting shadows just aren't there.

Is there anything to replace this loss of eager anticipation? Well, yes. I'm one of the lucky ones; for me reality has turned out to be immensely better than the fantasies I wove in my teen years. My career is deeply satisfying. Marriage is marvellous, full of humour and comfort and security. Sex has turned out to be infinitely more fun than even the most torrid of my adolescent yearnings. And the real children who allow me to share their lives are a great deal more delightful than the cardboard cut-outs I visualised.

And I have a degree of security that I could never have known would be possible. It's comforting to have achieved that career; comforting to know I won't die a disappointed virgin; comforting to realise I have my hope of immortality in my offspring. But I must be honest. Sweet as is the taste of security, it hasn't that special savour that anticipation had. It's a bit like the difference between a good wholesome treacle pudding and a soufflé surprise.

And what else must lie locked away with anticipation ? I shall miss enthusiasm. There was a time when I would go off at half-cock about all sorts of things – questions political, moral, social. A new cause was espoused with a burning eagerness that was marvellously heady. But there is something slightly ludicrous about forty-year-olds who rush about waving banners and crying, 'Woe, woe unto the nations.' Not for nothing do the words 'angry' and 'young' slot together so inevitably.

But at least I shan't miss that sick taste left behind when one of my enthusiasms fizzled out and died in a few damp and silly splutters. When I boil over nowadays, and I still do it occasionally, I can keep the fire burning with the fuel of rational thought, and keep it burning longer. Maybe even get some results.

There is one thing I shall lay away with a deep sense of relief; the anguish of looking wrong in a purely physical sense. Most of my friends of my age mourn the diminution of their girlish good looks. I don't because I never had any. The slightly sagging figure, the less upstanding bosom, the greying hair, the lining face – I welcome them for they are an undoubted improvement on the moon-faced hefty awkward girl I used to be. As my fortieth birthday comes zooming towards me, I can at last accept the matronly looks I've had since I was sixteen – damn it, I am a matron. And one splendid thing about having been undoubtedly fat all my adult life is that fat faces are rarely scraggy haggard ones! When you've always had dewlaps anyway, you've learned to live with them when you've reached my age.

I can't think of anything else to put regretfully away for ever. But I've found other things that come with age that I never knew would be so enjoyable. Like nostalgia. Wallowing in the music of the thirties and forties, swopping reminiscences of a wartime childhood with contemporaries while younger people look on, mystified, is fun. Being free of the agonising indecisions of adolescence, with the doubts about whether one is behaving correctly or not, all melted away, is delightful. Now, I know how little it matters if one makes a fool of oneself; that laughing at your own idiocies instead of weeping about them brings a new dimension to living. The pleasure of having developed a definite taste – to be able to say I like that dress, that picture, that music, without caring whether or not one is displaying philistinism–that's one of the unsung joys of maturity.

On balance then, it's great to be knocking forty. I'm not over the hill yet, not slithering hopelessly down the lower slopes into toothless senility. I'm standing on the peak, and do you know something ? The view is lovely.

THE UNIVERSE OVER MY HEAD   *David Scott Blackhall*

Mr Blackhall – a very popular broadcaster – is blind. He is the compère of the radio programme In Touch.

When I was a young man, up to the age of forty, I used to think vaguely what fun it would be to sleep in the garden. Now that I am six times a grandfather, and past forty, I realise that there's no reason why I shouldn't. This is my third summer, according to the calendar, that I have slept in the garden, a metal and plastic folding bed between me and Mother Earth, a down sleeping-bag for comfort and all heaven for a bedspread. It seems like wasting my life to go to sleep because the night intoxicates me and the farthest corner of the universe is within my fingers' reach and everything is twice as real and a hundred times more wonderful.

Because my garden is not completely secluded and because there are such things as neighbours, I compromise in the matter of sleeping apparel. I would feel a bit self-conscious in my orange and gold pyjamas, so I settle for denims, a sport shirt and, occasionally a pullover. The children next door can see me from their bedroom window and I'm told that they are under the impression that I am there to guard them. Anonymous inmates of two houses in the next road could also see me from their bedroom windows, if they were really determined. Good luck to them!

Merging and mellowing into the night, alone with the faint, sacred and slumbering noises of a world without end, I invent, out of my head and out of the darkness, a dozen or so glittering iambic pentameters which would have done credit to Shakespeare. Which, indeed, he would have written himself if he had slept out and given his mind to it.

I remember, for example, that tomorrow I am to give the address for morning service at a nearby Prep School, and in the twinkling of a star I am standing there majestically, an archetypal blind soothsayer, with golden precepts rolling from my tongue, the boys all wide-eyed and the masters agog. Never mind that tomorrow the reality will be a humdrum affair. Tonight it is magnificent, the experience of a lifetime, unforgettable.

Or I think, perhaps, that it's time I gave another talk for *Woman's Hour* and the words spill over me and every phrase is a poem, alive and shining with music and magic. And everything comes, as Keats said all poetry should come or not at all, as naturally as the leaves to a tree. And afterwards, listeners write to me and say enthusiastic and unexpected things, like, 'I wonder if you have ever broadcast before.'

I begin a sonnet, writing the flame-coloured words across the sky, and the very first line I shape says so much, and says it so clearly and so exquisitely, that the other thirteen lines would be superfluous, so I say the line over and over, and I am content with the only one-line sonnet in English Literature.

There is nothing in the world so romantic as hearing the first stir of feathers, the first call of the morning. Especially when you are there, sharing the earliest chink of day with an exultant thrush. For Browning, morning was at seven and the hillside was dew-pearled. For me, morning is when the stars die and the starlings come to life, round about half past four, and the sleeping-bag is dew-pearled, and I am snug and waterproof inside it and I wonder was it yesterday the world began, the sky no wider than my garden.

It is a shyly secret thing to dial the number of the London Weather Report and hear that the night will be fine and dry with long, clear periods. As I climb into my sleeping-bag, I am making a niche for myself in a corner of the sky. I pull the shadows in after me and I zip up the universe, not quite over my head. In the time of a falling star, in one rustle of a leaf, I hold the history of mankind in the palm of my hand and I am all the poets and prophets since the beginning of the world. Bright star, I whisper to my pillow, would thou wert steadfast as I am!

At a quarter past four, a cat jumps on to my bed and scares the living daylights out of me. It begins to rain. Every storm (I have discovered) begins with a single, small, sharp drop which falls with the uttermost accuracy into my uppermost eye. I fumble with zip and slippers, fold up my bed and totter indoors. I clothe my soul with a body, the light-fingered morning, night and the world are all thumbs again, and nothing, not even the weather report, is true any more.

MY DEATH WISHES *Rosemary Meynell*

I don't want my loved-ones to say, 'She wouldn't want any fuss.' It will be *my* day and I want a lot of fuss and trouble-taking to have everything just as I wish.

I want a nice plain coffin, not a mass produced chocolate-box affair; and I want it carried in and out of the church by four stalwart chaps, not wheeled on a sort of silver tea-trolley. My grandfather's bearers were his friends, but I am prepared to settle for professional undertakers who know their job because, let's face it, friends are apt to mismanage things, especially if they are feeling emotional and have had a drink or two to cheer themselves up. But, as I say, I want human bearers; after all I only weigh eight stone plus and it won't be a hard job for them. I don't want to be cremated. I know it is easier and tidier but I want to be buried in the country churchyard where I belong, facing east in the traditional way. By the way, I should have made it clear earlier on that I am not donating any part of what St Francis called 'poor donkey, my body', to medical science. I realise it is selfish of me but it just happens I don't want to. So no transplants, please. I want the good earth and the grass and flowers to have all of me.

I don't want the service to be ecumenical. My Roman Catholic and Methodist friends, and the agnostics too, must put up with the pure unadulterated 1662 Anglican burial service. There is nothing more beautiful or more basic. Anyway, it is what I want.

If an organist is available, I should like some music and a few simple hymns. But if the congregation is small and there is no choir, I should prefer them just to say the appropriate psalms including, of course, the Nunc Dimittis – 'Now lettest thou Thy servant depart in peace . . .'

I have a nasty feeling people will say, 'Dear Rosemary wouldn't want us to travel far, or go to any inconvenience or expense to get to the funeral.' In fact, I hope all my friends and relations who are not ill or infirm, will make an effort to come and I think they will be glad they came. I'll tell you why in a minute. Unless they have strong views about not wearing mourning, I shall expect them to be soberly dressed. Black ties please! After all they wouldn't go to a wedding in inappropriate clothes. For the women, I shall leave provision in my will for a small prize for the best blacked-out person.

The announcement of my death will not say, 'No flowers. Dona-
tions to etc.' I love flowers and I want them in profusion at my funeral.
I prefer simple cut flowers rather than wreaths but florists must live
and people must do what they like in this matter.

After the funeral, I want everyone who has bothered to come to
have a nice party with plenty of good food and drink. I want hosts and
hostesses appointed – is this asking too much ? – who will gather up
stragglers from the churchyard who may not have transport and con-
vey them to some appropriate home or hostelry, making sure of
course that they are people who knew me and not mere idle onlookers.
I have many friends, and I hope someone will go round and introduce
them all to each other so that no one is left out or lonely. And, in an
adjoining room to the party, I want a sort of White Elephant stall of
all my minor possessions; good clothes, silver, jewellery, books and
things not specifically mentioned in my will. And I want everyone
present to choose something to take away with them as a little
memento and reward for going to so much trouble. And no rushing
please, to get the best!

And then there is the question of a headstone. I am sorry but I *do*
want one, and my legatees will be expected to spare something from
what I leave them to pay for it. I want them to commission an up-and-
coming artist-craftsman who is good at lettering, and leave it to him
to produce something worthy of the churchyard and its old Norman
church. I don't want undertakers' marble. I want a good local stone
and a hand-made job. It will cost a packet, but never mind, it's what
I want!

Triumphs and Adversities

OPEN LETTER TO AN UNMARRIED MOTHER

I have often wished I could write this letter . . . on the baby's birthdays, on the anniversary of the day he came to us, at Christmas, and on all the occasions of all his achievements. The day he cut his first tooth, the day he walked for the first time, the day he learnt to ride a bike . . . many days.

Many, many days, I have wanted to share with you all the joy your baby has brought to us. In my imagination, I have tried to share too the grief of your decision. Secretly on his first few birthdays I cried with you; ached to tell you he was all right; happy and loved. And then, as the birthdays have passed, I have been glad that my grief for you has become more contained as time has distanced it from its occasion.

I have taken comfort from the fact that this is the way of grief, and of time, and, as the years have passed, I have dared to hope that for you too it has been like this – and that now we can smile a little at each other through our birthday tears, knowing that all is well.

Although adoption is, for us, solemn – in the way that any vows are solemn – we have never been able to feel earnest or pompous or weighed down by the responsibility of our adoptive state. Like other parents, we have learnt mostly from our mistakes . . . and most from our children.

As your baby has grown we have told him what we know of you – that you were young when he was born, and kind and loving and worried about what would be best for him. You had no house, we said, and no cot and no pram, and because you weren't married you had no husband to go out and work to earn the money to buy these things – and you said to yourself, 'If I go out to work, who will look after the baby ?''

And you knew, we said, how babies need a mother to look after them, and how little boys like to have a father to go fishing with, and you said to yourself, 'I don't want to part with my baby because I love him so.'

We told him then, how you were filled with courage and how you thought, 'But I mustn't just think of myself. I must think about what is best for the baby.' And you decided that life with a mother and a father, and a house and a cot and a pram and brothers and sisters would be best for him. And that was how it came about that he came to us, to enrich our lives and bring such warmth and depth to us.

Long ago, this was one of his favourite stories, but now time has given acceptance to him too, and he understands.

I hope you are glad to hear that adoption is not earnest for him either, and that he can cope.

One day, I heard another child say to him, 'You're second-hand you know.' I held my breath . . .

In a hundred years I should never have thought of the inspired answer that came bubbling cheerfully from your delightful child— and our delightful child . . .

'I know,' he said, and burst out laughing . . . 'I'm a priceless antique. Very valuable. Everybody wants me.'

And this was how I knew that it had been right not to guard him from the truth of his situation. He was only ten, but from not being shielded from the truth, he had learnt already to guard the truth against distortion. And to guard it—not with the ponderous armour of defensive explanation, but with the open grace of humour.

When you trusted him to our keeping, you hoped that when he grew up we would tell him that you loved him.

Most of all, I have wanted to write this letter so that you will know that we have . . . and that he knows.

ACID   *Diana Haydock and Molly Scobie*

Since this broadcast, Diana Haydock has married and is now living in Sweden.
As an attractive girl of eighteen she was disfigured by acid, thrown into her face by a jealous boy. Here she talks to Molly Scobie.

DIANA HAYDOCK: Like most eighteen year olds who are fairly attractive I was very, very vain, spent a lot of money on make-up, and clothes were my main interest. I spent much too much time going out having a good social life rather than doing what I should be doing.

MOLLY SCOBIE: What were you studying ?

HAYDOCK: Well, I was just doing a general education course. I didn't really know what I wanted to do when I finished, although I had a vague idea that I'd like to have a go at modelling.

SCOBIE: I believe you were whisked away quickly after the attack. Can you recall what you thought as it happened?

HAYDOCK: Well, as it happened I realised – I didn't know what had been thrown but I realised it was something that would disfigure me and my main concern was to get something done as quickly as possible to counteract this and so I screamed madly. Everyone in the College acted very quickly and they washed it with bicarbonate and one thing and another and then they sent me off to the local hospital where they just did as much as they could with the eye and sent me on to the burns unit at Roehampton. I had an idea from books and movies that I wouldn't be allowed to see a mirror and there didn't seem to be any around so I didn't dare ask for one. But within a few days I persuaded my mother to bring one in and she was quite willing and so I studied myself in the mirror from day to day then. As the time came for my going home I thought, 'Oh dear, how am I going to manage?' And then when I got home I thought, 'Well, the most important thing is to go out straight away.' So the first Saturday morning when it's very busy in the shopping areas I went out with my mother and everyone stared but having got that first initial outing over, I didn't mind it so much.

I think the most difficult thing to deal with was walking along a road when you'd be coming to a group of road workers and they'd see a girl walking towards them and start whistling and calling out remarks and then as you got nearer they'd realise what your face looked like and they'd be terribly embarrassed and you'd be terribly embarrassed and no one would know where to look. And this was really awkward. The thing that I resented most, I suppose, was when people would say, 'What happened?' And I'd tell them as briefly as I could and they'd immediately say, 'Oh, my God, your poor mother.' And I used to think, 'Well, yes, you know it isn't very nice for her but then it's a great deal worse for me.' And then they'd quite often make this worse from my mother's point of view, I thought, by saying, 'Well, have you got any brothers and sisters?' And when I said I had a sister they'd say, 'Oh, well, that's not so bad for her then.' As though, you know, this made it all right.

SCOBIE: Do you feel bitter towards the boy who attacked you?

HAYDOCK: Well, I don't think I've felt bitter. I knew nothing really about his background – I didn't know him very well. It seems that

he just had an obsessional crush on me – it could have been anyone else as well as me – the fact that it was me meant that I had to
deal with the thing. It's a fact that it happened and that's what I've
had to cope with.

SCOBIE: How has this affected your social life?

HAYDOCK: For the two years that I was in and out of hospital constantly I didn't have much of a social life except with very good
friends.

SCOBIE: You've been travelling quite a bit over the past few years –
have you found that attitudes towards you differ in different
countries?

HAYDOCK: When I'd been abroad I found that in France everyone just stops dead in their tracks and stares, and you just don't know
where to look. And I was in India a year or so ago and there it was
slightly different. Everyone was very uninhibited and people used to
come up and ask me about it and they asked in such a friendly way
that you just didn't mind and I sort of chattered away quite gaily
about it. But then in the Scandinavian countries I think people are a
little more inhibited and they don't register any sort of reaction at all.

One thing I rather miss now that things are much better is that I
got much better treatment in shops and on buses and amongst all
sorts of people when the whole thing looked very, very bad because
people felt sorry for you. And they felt that perhaps you weren't
quite all there anyway, because people have still got this attitude that
someone physically upset in some way is likely to be a bit mentally
retarded too. So that people would remember me in shops and give
me good service and bus conductors would be quite willing to change
five pound notes for threepenny fares and all this has gone now, so I
think – well, it did have some advantages.

SCOBIE: What are your plans for the future?

HAYDOCK: Well, I'm engaged to a Swede so I work for a few
weeks and save my money up madly, and then rush over there for
a couple of weeks.

Throughout all this period so many people just said to me 'Oh, you
should write a book about this' that I thought, 'Well, I will, I'll show
them, I'll get down to it and write a book.' But I keep putting it off
and don't really get round to starting. But I would like sometime to
try and either use the whole situation as the basis for a novel, or else
write a straight autobiography – I don't know.

THE WIDOWER *John Jarrett*

My wife and I had been married for nineteen years when she died. Suddenly, our lifetime together was sheared in two.

No one ever again can mend the break in the shared adventure of a marriage. No one else can know about times such as the night we decided to make our first baby . . . the day I came home with the news that I had lost my job, and she didn't fuss . . . the first Sunday we stepped inside the house we were building and it was plaster-splattered and damp and raw and all ours . . . those vigils every night for ten days when our first child sweated and suffered with gastro-enteritis. These moments I can only relive with one person, and she is gone.

But if you are faced as I was, with remaking a life, you carry on. I plan the meals, I put out the laundry, I shop, I cook, I sew. I'm lucky – I can do these things. Not that there aren't women kind enough to help. But it isn't easy to accept the idea of some other woman doing these things for me in her house.

And for endless months afterwards I found I was vulnerable. Out of a book falls an old shopping list, in her handwriting. A passer-by says cheerily, 'Haven't seen your missus lately. How is she ?'

The children recover. It's terrible, and merciful, how quickly they pick up their lives. But now, as well as authority and ruler, I am also comforter and buffer.

When my daughter, within six months of her mother's death, fell head over heels in love for the first time in her seventeen-year-old life, I was delighted. It was just what she needed.

But she also needed a mother. She needed a feminine reaction when, ever so casually, she pointed to him and said, 'Don't you think he's nice ?' There was only me, so I manoeuvred to get the two of them together under the right conditions. She needed a shoulder to cry on with great gulping sobs when the holiday came to an end and she waved goodbye to him as the car drew away. There was only me. I don't know if I did it well enough, but I tried.

I worked, how I worked, because while I was busy at my job, I could forget and laugh. And in the evening until the children went to bed, there were tears to be wiped, noses to be blown, homework to be checked, school scandals to be listened to and the cleanness or dirti-ness of underwear to be checked.

But when they were all in bed, the silence of the house closed in. I found that I was talking to myself a little and even though it seemed silly, I went on doing it. Because you need someone to tell about all the little triumphs and troubles of the day.

For instance, my wife was the driver in our family. An American, like all Americans she seemed born behind a wheel. Now I had to learn. It would have been nice to have told her proudly that I had passed my test, even at the third go. My younger daughter sailed into a good new school and neighbours said, 'Isn't she clever?' But it wasn't really their praise we wanted.

Everyone assumes that I will marry again. My wife had said she would want me to, it would be a compliment to her. But I am shy of facing up to seeing what kind of love a man of forty can offer the second woman in his life. Oh, men do remarry, I know, successfully. There can be a new physical excitement, a new building up of shared memories, even (I would hope) more children.

But you cannot drink twice from the same river, as the proverb goes, and however warm and gentle the new water is, it does not have the sparkle and brightness of the first stream of love. It's hard to settle for less, if you've had that. And although at moments, like many married couples, we made life hell for each other, we had, unlike many married couples, perfect, shining days.

And where and how does a widower find his wife or do his courting? Our friends were those we watched fall in love and marry and have families at the time we did. And even if I should meet some woman of the right age who is unmarried or herself widowed, a friendship is difficult because the question of marriage hangs in the air between us from our first word.

The neighbours who drop in say how well I manage and tell me that time is a great healer. They must be right, I suppose, or I couldn't laugh or look at another woman or talk about my wife. All I know is that I still wake in the night and fling out an arm to draw her to me in our bed.

I go downstairs, make a cup of tea, smoke a cigarette, read a little. It's hopeless to try to go straight back to sleep. And as I sit there alone in the quiet house, I wonder – how long do you go on being haunted?

LEARNING AGAIN   *Frances Newns*

The doctor was doing his rounds. My bed was the seventh in line and I waited impatiently expecting the news I had been longing to hear – 'Yes, you can go home now.'

How many months had I been wearing that calliper around my leg ? Was it three or four ? I'd got so frustrated at having to take everything easy. My life had been nothing but sports, athletics, swimming and horse-riding. I never worried about anything until now. I lay and dreamed of all the things I was going to do – for instance, practise really hard at running and perhaps reach international standards. Then I was sharply brought back to the present as the doctor came to my bed and sat down. He put his warm hand on my shin, looked into my eyes and in a matter-of-fact voice said, 'Well, I'm sorry – it's got to come off. There is a strong possibility that the infection will spread to the rest of your body. I am sorry, but it is the best thing to do, and it must be done tomorrow.' I closed my eyes and lay back and when I looked up he'd gone.

Time seemed to be going so quickly as I lay there, with the tears running down my cheeks, thinking of everything I had ever done, and would never be able to do again. Another doctor came to see me and asked if I would like to know anything. Oh yes, there were hundreds of questions. How long would the operation take ? Where were they going to take it off from ? Would there be a lot of pain ? Would I walk again ?

Yes, there would be pain but it wouldn't last for long and I would certainly walk again. The doctor sat patiently and kindly answering my questions for what must have been over an hour; I kept wriggling my toes and feeling my leg, knowing that tomorrow it wouldn't be there.

It was almost a relief to get on to the stretcher the next morning, my fear dulled by heavy tranquillisers. My last thought was, 'Please don't let me wake up.'

I shall never forget waking up. I opened my eyes and stared at the ceiling. It took me a long time to pluck up my courage to look down. When I did, it seemed ridiculous. It was just gone! I don't know quite what I expected, but it amazed me that there was nothing there.

The first day and night were the worst. It was nothing but pain. I couldn't feel the wound actually hurting, just awful 'pins and needles' in the foot and a sharp throbbing pain in the shin where the infection used to be.

It may sound funny, but the next ten days were very happy. Although now the pain was almost unbearable and I cringed every time I looked at the bandage-wreathed stump, people were so nice to me it seemed unfair to feel sorry for myself.

Ten days afterwards when some of the stitches had been removed, I was sent to the limb-fitting centre at Roehampton. Here I had my next biggest shock. People of every age and description – each with one or two, or maybe more limbs missing, were milling around a huge waiting room. The new arrivals, like me, sitting in wheelchairs and looking with bewilderment and horror at all the different types of limbs.

After the doctor had showed me the metal leg I would eventually be wearing – it looked so ugly and uncomfortable – I was measured for my first leg. Not the final one, just a metal frame with a socket that must be worn until the stump had lost its swelling and some of its muscles, so that the final leg would fit properly for a few years. This takes about three months – three months of people staring and children pointing; and hobbling and falling and still pain. The pain in the leg that is no longer there – an itch perhaps or even cramp, which was very bewildering. But I had already started to fit in with the leg-less group. Most of the people I had met at Roehampton were cheerful and called their stump some name and joked about themselves. It didn't take me long to get used to it and I soon found I could get around quite quickly. I wanted to try everything just to prove that I was the same as everyone else. I found I could climb trees and ride without my leg on, although I had a few spills, and I played cricket and football and all sorts of ridiculous things.

Then the long months of waiting were over and my new metal leg was fitted on. It felt like a lump of lead – but I was told it was one of the most up-to-date ones there were. There were no belts or straps any more, it stayed on by suction. I looked at myself in the mirror for ages, from every different angle. Admittedly, it was metal, but it was a leg; it bent at the knee, was the same shape and made me look – well – almost normal. I felt like a girl again. This, of course, was terribly important. What would men think of me now ? A girl to me was soft and gentle, should walk with poise and at the same time be able to do most things that a man can, but always remain graceful. I thought I'd never be able to do it with this hard, cumbersome object clinging to me. But I was going to have a damned good try. So I learned to walk again properly, with hardly any limp and no sticks or anything. I had to learn to get on and off buses, escalators, up and down stairs, and to get up if I fell. It was good fun really, learning all these things and becoming over the weeks happy and cheerful. I am twenty-one now, and it's almost six years since the operation. I am still finding out about things like what sort of stockings to wear. I'm perfectly happy. I've learned to ride again, bicycles and horses, which has meant more to me than anything, and I go for long walks and dance all night. There are compensations. Maxis for instance. And in the evenings, I show one leg in a long dress or my bare mid-riff or back. And of course, there is always the funny side. I bet you have never got up in the morning after a wild party the night before, where you ended up rather merry, to find a dent the size of an apple in your shin.

So my life, even with all its problems, and frustrations, is probably fuller than those of a lot of people. Because, when you lose something like this, you realise the value of life, of friends, of people who want to help you, and I know it may sound absurd but I sincerely believe that I have benefited, not lost.

IT DOESN'T HAPPEN TO PEOPLE LIKE US *Nancy Richards*

Most people would agree that Shelter is doing a marvellous job. Many would qualify this with the thought that it's a losing job – those they help will just go on needing help – they're that type. Homelessness doesn't happen to ordinary people like us, does it ?

I've just gained a teaching certificate and started the final year of a B.Ed. course. My elder son has gone up to university this term. My younger son is an intelligent handful. Several autumns ago, we were destitute and homeless.

My marriage was irrevocably broken; the situation, both materially and emotionally, had reached a stage where breakdown for me, and separation for my sons, seemed inevitable. A member of the Samaritans had arranged for me to take a job as housekeeper to a widower with two children. I'd refused to consider the post unless it offered reasonable security, which my sons, particularly the younger, badly needed.

The work was hard. It included cleaning a four-storey house, personal laundry, and cooking and serving a formal lunch every day. I took the younger child to school, collecting him in the middle of preparing lunch.

My elder son joined us at the end of the first week. At the end of the second I was given a week's notice. I was told I was an excellent housekeeper and an exceptional cook, but my employer felt that my elder son just would not fit. Fourteen is not the most ingratiating age in a boy's life, I admit, but a week hardly seemed a fair trial. My employer was sorry, but he couldn't possibly give me longer notice – he'd engaged another housekeeper and needed our rooms.

I learned later that I was one of a succession of housekeepers in this post and my predecessor had been given equally short notice. There appears to be no legal protection for a woman in this situation – few of them are in a position to insist on a written contract when they take a post.

The following week was grim, as I'd no extra time off to find accommodation. First I tried the domestic agencies. One employer would have welcomed my elder son – but didn't feel that he and his wife could tolerate a small boy. The matron of a girls' boarding school was quite happy about the younger one – but didn't think that a teenage boy was suitable.

The council housing department were willing to place my name on their list, which made me eligible for housing in twelve months' time. No, they had no temporary accommodation. All those big empty houses ? Part of the redevelopment scheme and not available for letting.

In desperation, I rang the Salvation Army. Very distressed, the warden of the local girls' home said she just hadn't any accommodation at all for the boys – but we were all welcome to a meal at any time. Her kindness nearly broke me and it was some time before I felt able to face my sons again.

The next day at one o'clock, with all our belongings and just four pounds, we drove away in a taxi – with no idea of where we would sleep that night. The taxi-driver was the first link in the chain which rescued us. He took us to a clean, friendly boarding-house whose owner, married to a refugee, was willing to take us in at cut rates. One always finds kindness, in any situation, but this was constructive help of the kind we badly needed.

During the next week, I walked the streets of that lovely town, golden beneath its turning chestnut trees and apparently completely indifferent to our misery.

Outside almost the last estate agent's, I was approached by a man who had sensed the desperation in my inquiry. He knew of a flat, not much of a place, but it might do. He took me round to the address in his car and the woman said, yes, I could have the flat if her husband agreed when he came home. That endless seven hours! But the old-fashioned key was the most magnificent present I'd ever had.

There were still hardships ahead. The National Assistance Board, as it was called then, refused to help me pay the necessary week's rent in advance – so my engagement ring went. My small son became ill and so I couldn't take a job. My landlord became difficult when he found that I was living on National Assistance.

Only during the last year have the skies seemed to be clearing – but nothing has equalled that nightmare of homelessness, when there seemed to be no organisation, official or otherwise, with both the will and the power to help us.

Homelessness can happen to 'people like us' – and there was no Shelter when it happened to my sons and me.

TOO OLD *John Parsons*

I must tell you that to be abruptly taken from the mainstream of active business life and to walk up and down in the open prison of Not Belonging is a grim experience. After twenty-four years with the same company I enjoyed the satisfaction of being an efficient executive. Then, without warning, in direct consequence of a big take-over, the Division in which I'd worked for so long was closed down and disbanded. Fifty of us, from junior messenger boys to senior executives, were out on the street jobless. We seniors had nothing to show for our long service but a redundancy pay-cheque in the bank and – a 'frozen' pension payable, I quote you, 'on your sixty-fifth birthday.' I was unbelievably faced with the problem of finding another executive job. It was hard to grasp that I was heading for unemployment. To me it was unthinkable, incredible. I felt I was in a dream, but we all woke up at the end of the month! The fortunate few left in other departments, those not sacked, and feeling for the time being secure, were awkward and embarrassed. 'Ah, hello!' they said, 'Are

you fixed up yet ? Found yourself another job ?' The forced heartiness
and maddening bonhomie, only thinly hid the individual's relief that
he was untouched by the close-down.

'No,' you say, 'no, indeed, it's not easy at fifty-six to find another
job – no-one wants to know if you're over forty.' They'd frown sympathetically, nod, shake their heads, and deplore the situation. But,
what could they say ?

Suddenly comes the Monday morning when there is no train to
catch, no office to go to, no work. Suddenly one is not anything at all.
The essential work-rhythm of life is broken off. There was, of course,
the immediate need to take some specific action. I contacted people
connected with my work by telephone and by letter. There was a great
deal of earnest sympathy. 'I'm so sorry, I'll see what I can do,' they'd
say, or, an easier one, 'I'll let you know if anything comes up.' For the
first week the telephone rang busily. There were frequent calls from
friends regretting the abrupt change in my circumstance and wishing
me good luck. A few actively tried to help. In the second week there
were only one or two calls. But there was always the vague suggestion,
'Why don't you write, or something ?' I'd patiently explain to them
that to write to earn enough to make a living one has to be trained –
I'm not. Of course one does write . . . letters! Some are replied to,
none with anything tangible to offer. Some don't even bother to reply.
I know what happens – they lodge in a pending tray, and are slowly
lost to mind under a pile of unurgent papers. A pending tray absolves
the conscience! The inference to the owner is that anything in it
will be dealt with sooner or later. But it's later, and then it's too late,
so it's filed! Some answers came in the form of those involved official
application forms. Four foolscap pages of questions asking about one's
early days onwards in the world of commerce. Always the key questions are: date of birth ? age ? I'd fill in the forms and wait. The replies
came in slowly. There are the formal regrets, blunted a little by the
polite, 'Thank you however for writing,' but all say, more or less,
'We regret to have to tell you that your application was not successful.'

Now I'm extremely fit and blessed with vitality and mental alert-
ness, but although I have a worthwhile record of expertise and
efficiency, there is a barrier to my hopes of interesting other and new
employers. That barrier is the year of my birth! I am fifty-six years
of age and can't do a thing about it. On paper that has a compulsively
psychological effect on employers. It reads 'old' to them, and so often

defeats the possibility of even a semi-permanent engagement. On Thursdays I visit the Labour Exchange and see a number of other executive types – they are all over forty, and call it what you like, we are all on the dole, which gives one only the bare bones of creature living.

Obviously I shall have to give up thinking of myself as a production executive. I'll have to settle for a big drop in earnings and a more modest standard of living. But I'm perfectly prepared to try something else; in fact a new field might be rather stimulating. Like Mr Micawber I am alertly waiting for something to turn up.

FROM MY WHEELCHAIR *Molly Holden*

Mrs Holden is a poet: in 1968 Chatto & Windus published her book of poetry 'To Make Me Grieve.' The same publishers are bringing out another book of her poems this year (1971).

When I was a girl I grandly convinced myself that I would commit suicide before I became old and useless. Well, now that I am useless (though not old, which makes it all the more bitter) why do I not do as I promised myself I would?

It seems obvious enough. I was thoroughly disabled by multiple sclerosis four years ago, when I was just thirty-seven (my children were eleven and eight), having struggled against its encroachment for eleven years. I now spend all day, every day (except Saturday afternoons), in a wheelchair or an armchair, in one room, looking at the same view – my garden, rooftops, a church spire – from the same window for eight to twelve hours a day, according to the light and time of year. I exist from one course of cortisone injections to another. Apart from my husband, one very good friend who comes to see me regularly, and two or three other friends who come when they can, I am quite isolated from my contemporaries. I do not choose to be taken to a club for the disabled (the pain and the effort are too much, nor, as I was not a 'clubbable' person before, do I see why illness should make me so), much entertaining at home simply involves my husband in more chores and in any case, most able-bodied visitors stay too long for an invalid's strength. Pain, in the very nature of things, is not something one can get used to – this pain is very curious – burning, granular and spasmodic, almost impossible to describe.

These are the obvious miseries. More subtle tortures are devised for the disabled woman. Nearly all my instincts are rebuffed or frustrated – I cannot look after my family, cook for them or care for them if they are ill; I can no longer achieve any sexual satisfaction. I cannot contribute anything tangible to the family economy – in fact somebody must be paid to do the work that I once did for love. As I was a full-time wife and mother when I was disabled I get no sickness benefit. Bringing up a family and looking after a home is not, apparently, productive employment. My husband gets an increased personal allowance because of my incapacity, but this does not amount to sufficient to cover the cost of the insurance stamp we must pay for necessary help; the sense of guilt that any disabled woman feels on watching her family look after themselves for much of the time is thereby increased. So I sit and watch another woman looking after my home, doing her best, but necessarily disarranging the pattern that I took such pleasure in making. I cannot put pictures straight, I must ask for things to be done that I once did without thinking.

I still care a little about make-up, but only out of self-respect. I still try to go on short holidays with the family but really only because the children say, 'It wouldn't be the same without you.' Hotels with ground-floor rooms are fairly rare and normal toilets hellishly difficult to use – it can all be very humiliating. A terrible sense of isolation and irrelevance possesses me at times, especially when I hear anyone speaking of all the normal, active things that I used to do, or as I read of them.

People sometimes say, awkwardly, on meeting me for the first time since this happened, 'I suppose you must get used to it,' or 'Perhaps there are compensations.' The straight response to both these remarks is 'No.' However, if you wish to spare them awkwardness, the reply is a slight shrug and a change of subject.

This is an objective statement of facts, not a self-pitying complaint. What then makes this reduced, this quarter-life still worth living ?

Well, first of all, of course, there is the painfully achieved and painfully retained knowledge that I can be of some use still to my family. I can arrange for food to be cooked, keep a distant check on the airing of clothes, listen to problems or grievances, help sometimes with homework. I am there, a certain centre in the house to which they return. I see that they need to love me. To remove myself deliberately would be treachery. I can still share a great deal with my husband and help him in many ways. And I also, for the moment at least, am at home and have my eyesight still, so that not only do I have the delight of watching young bodies grow and familiar faces smile, but I can watch from my window the procession of seasons and natural beauty in which I once used to take so passionate a part. Even the very indifference of nature is sometimes a comfort in that I know my own and others' unhappiness to be quite irrelevant to sunrise and the thrush in the sycamore. I can read, preferably books in which I do not get too emotionally involved, and listen to music, which is beautifully impersonal and universal, and I can write – all this on my better days!

There is, therefore, something left, although there is no compensation for the greatest losses; nor will I ever get used to the blank impossibility of natural reaction to an instinct – not to be able to walk into the garden when spring comes, not to be able to get up and prepare a meal for my daughter when she comes home late from her school choir. Anyone disabled, if really honest, will admit to this sense of loss.

There is obviously no point in stressing this – the able-bodied do not like to think too much of unhappiness and much prefer, naturally, the 'cheerful invalid' act that one instinctively puts on for them. Of course I am pleased to have visitors, to know that someone remembers me; besides, if I am too truthful, they may never come again! Some former friends have not come at all or have come once to feel that they have done their duty, and never again. They, perhaps, are afraid. I doubt the excuse of being too busy. It does not hold water for long. Such omissions hurt though, as does the lack of imagination of some others – the young man who spent half an hour telling me how he was once in bed for six weeks (but he meant kindly!) or the neighbours who put up a six-foot fence in front of what was then my only small view because they objected – a year before it was built – to an extension we planned to increase my outlook. I still find myself unable to forgive this lack of human charity.

Finally, many others more unfortunate than myself are quite unable to express their feelings of desolation and still retain human dignity; because I am still articulate I feel a certain uncomfortable responsibility to give some expression to this curious experience so that the able-bodied can have some true idea of what it is like. You may not like the thought of us because we remind you of sorrow and the dark side of life, but we merit the same treatment as yourselves.

So love and obligations keep me alive yet awhile. Any further deterioration and I may decide to withdraw in comparatively good order. For the moment, although certain actions of others bring old sensations unbearably to mind – the woman over the road pulling the front door after her as she goes out shopping on a sunny afternoon, my daughter tightening her stockings and turning herself about in her new coat – I do try to keep as quiet as possible about these griefs and do not cry more often than I can help. There are many like myself.

Children

INDIAN SCHOOLGIRL   *Margaret Goodall*

She had huge eyes like brown pansies, but the expression in them was like that of a rabbit in a trap. I was told that she was to join my class the following day. Of course she needed special lessons and teachers, but at that moment there was no vacancy for her, so we had to do our best. That afternoon I delivered a prepared speech to my band of villains. I told them that we had been chosen from all the second year forms for the special task of welcoming Ravindar to England. I spoke of her life in India, and why she would be wearing trousers instead of school uniform. Suddenly I realised that they were all listening, really listening, so on the spur of the moment I abandoned my idea of choosing one girl to look after Ravindar, and swore them all in as deputies.

The girl I fetched from the office the following morning was very thin; arms and legs and plaits stuck out in all directions so that she looked all odds and ends and corners. Yet she had great dignity, so much that I did not take her hand, but ushered her along the corridor as if she was some visiting VIP. She was received with cries of delight, clucked over, patted, shown her books and desk. Ravindar had joined 2N.

My form are quarrelsome, but nobody has ever quarrelled with Ravindar, or, more surprisingly, quarrelled about her. She became their living doll, to be petted, spoiled, cherished and protected at all times. Of course, her writing was very odd, and she did not attempt to speak, but she tried hard to fit in.

The second week she was with us she did say one word. This was 'eighteen', her number on the register. This number calling was a twice daily ritual, and has always been a problem for 2N. Those who call first get bored with the proceedings once their part in it is over and interrupt the ones who are still calling until we all forget what we are about. Now there was silence. We strained our ears to catch the word 'eighteen', then pandemonium broke out. 'Oohing' and 'Aahing' and cackling like nineteen hens with one chick between them they clattered off to lessons with Ravindar firmly wedged in the middle for protection.

The weeks passed by, and still the novelty of looking after Ravindar did not wear off. We clubbed together to buy her her first Easter egg. Then she had a spell in hospital; when she came out again she looked better and began to fill out a little. Occasionally she treated us to a glimpse of her smile, like a moonbeam in a dark room. Then she got a place in a special school, and she belonged to us for the morning only. But she brought us her work, pictures with wobbly letters underneath them. We put them on the notice board with great pride, and showed them to everybody who came in.

A new year began and we were 3N. Ravindar's smile came more readily now, and she took her turn at watching for me to come along the corridor, running to warn the others with her red-ribboned plaits stuck out behind her. Christmas came and went, and it was 3N's turn to read in Assembly if we wished to do so. As usual, the girls volunteered, and we set about choosing readings and writing prayers. Then, to my amazement, the girls said that Ravindar wanted to take part. This seemed so far beyond her capabilities that I did not know what to say, but when she quietly said 'Yiss, pliss' I did not have the heart to say no.

Had we the right to ask a Sikh to take part, anyway? I decided that this was not the point; Ravindar wanted to join in this class activity and so she should. But how? The readings were beyond her, it would have to be a simple prayer. Then I remembered that when we had prayers in the classroom we always said the Lord's Prayer. She could say that. At last the day dawned. As I made my way to my place I prayed that all would go well. It would be a tragedy if Ravindar became a figure of fun before the whole school. The Headmistress explained to the school that when Ravindar had joined us, nearly a year ago, she had not been able to understand or speak a word of English. Now she was going to read to us, and we were to listen, but first the Headmistress would like to thank 3N who had helped Ravindar so much. Ravindar's face was its usual study in Eastern calm, but 3N were nudging one another and giggling, their faces like tomatoes. I need not have worried, every word Ravindar said was clearly heard and she did not falter once. Nobody coughed; nobody shuffled; nobody busied themselves putting their pile of hymn books on the chair in front for some unsuspecting girl to sit on. All listened, and all said Amen.

Back in my room Ravindar came to my desk. 'Jane iss awaiy,' she

said quite distinctly, 'iss no regisser – I fetch.' She sped off at a rate
expressly forbidden by the school rules, but I did not stop her. It was
obvious that reading in Assembly was going to have more than one
effect.

Ravindar still goes to special lessons, but we hope to have her for
the whole day before long. She laughs a lot, and speaks quite clearly,
and has been register monitress this term. She is so conscientious and
eager to please that she is ready now to be Form Captain if she is
elected. Ravindar owes much to the special lessons she has been able to
attend, but I like to think that the kindness, patience and friendship
she has received from 3N has helped.

NEWS FROM HOME   *Maureen Vincent*

With our seventh child now firmly dug in to *Janet and John*, the most
intimate details of our family life can scarcely be said to hold any
more surprises for the staff of the local Mixed Infants. But it still
sends a chill down my spine when, among the neat array of copy books
on the youngest's desk on Open Day, I see the dread title, 'My Own
News'.

Our first encounter with our lives as seen through my eldest son's
eyes should have given us fair warning of what was to follow: '17th
March. It is St Patrick's Day today and my Mummy and Daddy are
going up to London to get Married.'

Blushingly, I felt the need to explain that, to a five-year-old, the
splendour of full evening dress laid out ready for the Irish Club dance
might well appear only suitable for such a very important occasion as
one's wedding day.

And I felt that my explanation had been accepted. But how could I
explain, or indeed attempt to live down, this ? –'On Monday my
Mummy does the washing. If it is raining when she wakes up she
says oh blast and goes back to sleep.'

But News Books do have their uses. For instance: 'My Mummy
and Daddy never get cross unless they have a reason for it, or they
are tired.' That impelled us to take a good look at ourselves and try,
for the future, just not to be *that* tired. Oh, dear, the resolutions one
makes! 'My Mummy is not fat, but again she is not thin. My Father
is quite fat.' That graphic piece of descriptive writing triggered off

some pretty frantic dieting, I can tell you.

'When Mummy and Daddy have a visitor to supper we get the left-overs,' sounds pathetic. I wondered if I should mention casually that the children are fed before visitors arrive. Better to leave it, perhaps. But what about, 'Usually if Mummy and Daddy are staying in we get some of their supper.' Usually ? No wonder we're fat!

'My Mother is nearly always happy and so is my Daddy,' makes up for, but does not quite blot out the guilty memory of, 'When you come to visit our house you will find the gate open. It is always open because it has stuck.' A friend and I read our offsprings' versions of 'My Home,' pinned on the classroom wall for all to read. She sighed, 'Mine sounds like a cross between Buckingham Palace and a slum.'

At times I have resorted to low cunning. 'What are you going to put in your News Books today ?' I inquire cheerfully, then go on to suggest some item which will not discredit us for once. But it's no good. What goes into the News Book will always be what seems most interesting or important to the child. Any suggestions you make will have been forgotten long before pencil is put to paper.

The one crumb of comfort is that quite possibly teachers become so inured to all these revelations, that most leave them unmoved. They're probably more interested in the spelling and punctuation of the offering than in its news value. But one extract from our nine-year-old's recent essay on 'My Parents' must have raised a few eye-brows in the Staff Room. 'My parents are not shy at all. My Mummy has seven children.'

You can learn quite a lot from 'My Own News'. It gives you an unequalled chance to see yourself through the eyes of those most important others, your own children.

BIG BROTHER *Joan Goldman*

When our son Bill was twelve we presented him with a baby sister. He received her with mixed feelings, the predominant one being, 'How are the fellows at school going to take this ?' Being an only child at the time, he would have welcomed a little brother, but he regarded the arrival of a little sister as rather embarrassing; and when asked if he would like to choose a name for her, he said he had no interest whatsoever in girls *or* their names. His world was one of football, train-spotting and the printed output of Frank Richards. Girls were an irrelevance – including this latest addition to the gender right inside his own home.

When Emma, as we called her, was two years old another child was added to the family: a girl called Joanna.

Naturally there was some apprehension on our part as to how Bill would react to this second irregularity. He was almost fifteen and had come a long way since his Billy Bunter days. He now had an opinion of himself as both knowledgeable and sophisticated, being a chap with eight 'O' levels under his belt and hair long enough round the back to cover his collar. He not only by now acknowledged the existence of girls but found them a decorative addition to the scene. Older girls, that is – not our two whom he still looked upon as totally without a reason for existing. He was, however, prepared to be tolerant and, provided the girls were kept in suitable subjugation, to settle for peaceful coexistence.

It didn't turn out as easy as that. Peaceful coexistence never does. The girls proved to be lively, inquisitive creatures for whom Bill was a source of unending fascination and they couldn't leave him alone.

Emma, the elder girl, had at first taken him to be some kind of third parent and, for a short period, paid him a rather flattering obedience. But it was inevitable that she should witness his occasional skirmishes with her actual parents and draw the inevitable conclusions – unhappily for Bill's authority. By the time she was four, and Joanna two, their nuisance value to him was plain to see and he blamed it on our muddle-headed views on child psychology with its nonsense about setting-them-a-good-example and true-discipline-coming-from-within. What they needed, as he saw it, was the firm hand of retribution sharply administered on the bottom. Emma's in particular. He saw her as having built up a pretty impressive list of punishable offences, chief among them her behaviour with the telephone. She rushed to answer it every time it rang and her 'Hello! What do you want? Goodbye!' was no encouragement to callers. As most of them were Bill's friends he took what is called exception to the procedure. When told that we were training her to use the telephone correctly he said, 'Why must she learn on my calls?' 'We can't know beforehand that they will be yours.' 'You jolly well know they're not hers!'

We suggested he rush to the telephone himself when it rang but that wasn't an easy solution, either. He played Pop records in his room so loudly that it drowned all other sounds, including that of the telephone. He was addicted to the music of a gravel-voiced singer called Bob Dylan, whom Emma had heard mentioned so often that when she opened the front door to Bill's friends she would call out, in all sincerity, 'It's that old Bob Dylan come to see Bill.'

None of this was to Bill's fancy, sensitive as he was to his newly acquired status as young man of the world.

'I shall kill those two kids one of these days!'

'Never make a threat you're not prepared to carry out,' he was advised.

'And who says I'm not ?'

If he intrigued them, there were occasions when they intrigued him, notably in their manner of talking. As fond parents we found their quaint use of English charmingly endearing, but this youthful babbling only served to convince Bill that they were deranged.

'It is possible,' he maintained. 'I read in *Reader's Digest* that the children of elderly parents run that risk.'

Now a year later, with Emma attending infant school and Joanna nursery school, their speech has acquired some kind of normality and their sanity seems no longer in question.

Expanding horizons have brought endless questions and with these they turn to Bill, he being a sixth former and the fountainhead of all knowledge. They listen with deference to his answers and he expends upon them the rhetoric of a man who has waited a lifetime to come into his own and find an audience . . . 'Now, girls, to begin with, the Earth isn't flat. It feels flat but it's really shaped like a ball and it rotates in space, on its own axis at an angle of twenty-three degrees, inclining towards the sun. Got that ?'

They nod spellbound. He doesn't question their comprehension. If they listen, they qualify as an audience so far as he is concerned. Indeed, their very lack of comprehension strengthens his position. Nobody talks to them like Bill and they are bewitched by his brilliance. Who but Bill could eat a stinging nettle, put his finger through a lighted match, make a telephone out of cocoa tins ?

Emma tells him, 'You're the cleverest brother in the whole world. We've never heard of a brother as clever as you, have we Joanna ?' And Joanna shakes her head gravely.

He can't pretend they constitute the ideal in fan-clubs, but it's an imperfect world and he's not the first who's had to compromise. There is even at last a hint of affection towards them. 'They're not bad little kids really,' he informs me. 'A bit thick but I suppose they could be worse.'

LET'S ALL MOVE AND GROW! *Vera Michaelson*

I was taking my class of infants for a nice, quiet writing lesson, doing nobody any harm, when, out of the blue, the Physical Education Expert arrived. It was a fine, sunny day and this dedicated lady didn't exactly ask why we weren't 'Moving and Growing' in the square which does for a playground in our city school, she just looked at the timetable, sighed and said it was a pity that so many teachers didn't realise the importance of physical education.

During the mid-morning break, she gave all staff a little lecture on the latest developments in this field. She also made quite a few suggestions and left us with a veiled threat to come back and see if they were being carried out.

It's a pity she didn't touch on the problems of undressing and dressing forty five-year-olds. Until then my charges had been perfectly satisfied with a run round the playground. When I told them the next morning that we were going out in the playground to learn how to 'Move and Grow', they were unimpressed.

'We'll start right away,' I told them brightly. 'Now I want all woollies off and everyone changed into plimsolls.'

There were instant howls of protest.

'My mummy says I mustn't take my cardigan off.'

'I can't find my plimsolls.'

'This isn't a woolly, it's my blazer.'

'I can't undo my back buttons.'

I took a deep breath, counted three and plunged in.

Eventually we were ready to go forth and start to build the body beautiful, but by that time Miss Peters' class was in the playground. So I led my shivering flock back to the classroom and spent the rest of the morning sorting out clothes and doing up laces.

Next morning a queue of angry parents was waiting for me. First Mrs Jones wanted to know why Johnny came home with two left shoes, neither of them belonging to him. After that, Mrs Johnson's problem was simple and all I had to do was to promise to look for Ian's pullover. I couldn't explain to Mrs Page why Jimmy had a little girl's petticoat under his shirt, but at least it got rid of Mrs Daley who said it was Susan's.

Well, all this called for a compromise, so half an hour before the next physical education period, I told my class:

'Only one woolly off and if you can't tie laces, don't bother about plimsolls.' You can't please everyone and after all, there are more irate parents than keen Physical Education Experts.

Once out in the playground, I started on the suggestions. The imagination has to be 'stimulated' first so we all became little butterflies dancing round the flowers, until Johnny revolted and said it was cissy. I saw his point, but discipline had to be maintained.

'But I'm going to choose the best butterflies and turn them into lions in the jungle,' I told him. This stimulated Johnny's imagination to bursting point. He just couldn't wait for my magic touch. He straightaway became a roaring lion – followed by the entire male section of the class.

By this time an interested audience had begun to gather at the school gate. There were three busy housewives, complete with prams, a postman, two labourers on their way to their tea break and one large Alsatian dog. Just then, a butterfly being chased by a roaring lion became separated from her plimsoll. It took gracefully to the air and sailed over the gate. One of the busy housewives neatly caught it and the postman chivalrously opened the gate for the lady to bring it back. That was the moment when the large Alsatian dog streaked past the front row of spectators and into the playground to join in our jungle revels.

Have you ever tried to tell forty screaming infants that a savage-looking dog won't hurt them if only they'd stand still and stop screaming? No, and I don't suppose a Physical Education Expert has either, because these things aren't supposed to happen when they're 'moving and growing'.

The events of the next few minutes have become mercifully vague, but I dimly remember being joined by the postman, the caretaker and the two labourers who managed to grab the dog's collar.

Once back in the classroom I checked up on possible casualties. Thank goodness there weren't any – only my damp nylons where the dog had licked them to show there were no ill feelings.

Miss Peters took over my class while I attended the post mortem in the Headmistress's study. She explained, quite reasonably, that when a passer-by phones the police to say that small children are being tortured by teachers with savage Alsatian dogs, the Education Committee is sure to ask questions.

I tried to tell her about the butterflies and the lions, but she patted me kindly on the shoulder and said, 'Go home and have a good rest. Tomorrow, I'll arrange for Miss Peters to take your class for physical education, and you can take hers for a nice, quiet writing lesson!'

ADOPTIVE AUNT, ADOPTIVE MOTHER *Kathleen Hek*

It all started one Sunday morning, when one of the Priests at my church made an appeal for people to take an interest in the local Children's Home, and become adopted aunts and uncles to some of the children. If we couldn't foster or adopt these children, he asked us to visit them, take them out, give them holidays, and remember their birthdays and Christmas. Some of them had no one in the world – and no one ever visited them or took them out. My first reaction was that 'I would love to do it.' I was working as a secretary at Bristol University and although single women with jobs are ostensibly career women, I must be honest and say that fundamentally I am not. I have always thought the career of a wife and mother must be so much more satisfying and real. As the days went on I became more and more convinced that *if* I could possibly manage to undertake this project I would.

One evening after work I went to the Home and was shown around by one of the Sisters. I was taken into the young children's dormitory, and they came milling around me, craving for attention. I noticed Peter at once, he was so pale, silent and withdrawn. The Sister told me no one ever came to visit him, and he never went out. He was then three and a half years old.

'Would you like to come for a bus-ride with your Auntie one day?' I asked. He didn't speak, just nodded his head slowly twice, without a smile on his face.

The next weekend I took him home for the afternoon to tea; my father and mother were intensely interested in him. But Peter was still very silent, very white-faced, ate enormously, and hung his head and kept on chanting in the same tone of voice, 'More bread and butter, more bread and butter!' He'd never tasted butter before.

From the first afternoon I tried never to fail him. Each Saturday he grew brighter, and would rush to meet me when I called for him. He became talkative, but his talk was very garbled, indistinct and still in the same dead tone, well below the standard of a normal four-year-old. A few months later my father died, and my mother and I started having Peter for a whole weekend, and after this we never considered having him for a day only – he always stayed one or two nights.

Gradually as this first year wore on I got him to speak more clearly. He thrived and began to grow confident and happy.

Then began the most troublesome and heartbreaking time for us all. By now our emotions were completely involved in his.

He cried bitterly when he went back to the Children's Home after his visits, and I really don't know *how* I managed to get him back. I'd hear him sobbing and see his tear-stained face at the window watching me disappear down the drive. I managed to harden my heart every Sunday night until he was five – and then at that age I knew if he were not adopted or fostered, he'd have to transfer to the Boys' Home nearby. By now my mother and I had come to think of him as ours. We couldn't bear the thought of him going into this huge Home among all the toughs up to the age of fifteen. In desperation I went to see the Secretary of the Adoption Society.

He told me I could certainly have him as a *foster* child and said there was no objection to a single woman fostering a child (even if she were at work) provided there was someone suitable at home to look after the child when she was not there. I would also receive a weekly allowance for him.

My mother and I scarcely stopped to think, we were so anxious to get him out of the Home, and one never-to-be-forgotten day I fetched Peter home as my foster child.

And now we'd taken the plunge, everything seemed to be added to us. Friends rallied round and gave me clothes, toys, helped out with baby-sitting; and the University, where I was still working as a secretary, showed me great consideration and sympathy.

As the weeks sped by and Peter went to school, I was astonished and delighted with the improvement he showed. His voice began to lose its dirge-like dead level quality, and he started to enunciate his words more clearly. He made good progress at school, passed his eleven-plus, and his conduct was excellent. He stopped calling me 'Auntie' and reverted naturally to 'Mummy' and 'Granny', and there we were, a granny and mother after all!

From the age, then, of five until eight and a half, he was my foster child, and I was visited periodically by the Foster Home Visitor, and got a small weekly allowance. Then I had a rise in salary and began to think about legal adoption. And the more I thought about it the more I realised that he would never be really secure until he was legally mine, and that as a foster child there was nothing to stop any belated relatives claiming him at any time. So the wheels of adoption were put into their slow motion, and I eventually attended the Magistrate's Court with him and passed out of the doors at Bridewell Police Station as his legal mother. Now no one could take him away.

Peter, today, is a young man of nineteen, and a trained chef from Bath Technical College. He was chosen out of all the students of his year to be Master of Ceremonies and Toast Master at a notable banquet at the Guildhall attended by about 170 guests. It was a great success, and the President and Mayor called for a special round of applause for their Master of Ceremonies. A very far cry indeed from 'More bread and butter'!

Peter is now in his first job at a University Hall of Residence, and at present lives at home.

Need I add that if, in the beginning, I had hesitated, worried too much about the real or imagined problems, been put off by the fact that he was somebody else's child, perhaps wondered about unknown inherited characteristics, I should have lost for ever the deepest human experience and the most treasured possession I have.

BOYS IN CLOVER *Leslie Gardiner*

I've been playing host to half a dozen boys from a youth club in the city. On the telephone I told the organiser I lived alone and only had one of everything, and he said that was all right, they'd fend for themselves. And he'd look in during the weekend to see everything was under control.

It was to be a competition camp weekend, for gymnastics and initiative tests and such-like. My place, three acres of wild garden, is ideal for that kind of thing. The organiser came down early to approve the site. I showed him the cricket pitch, the tangled wilderness of rhododendrons, the trout stream, waterfall and log bridges; also a patch of velvet lawn screened by birches where my deckchair, and nothing else, goes.

'Nice little place you've got here,' he said, with city superiority. 'Could have done with more space, but I suppose we'll manage. They're only wee chaps.' I didn't see the wee chaps arrive. Their first task had been to get in without being detected by the owner. The first sign was a spiral of smoke above the birches, that sent me running down to the garage for the fire-extinguisher. Heath fires are a constant menace in our parts. But it was only the club, cooking its supper on a fireplace of boulders they had rolled off the boundary wall. I wondered whether there was any point in asking them to move off the lawn bit, where my deckchair and nothing else goes. But I didn't like to strike a churlish note so early in the weekend. Besides, a tent and a flagstaff make little permanent mess and the scorched earth under a camp fire, if you give it time, will produce a picturesque crop of daisies.

That was Friday night. By Saturday morning the wee chaps, gastronomically speaking, were split down the middle. Three were occupied in my kitchen, turning out batches of Egyptian Eyes, whatever they are. Whatever they are, they require your cooker for the whole forenoon and both your frying pans.

The rest had decided on fish. One boy lay on the bank of the stream, guddling. Another splashed up and down in his boots, trailing a worm on a piece of string. The third actually boasted a bite – from a water-rat – and sat sucking his fingers. Higher up, they'd already erected a mud battery and sunk a flotilla of soup cans and wine bottles borrowed from the dustbin.

The club leader arrived in the afternoon – dramatically, with a piercing jungle shriek and a crash of undergrowth. Until I saw him in his shorts and singlet, I never realised how monstrous and yet agile he was. He thrust a clip-board of neatly-typed competition record sheets at me and the next moment was hanging from the top of a young poplar, piping some kind of bird-call. None of the boys paid the slightest attention. He ran the woods all afternoon, laying paper trails and uttering the warning cries of various wild creatures. The cows next door went into a huddle at the far end of their field, but his young charges remained wrapped up in their own pursuits.

After he had gone, unmissed, and we had had a game of cricket and with great presence of mind I had pleaded pressure of work to avoid the grand farewell supper of Egyptian Eyes – which turned out, incidentally, to be fried eggs dropped in holes in fried bread – after all that, boredom set in.

'What can we do for you, mister ?'

'Would you like to chop down a tree ?'

I found saw and axe and showed them the decaying chestnut. In ten minutes they were all back at the house, to watch the bandage applied to a knee-cap laid open by the axe. But the tree was down – well, half-down, half blocking the stream. If the farmer will lend me a couple of men, I shall shift it in no time.

An hour to go.

I said, 'See those fir-cones ? I pay a shilling a hundred for them, but there aren't many about.'

They scampered off in all directions. They were away about half an hour. It cost me three or four shillings, but it was worth it.

Their van arrived. They bundled the tent in and some of the litter. Then someone said: 'Where's Colin ?' We were listening to the eleven o'clock news when he burst in. From a sack and a couple of carrier bags he poured out enough fir-cones to make a forest. Two thousand eight hundred and something, he said, and I didn't dispute it. I paid up and looked pleasant, but not nearly as pleasant as Colin.

As they turned into the road, the van window came down and the wee chaps looked out. 'Be down next Easter, mister. Definitely. Be all right ?'

Yes, I suppose it will be.

BREAST FEEDING   *Eric Stroud*

Professor Stroud, of the Paediatric Department of King's College Hospital, is interviewed by Carol Marsh.

CAROL MARSH: Professor Stroud, what are your own views on the disadvantages and advantages of breast-feeding ?

ERIC STROUD: Well, I think that there has been a lot of misrepresentation on this, that some people feel that it is completely safe to bottle-feed all babies. This isn't quite true. The vast majority of babies can be quite successfully and safely fed with bottle feeds. On the other hand, there is a small group of babies who are put in danger by bottle-feeding. In particular we see a number of babies with gastro-enteritis each year, and some of these babies die. Very few of these babies would have gastro-enteritis if they were breast-fed. The other big danger of bottle feeding is the way that mothers slavishly follow the directions on the packet, so that one sees overweight babies being fed on milk to which sugar has been added, making them even more overweight, and we know now that if you overfeed a growing animal at a very young age, you actually increase the number of fat cells in his body. It is probable therefore that fat babies lead to obese adults and we know the dangers of that. However, these are obvious disadvantages.

There are other results of biochemical investigation which suggest that bottle-feeding may not be as safe, particularly in the first two weeks of life. It has been shown, for instance, that babies fed on cow's milk and cow's milk preparations during the first two weeks of life very often have rather low levels of calcium in the blood and just occasionally this can lead to convulsions in the first two weeks of life which would not occur if the baby had been breast-fed, so that all these are, if you like, disadvantages of bottle-feeding.

If one looks at the direct and obvious advantages of breast-feeding, then the first is, of course, that it is far less trouble, and it is rather surprising to me that so often a mother will say she bottle-feeds because it's too much trouble to breast-feed, although the breast milk is already made up. It's already the right temperature, it's readily available, and there are all sorts of humorous advantages such as the cat can't get at it and so forth. Quite seriously, though, there are very great advantages of breast-feeding and perhaps the most important of these are the psychological advantages. In response to this, the mother might say, 'Well, you can't say that my baby is at a psychological disadvantage because I bottle-feed him because I know that I love him and I love him deeply.' I think that this applies to most mothers who do bottle-feed their babies. Nevertheless, I have seen mothers who haven't been very excited about having a baby and who have, so to speak, fallen in love with their baby while they breast-feed him and certainly it ensures a very close and emotional contact between the baby and the mother.

MARSH: What about the woman who decides that she definitely doesn't want to breast-feed her child or for some reason or another can't breast-feed her child ?

STROUD: I think these fall into two groups. Firstly, there is the mother who really can't breast-feed her baby because she can't produce enough milk, and I feel sorry for those mothers when they have quoted against them the fact that in primitive society all mothers breast-feed their babies. In primitive society, the poor milk producers are bred out of the society by the death of their babies because, as those of us who have worked in the tropics know, if a mother doesn't breast-feed her baby in the first year of life, he will almost certainly die of gastro-enteritis. As a result of this, the poor milk-producing mothers in those societies don't give rise to further mothers, whereas in our society, for a number of generations now, we have been artificially feeding children and producing a certain number of women in society who cannot produce enough breast milk for their children. Unfortunately, we tend to exaggerate the number of these, and the vast majority of mothers who can't breast feed are unable to do so for a variety of reasons, many of which are dependent on mass psychology.

MARSH: If you do breast-feed, how long should it be for ?

STROUD: I think that the important period for breast-feeding is the first month of life. After that, the advantage of breast-feeding isn't so overriding, but I think the prevention of obesity, even though it does occur occasionally in breast-fed babies, is still a very great advantage. I think, however, that a large number of mothers decide long before they're married, or long before they're having babies, that they won't breast-feed their baby and this has to do with all sorts of vague social attitudes, including an attitude to what we call the female figure, and the figure is very important for most women. Whenever you go up and down in the underground, you're assailed by what is supposed to be the perfect bust, and this seems to be every woman's ambition. As a result, many of them are scared stiff to breast-feed.

MARSH: Is this so ? Does the figure suffer from breast-feeding ?

STROUD: Well, I know many, many mothers who've breast-fed babies and still have excellent figures.

MARSH: But there are some women who actively dislike the whole idea of breast-feeding a child. What would you say to them ?

STROUD: Oh, indeed there are, and some women find it quite nauseating. Some mothers have told me that they feel that it's too animal-like. Whenever one deals with a mother who feels in this way, I think it's the duty of the paediatrician to try to find out, if possible, why a mother feels like this. I've known a number of mothers who are sure that they feel that they would dislike breast-feeding, yet when it comes to the point, find that it gives them a great deal of joy and they really get to know their baby through breast-feeding it. On the other hand, if a mother continues to feel nauseated and repulsed by the idea or the sensation of breast-feeding, then I would be very happy to help her with successful bottle-feeding of the baby.

Animals

A MOLE IN THE FRIDGE *Patricia King*

It may have been the mole in the fridge that started me wondering if the pet situation wasn't getting out of hand! Not – I may say – that this particular mole was alive. 'Darling,' my mother had called from the kitchen, 'what's that in the foil wrap in the fridge?' 'A mole,' I called out. Her laugh turned into a shriek as she unwrapped it, and she appeared to be in a palsy. She paid very little attention to my explanation that my small daughter had found it in the garden dead, but freshly so, if you see what I mean, and had begged me to keep it. 'You *can't* keep dead moles!' I protested. 'But Mummy, you could have it stuffed!' So into the fridge it went to await stuffing.

We never did have it stuffed. My husband dialled a taxidermist's number from his crowded office on the following Monday, and said into the phone, to the intense interest of the office, 'How much to stuff a mole?' And a voice replied, 'Moles, three pounds ten.' He then phoned me and ordered us to bury it!

There's no doubt that, though the kids and I are the really pet-mad types, my husband does get involved. The time my daughter's chipmunk decided to make friends with the cat and was abruptly annihilated my daughter became hysterical. Something clearly had to be done, and it was decided to replace the chipmunk immediately – but nobody had one.

Suddenly, in this crisis, I remembered the famous London store equipped with a zoo department whose proud boast it is that they can supply anything. I phoned them. Yes, they said, they had chipmunks, but could I possibly come into the store to choose the animal? My husband commutes to London every day, so it was agreed he should go and choose the animal in his lunch hour. Now my husband's the quiet type and, unlike myself, not given to flamboyant behaviour, so, when he walked into the store and asked for a chipmunk and was told they didn't have any, he didn't panic but calmly roamed the cages until he came to one marked 'Japanese Ground Squirrel', peered at what appeared to be one sleeping ball of stripy fur and pronounced, 'This *is* a chipmunk, I'll have that one.'

'Oh, dear,' said the girl. 'How do I get it out, suppose it bites?' She fetched a butterfly net, opened the cage and prepared for battle. What she didn't know was that the little bundle of fur was a decoy, set up by the gang leader, an arch chipmunk, who, on a given signal, flew out of the door of the cage, followed by his entire gang of accomplices. There were chipmunks everywhere! The store went mad. Women jumped on to chairs, shrieking and holding their skirts. Assistants, grabbing nets, flew in all directions making swipes at the floor. Gentlemen threw their bowlers to try and capture the flying creatures, while my husband – ever calm – said, with perhaps just a touch of impatience, 'I really can't wait all day!'

It was left that the chipmunk would be dispatched to me the following Thursday, but on the day – no chipmunk. I phoned the store. There was a silence, then a voice I can only describe as broken said, 'Your chipmunk, Madam, is in Gents' Underwear.' It emerged that one chipmunk – mine – had escaped to the gents' underwear department where he was holed up (and I use the word advisedly) and no one could budge him. My mind boggled at the picture that presented itself of a very respectable gent trying on under-garments while a little lump travelled slowly up him, so I reassured the girl that I would take *any* chipmunk. Eventually one arrived and lived with us for three years, eating grapes, nuts, fingers, pyjama bottoms, and bowler hats.

Then there was the jackdaw that flew down from the sky on to my daughter's shoulder as she walked up the garden from school and said 'Hello.' He soon came inside, and proceeded to take over and reorganise the house. He loved the girls and would permit them to stroke his breast feathers as he sat on their shoulders and he'd say 'oooh!' But let one of my sons approach him and he got pecked! He slept on my bedroom window latch until six on the dot, when he'd wake, fly to my bed, pull my hair and bellow 'Hello' in my ear. He would then proceed to walk up and down my bed. It's very difficult to sleep with a jackdaw walking up and down your stomach – though some people would, I suppose. Each day we would turn him out and he would fly away, returning at dusk, when he would rap his beak on a window until we let him in.

Things went on like this for weeks. We were all knee deep in droppings. He terrorised the cats and picked fights with my son's sandals, which he fought to the death.

I think it was I who thought of taking a photo. 'Wait,' I said as it pirouetted on someone's shoulder, 'I'll get the camera, but,' I warned, 'it may be frightened of it.' Frightened, my foot – I have never seen anything so disgusting. As soon as it clapped a beady eye on the camera it was like a film star at a press conference. It posed, turning its best side to face it. It dominated all the photos; mind you, it was a George Raft type, all oiled hair and spats – but what a performance!

The photos were rather good so I sent them to a local paper and they published them. But, when I phoned a week later and reminded them they hadn't paid me for them, they replied that they didn't pay for items sent in by local residents! 'What nonsense,' I said, 'You paid me for photographs of the fire I sent in last year!' 'Aha,' said the man, 'there you have it, we *do* pay for fire photographs!' So if a jackdaw should fly out of the sky on to your shoulder and say 'Hello,' *before* you photograph him for the local paper, *set fire* to him, or you won't get paid!

PIGS IS EQUAL   *Harry Whitelock*

To pig or not to pig ? Some years ago that was a question I answered in the affirmative, and if I didn't make very much money at least I met some nice pigs. To be truthful I also met a few not quite so nice.

I think the most interesting thing about pigs is their individuality. I know, of course, that all animals are individuals, but pigs are more so. You may have heard the saying, 'dogs look up to you, cats look down on you, but pigs is equal.' I think this is true, the only thing I would add is that some are more equal than others. Possibly it depends on who or what they have to be equal to.

I once had a pig called Henrietta who, because of a sickly childhood, was brought up in a pen of her own. She was the only pig I have known who had a fan mail. Her fame spread rapidly, and at one time she had more visitors than I. People would call at all sorts of odd hours and ask to see Henrietta. Her repertoire included coming when her name was called, no matter who called it, saying please and thank you for tit-bits, jumping through a hoop, and a peculiar sort of porcine curtsy. Hers was an affectionate and gentle nature, and her passing was mourned by all who knew her.

The other side of the coin was typified by No. 1 – more often referred to as that blasted old No. 1. Her prosaic and unimaginative name suited her selfish and determined nature, but as a prolific mother she lived to try our patience for many years. Despotic, calculating, and with her beady eye firmly fixed on any opportunity for private gain or human irritation, she lived an egotistical, uncooperative life, enjoying every moment to the full.

Her size and physical strength were tremendous; fences, walls, oak doors and solid steel bolts merely provided her with an opportunity of demonstrating her expertise in escapology. I once saw her deal with a new, extra strong, woven pig wire fence that was supported by oak posts, and fixed to the ground every few feet with twisted metal stakes. Strolling casually up to this new barrier, she inspected the field of lush, young grass the other side. Mouth watering, she came to an instant decision. Placing her nose in the centre of the fence she leant her vast weight forward and pushed. The fence parted round her, unhurriedly she walked a few yards into the field and calmly began to graze.

A fierce and jealous mother, she usually had about fourteen strong, healthy piglets at a time. Should anyone be unwise enough to go near them in the first few days, she would show her intention of keeping the family exclusive by eating the lot.

Only once did we succeed in persuading her to farrow indoors, and that was when we were concerned at the effect on the piglets of being born in the snow. The winter was exceptionally cold, and we felt we could not allow her to follow her usual practice of farrowing wherever her fancy dictated.

At the time she was living in a hut so small she could barely get inside. Placing a larger hut in the paddock, we blocked the door with rocks and put a fence all round, leaving a heap of straw inside the wire. As expected No. 1 found the challenge irresistible. Breaking through the fence she removed the rocks, and made a nest of the straw which she carried into the hut. When we fed her on the evening after this achievement, she gave us one of her fierce, try-to-shift-me-if-you-dare looks, and we crept away, secretly congratulating ourselves on our guile.

The young pigs flourished and some weeks later we had to castrate them, an operation which is supposed to prevent their flesh being tainted when they are killed. One man lured No. 1 to the far end of the paddock, with a plentiful supply of food, whilst I and a helper slipped into the hut unobserved. We had just finished dealing with the last of the piglets when a shout from outside made us look through the small window.

Like a charging Rhino No. 1 was hurtling across the paddock towards us. The stout hut door was firmly secured by two inside bolts, and we felt the worst that could happen might be a lengthy siege. The door was struck as if by a battering ram and splintered at the first blow. The second attack brought the great head and foam flecked jaws into the hut. My helper and I dived simultaneously for the window where we remained ignominiously jammed shoulder to shoulder with our legs kicking ineffectively. Fortunately No. 1 was also momentarily jammed, and our friend outside was able to haul us through the window. After which we all took to our heels, only stopping when safely over the paddock wall.

When she died, which she did on the farthest field on the farm, thus causing maximum inconvenience, she had given birth to a total of 160 pigs.

Looking back over the long drawn out battle which she waged so effectively against any kind of discipline, and counting the cost of buildings and equipment destroyed en route, there is no doubt in my mind that she was the winner. That is probably why, as I surveyed her inanimate body with mixed emotions jostling my mind, I thought I detected a faint, self satisfied smile on the one time fierce and obstinate features.

In between the extremes of Henrietta and No. 1 I have had pigs of all degrees. Intelligent, fascinating, rewarding and frustrating they have come and gone – enriching my life with the pleasure of their brief company.

GULLY   *Betty Sells*

His full name was Unus Premier, according to my son and his friend, who found him during a gull count on one of the small islands in the Bristol Channel. Apart from knowing that gulls ate fish, and lived on and near the sea, I hadn't a clue how to bring him up. He was about three days old when he arrived; a ball of yellow fluff, with black spots, and a huge beak. Unlike the land birds, his eyes were open, and he could stagger around on his large webbed feet, although every now and then he would subside on his backside as his legs gave way.

At first he spent his days on the kitchen draining board, in a cardboard box, laid on its side, so he could get out easily, and walk about. He soon discovered the sink, and had a wonderful time paddling about in the water, in between my washing-up sessions.

His appetite was enormous, and he gobbled vast quantities of fish. It was astonishing how tame Gully was with all of us, and his conversation was quite comic.

We soon knew if he wanted food, company, a paddle in the sink or just a chat, by the noises he made.

After a few weeks, life was becoming very difficult in the kitchen and we considered it was time to get him out of doors. We got out hammer and nails, collected odd pieces of wood, wire netting, and an old tea chest, and set to work on a cage. This contraption was then laid on the lawn, my largest casserole dish was filled with water for his paddling pool, and some tasty raw herring laid beside it. Gully loved it. By now his fluffy down was beginning to disappear, and some semblance of feathers and quills along his wings were appearing. His boisterous squawks, and mutterings, made us fear complaints from our neighbours, but they were so intrigued that they used to come in to see how he was getting on, and the more people that came, the better he liked it.

We had a raised pool in our garden, which was perfect for his first lessons in swimming. He found it most unpleasant the first time, but after a few days he could hoist himself up, and flop in and out by himself.

Our dog had a go at him a couple of times, until he got a good peck from that huge beak, and he gave him a wide berth from then on. Gully never seemed to fear anyone or anything.

A few weeks later, he decided that he didn't want to stay in his cage during the day, so we left him to roam about the garden. He now began to refuse the fresh herrings and mackerel we bought him daily, and we discovered that he was foraging on the compost heap, and among the bushes. Another hurdle was over, as it was clear that he could now fend for himself. Whenever we came into the garden and called, he would come running, neck out, and make straight for us, talking all the time. His curiosity was endless. If I was hanging out the clothes, and left the peg bag on the ground, in would go Gully's head, and he'd swallow a peg in a trice. I got quite used to forcing his beak open and pulling out the most extraordinary objects.

The most endearing habit he had was one that had to be seen to be believed. He would sit in our laps for hours at a time. If we stretched out on the sun beds a great speckled body would flop onto us, and rather like a cat, would curl up and snuggle down. If he could have purred he would.

His flying wasn't too good. Our garden wasn't open enough or wide enough to give him a proper take-off, and he spent hours making practice runs and taking off at shoulder height, but he wasn't happy at his efforts, and made a furious din in his angry attempts. He was eight weeks old now, and ready for the wild again. So early one morning, I took our two children, with six of their friends, and Gully, much to his disgust, in an enclosed cardboard box, and sailed over to the island where he had been found, and there opened the box, and let him out.

It was a tense moment. He emerged, and spent some time swearing at us for confining him in such an undignified manner, and then he looked around. Deliberately he picked up a white feather, and before our amazed eyes he took off, and soared high above us. We couldn't believe it. There was Gully high above us, winging strongly over the sea, as if he'd done it always. Round and round he went for a full five minutes, while we stood and watched. At last he came down to the sea, and still holding the white feather, landed smoothly on the water.

We left him there sitting on the tiny slip-way, as our boat moved off, unmoving and dignified. He knew he was home at last.

THE DIPLOMATIC OTTER   *Estelle Holt*

The otter was called Weasel, which confused everyone. He had been named Weasel by his owner, Fred Warner, who was then British Ambassador to Laos.

I had given Weasel to Mr Warner as a peace-offering. This was not really necessary, for he is a most forgiving person but at this time I was writing a newspaper column and this is exceedingly difficult to do without occasionally annoying ambassadors. What had happened though was not my fault. I had captioned a picture of Mr Warner at a Laos ceremony. The ceremony of New Year in Laos is a water ceremony and the better liked the person is the more water is poured on him. I had written, 'As a result of his popularity Ambassador

Warner has been completely soaked on all occasions of the Lao New Year, and somehow the last words were dropped. It read, 'As a result of his popularity Ambassador Warner has been completely soaked on all occasions.' A peace-offering seemed in order.

It was a hunter who found Weasel, an orphaned baby otter, in the jungle. I gave him to the ambassador whose finger Weasel bit to the bone. His diplomatic career got off to a bad start. Mr Warner called him Weasel because he said that was how he behaved, but within a few days they were deeply attached to each other.

At first Weasel lived in a small bathroom at the Residence until he had scared too many guests into screams of 'Rat! rat!' Then he had his own little house with a private swimming pool. He also used the Embassy swimming-pool. It was Mr Warner who encouraged him to swim. In the beginning he was terrified of water. Later they spent hours swimming together. Weasel loved riding on his master's back and the ambassador's shoulders were often interestingly lacerated.

But Weasel really adored Mr Warner. He crooned love songs to him. When, because of an accident, Mr Warner had to stay in bed, Weasel's wails were so piercing that he had to be carried up on hourly visits, was sometimes forgotten and would disrupt meetings by suddenly appearing from under a pillow. He had no atavistic instinct.

Then there was tragedy. Mr Warner was re-posted as Deputy Chief of the British Delegation to NATO in Brussels. Weasel, left behind in Laos, was heartbroken. I tried desperately to find him a mate. I appealed for one in my column and a sub-editor put up the headline WANTED: FEMALE OTTER TO REPLACE BRITISH AMBASSADOR.

Weasel was an alcoholic. Whisky was his drink. Any unguarded glass he'd snatch in his tiny webbed hands and swig at a gulp. Mr Warner insisted it was the ice-cubes he liked but no one else believed this at all. Weasel would down as many swigs as he could snatch and then stagger, jubilant, to his swimming pool.

After Mr Warner left, the Chargé d'Affaires gave a sherry party and I was allowed to bring Weasel. He travelled round the room in my arms with a polite squeak for each guest. To the Russian ambassador, a particular friend, he was especially charming. Then he spotted a glass, was out of my arms in a flash, and took a long swig. But it was sherry. Not whisky. He spat it out, said 'Beauh!' quite distinctly, and trotted crossly out of the room. Some of the other guests seemed sympathetic.

Then I found him a wife and cabled to Mr Warner in Brussels: WEASEL MARRIED THIS MORNING TO ATTRACTIVE VERY YOUNG OTTER BELIEVED TO BE VIRGIN.

'That cable,' said the head of the political section of the US Embassy, 'will go through the computers of every Warsaw Pact country.'

A Canadian colonel thought it wouldn't be necessary to use computers. He explained that 'Weasel' was a known code name for a single jet-engined fighter aircraft and 'otter' meant any plane fitted with snow-landing equipment. The question, he said, would be why was the Deputy Head of the British Delegation to NATO getting news from Laos of this new plane – 'believed to be virgin'. Where were the British planning to land ? The Yunnan ?

That evening I suggested to the Russian ambassador that he should warn his intelligence people that there really was an otter called Weasel who had been found a virgin wife. 'Ah, that is a very good joke,' said the Russian ambassador. 'This I will do nothing to prevent.'

But the new British ambassador did not take to Weasel. Neither did the ambassador's wife. The atmosphere at the Residence was changed. There was now a beautiful garden and plants being potted for charities. Instead of the gay Sunday-long parties at the swimming pool with laughing Lao guests and Weasel squealing with joy, there were garden parties with tea and flowery hats and sandwiches. It was no setting for hard-living drinking otters.

Finally, the ambassador's wife told me they had to go. The Prime Minister himself offered to take them but was, I suspect, dissuaded for fear their squeaking would interrupt his cabinet meetings.

'And another thing,' said the ambassador's wife, 'that "Wife" of Weasel is male.'

I cabled Brussels again, WEASEL'S WIFE SUSPECTED TO BE MALE SORRY, and got a reply, BAD LUCK BUT DO NOT REPEAT NOT CONSIDER THIS SERIOUS SECURITY RISK.

I asked the Russian ambassador if he would take them. 'Estell-ushka,' he said sternly, 'all you wish is to write a paragraph – "Two homosexual British otters defect to Russian Embassy in Vientiane" and I will not give them asylum.'

So the end is sad. I got ill and the ambassador's wife was very kind and invited me to recuperate at the Residence where all day I was allowed to play with the otters. Locked up for so long they were, of course, wild with excitement, bit everyone – including visiting heads of missions – and even during meals their little faces were pressed to the window looking – I am really sure – for Mr Warner.

Then they were taken to another house where a home had been offered and they both died. I think Weasel's heart just broke with homesickness and the fear that now he could never see his own loved ambassador again, and his friend died from the loss of Weasel.

Mr Warner and I still deeply mourn Weasel. And at the British Residence in Vientiane with its new beautiful garden, visitors still ask 'But *where* is the ambassador's otter ?'

THE STRANGE LIFE OF THE HEDGEHOG *Dr Maurice Burton*

Dr Burton is a naturalist, author and journalist.
The hedgehog appears to exercise a strange fascination over listeners –
any broadcast on the subject is immediately followed by a spate of letters.
Dr Burton talks to Brian Wallworth.

DR BURTON: The hedgehog is probably one of our most common animals, not necessarily the most numerous but it's evenly distributed over the country. It is an insectivore – it belongs to the same class of animals as shrews and moles and those indeed are some of the earliest mammals that appeared on the earth, so the hedgehog is very much the oldest inhabitant we have in this country. It still retains the sucking reflex, in other words like a baby that doesn't get out of its babyhood, it is still capable of sucking, which is unusual. And the other thing that is very noticeable about the hedgehog is that it seems to have a petulant nature – it very readily throws itself into tantrums if it can't have its own way, for example if it tries to get through a fence and finds its way blocked, it will throw itself on its back and wriggle about and scream like a naughty child. This is because mentally it hasn't really grown up, physically it probably hasn't either. It has been the subject of many legends. The most longstanding of legends, in this country anyway, is that hedgehogs will take milk from cows, and cowmen have been saying for centuries when they bring a cow into the stable to milk it and it gives no milk, that the hedgehog has been at the cow. Now not very long ago I was discussing it with a friend and she went so far as to test a tame hedgehog she had by getting a calf-feeding teat and the moment she put this near her hedge-hog it immediately grasped it and sucked it dry; she tried this on a number of occasions always with the same result. And at about the same time my attention was drawn to the fact that in the *Veterinary Review* there were two articles about vets having been called in to treat cows whose teats had been damaged. So that the idea that hedge-hogs take milk from cows which has been pooh-poohed by the zo-ologists, but has been believed in for centuries by the countrymen, is now known by at least some vets to be correct.

BRIAN WALLWORTH: But how do you think they do it, how do they actually get the milk?

BURTON: I think it could be done while the cow is standing up. If you measure the height at which the nose of the hedgehog would be from the ground when it stood erect on its hind legs, you see immediately that there would be no difficulty in a hedgehog rearing itself up on its hind legs and seizing the teat of a cow that was standing up. We know from tame ones that hedgehogs will sometimes stand on hind legs. Now there is another legend, and that is of the hedgehog rolling on apples in order to impale them on its spines to carry them off. To give you a better explanation of this I'd like to go on to another feature of hedge-hog behaviour which has interested me very much – it's that the hedgehog will select something to lick and it licks and licks and licks and licks, and its mouth fills with a sort of soapy or foamy saliva, and then suddenly it throws itself into contortions and puts its head round, throws out its tongue on to the spines of its back and puts a dab of spittle on the spines. Having done that, it returns to the object and starts to lick again – licks, licks, licks, mouth with saliva, throw into contortion, spittle on the spine and so it goes on until in some cases the hedgehog is just covered with spittle. Now when they throw themselves into contortions like that, the spines on one side will get stabbed into the ground and I got the idea that perhaps this legend about hedgehogs taking apples on their spines may have something to do with self-anointing, so when I happened to have a hedgehog that did self-anoint regularly, I took it out one autumn when the crab apples were on the ground, and put it down among the apples and got it to self-anoint, and sure enough it stabbed one of the apples and carried it away on its spine and it did that several times. So it's just possible that again this legend which goes back two thousand years is correct.

WALLWORTH: Do you think this is anything to do with the mating ceremony?

BURTON: It may well be. Though there was one story I got from a lady who wrote to me saying that a gipsy had told her that if you put two hedgehogs near together and one of them goes over and puts spittle on the spines of the other one, then you have got a pair and they will mate and live happily ever after. Of course the gipsy was a bit out because they don't mate and live happily ever after; they mate and then go their separate ways and the female has to look after the family.

WALLWORTH: The gipsies seem to have a lot to do with hedgehogs.

BURTON: Well, they do, because they used to eat them and they probably still do.

WALLWORTH: How do they get the spines off?

BURTON: I'm not very well versed in this, but they're always said to bake them in clay so that when the hedgehog is cooked and the clay is taken off, the spines are taken away with it. But I've got an idea that probably that is not absolutely correct, I don't know.

WALLWORTH: And you haven't, in fact, eaten one yourself?

BURTON: I've never eaten one myself. For one thing I'm a vegetarian and apart from which I'm so fond of hedgehogs I don't think I could anyway.

WALLWORTH: Are they very easily tamed?

BURTON: Oh, they're the easiest thing in the world to tame. You see, when a hedgehog is frightened, it raises its spines. If you can push those spines down, it is no longer frightened. If you want to tame a hedgehog, what you do is to stroke it from the head backwards – from the head along its back towards the tail, stroke, stroke, stroke, get the spines down and when you've done that, then the hedgehog is tranquil.

Thoughts on Living

The following three articles, together with thirteen other talks from the *Woman's Hour* series, also appear in the book *Personal Philosophy*, published by the BBC.

PERSONAL PHILOSOPHY: 1 *Archbishop Anthony Bloom*

Archbishop Anthony Bloom advises Jocelyn Ryder Smith on how to achieve inner peace.
Archbishop Bloom is Head of the Russian Orthodox Church in England.

JOCELYN RYDER-SMITH: Is there any way in which we can live busy, demanding lives, but have inner quiet?

ARCHBISHOP ANTHONY BLOOM: I think the first thing we must learn is to make choices. We all know how to forget, because we do it quite naturally, spontaneously, and we also know that we forget selectively. What we must learn is to select intentionally what we are going to forget, and then we will have got rid of a great many of those things which clutter our mind.

RYDER-SMITH: What are the sorts of things that we tend to hold on to that we really should unload?

BLOOM: Usually it's things that affect us directly: we're told something kind or unkind, we have been hurt, we have been impressed by something. We retain those things which are of no importance except that they have touched our own lives, and we forget other things which in themselves we would value a great deal more, but they are superseded by this short-sightedness of ours. We must learn to readjust ourselves – the way in which we focus when we look at things. We must learn not to look too close, and to have a sense of perspective.

RYDER-SMITH: It is sometimes difficult to control the thoughts that stay in our minds, or keep returning to them. How can we learn to let trivial things go, and turn to the things that are truly important?

BLOOM: It's partly a question of discipline. Anyone who has studied, for instance, or is doing a piece of work of any kind, has got to learn to get rid of parasitic thoughts. And there are a great deal of parasitic thoughts in our minds, so we must learn to let go of thoughts, even when they are very interesting, and say, 'For the moment I'm not busy with this.' If we practise pruning our thinking, quite soon we can do it. We can learn.

RYDER-SMITH: Once we have learnt, and we can drop unnecessary mental luggage, how can we then achieve inner quiet?

BLOOM: I think first of all we must learn to see things in proportion and with a certain sense of humour. If you have got a sense of humour, you will quite easily realise how ridiculous it is to feel that you are the absolute centre of things – life is so rich, so complicated and at times so tragic, or so glorious. Also we would feel less worried about what we do and how we do things, if we realised that ultimately, for a believer, an action should be an act of God through us. Unless we are still and quiet, unless we are capable of listening to what God says to us, we will never be able to act with sovereign freedom. This is something that can teach us inner quiet, because it will compel us to sit back and to look as long as we need to look, and only then to act with a certainty which frees us from unnecessary emotional or intellectual burdens.

RYDER-SMITH: Can you tell me finally, if we learn to have an inner quietness – what does this give to our lives?

BLOOM: It gives you depth, and stability, steadiness within you. And when you have a deep serenity and silence you are then capable of looking round, listening, seeing things for what they are, and not projecting yourself outward; this gives you a sense of intensity of life and of depth of life, not only of your own but of everything around you. And if you think in terms of action, it is only that steadiness, that inner silence, that allows you to see and to hear objectively, that enables you to act with certainty and act in an objective way – not only expressing yourself but acting to achieve a given purpose.

2   James Hemming

James Hemming talks to Jocelyn Ryder-Smith about self love and selfishness and the distinction between the two. Dr Hemming is the well-known educational psychologist.

JOCELYN RYDER SMITH: Most of us grow up being told that we must not be selfish, we must learn to consider others. Would you say that selfishness is, in fact, the same thing as self love?

DR JAMES HEMMING: No, I think there are very important distinctions, because, unless the personality is founded on a proper valuation of oneself, unless there's self-respect, self-liking, self-regard, then it's very difficult to love others or consider them. In fact, the self-haters are typically miserable people. Psychopaths, for example, those *un*moral people, are nearly all self-haters. I'd like to remind Christians that what Jesus said was 'Love your neighbour as yourself.' In our kind of society we're a bit puritanical still; people regard this advice of Jesus as though it was 'love your neighbour *instead* of yourself,' or '*better* than yourself'. But it isn't; it's *as much* as you love yourself. The love of others begins with the proper love of yourself.

RYDER-SMITH: So what would you say selfishness means?

HEMMING: Blindness to the needs of others, lack of imagination in understanding what people need. It's manipulating others, treating them as things, and putting your own concerns first all the time. It's going on as though other people aren't there, or have no feelings. That is what selfishness really is.

RYDER-SMITH: If somebody recognises that they have got themselves set into a selfish pattern, what are the things they can do to get themselves out of it, to make themselves more understanding of other people's needs?

HEMMING: I'd say, think about people, wherever you are, whoever is around you. Look at people and think about them. Ask yourself what they're doing there, what they're thinking about, so that you will wean yourself a bit from just having the focus all the time on yourself.

RYDER-SMITH: What sort of a life do you think the selfish person ultimately lives – the selfish person who is always trying to get things for himself, first and foremost?

HEMMING: Well, we're all a bit selfish. If you're talking about the characteristically selfish person: he gets driven into isolation. Other people soon rumble the fact that this particular individual, this unfortunate individual we're talking about, doesn't care about them really, that all he is interested in is himself, so other people don't trust him, and you can't get far without trust. Trust is at the basis of all human happiness really.

RYDER-SMITH: What happens to a selfish person of the kind you've talked about, in marriage?

HEMMING: I think that selfishness is probably the great wrecker of marriages. It may break a marriage up or it may force the other person just to give way, which also wrecks a marriage because marriage should be a reciprocal affair. Many young men are still trained in selfishness by their mothers. A really selfish partner in marriage just wants every decision made in his favour. If this happens resentment builds up and builds up in the other person, even if the selfish demands are accepted.

RYDER-SMITH: Do you think, within a relationship where one of the partners is a giver and the other one is a selfish taker, it's possible for the giving partner to do something to break this pattern down?

HEMMING: Oh, yes! If, for instance, an unselfish woman is married to a selfish man, I think she can do a great deal to educate him, by making him more aware of how she feels, and she can take the scales off his eyes to show him a bit of what is happening in other people's worlds as well as in his own. She can do this just by little things that she says – 'How do you think Doris looked tonight?' 'Well, I think she was upset about something.' 'Oh, was she? I didn't notice anything.' You know, a woman can bring things in which gradually alert her husband to the needs of others.

RYDER-SMITH: People often talk about the need for give and take in a relationship. How can we strike a balance between these two for ourselves?

HEMMING: I think this is very important because people quite often think that unselfishness means being a doormat, whereas it's extremely bad for other people if we make no claims for ourselves. We should make legitimate claims for ourselves, being aware all the time of the needs and feelings of others. It always makes me appalled when I hear a nice mother saying, perhaps in a court, that her daughter has had everything she wants, and now she's gone wrong. But of course, giving someone everything they want is the way to train them to go wrong, to train them to be selfish.

RYDER-SMITH: How important would you say is it to work things out together, to discuss together the problems in a relationship?

HEMMING: Very important, because the whole value of discussion of any kind is that it takes away the blind spots from our own thinking and feeling. So I would consider discussion to be vital – even for instance with quite young children, not preaching at them, but discussing with them.

RYDER-SMITH: People often say of young children that they are naturally selfish; would you say this is true?

HEMMING: Young children are naturally everything, right from angel to devil. It's quite wrong to suppose that they're only selfish. They are demanding because they've got to carve out their own identity in a world that wasn't made by them; they've got to find themselves. So young children and adolescents are often demanding and brash, but they are also capable of spontaneous loving, spontaneous thoughtfulness, spontaneous giving. We can train them by appreciating these things. This helps them to think of others, so that we can get the balance on the right side in the end.

RYDER-SMITH: Is being self-centred the same thing as being selfish?

HEMMING: No, there is a very definite distinction. You see, you can have a person who is very outgoing, extroverted, who is, in fact, thoroughly selfish. The self-centred person may be unselfish but he drives people away because he or she regards any little thing affecting himself as an enormity, whereas other things affecting other people are disregarded. This makes people reject the self-centred. The self-centred person lives life out of perspective.

RYDER-SMITH: Can you sum up how we can find a balance for ourselves in our own lives between giving to other people, and meeting our own needs?

HEMMING: It's a matter of thought and sensitivity. Thinking through situations, deciding how we ought to behave so that we don't manipulate or dominate others, but at the same time making proper claims for our own needs through sharing and co-operation.

3 Eleanor Deeping

Eleanor Deeping talks about living with pain.

I live with pain. Like so many other people past middle age who have a chronic physical disability, I live with pain and it walks, sits, and lies with me as a constant companion.

When I first realised our partnership was indissoluble it was quite a blow, and I must admit I reeled under it. Until then, I'd always managed to regard my pain as a rather difficult temporary visitor, who would depart in due course, but the dawning of the certainty of its permanent presence was quite another matter.

When I started to take stock of the situation, of course, I gradually realised that somehow I was going to have to come to terms with it, if life was to be more than just an intolerable burden.

Being by nature a rather practical person, I began by taking a very close look at the ways in which other people cope when they are faced with pain in a fairly continuous form, and as one would expect, I found their reactions to it as different as the people themselves.

Some try turning their faces from it with a terrible courage, in an attempt to ignore its existence – like Emily Brontë – isolating themselves from all consolation. In others, it seems to breed a bitter resentment, twisting the mind into a perpetual question mark . . . the cry of 'Why me ?'

Then there are the sad neurotics, who use their suffering to manipulate others into submission to their every wish, but they seem to be in a very small minority.

I wondered how I would meet the challenge.

My guess was that, like most people, I would try hard, but fail often, in the battle against self-pity and depression which always seem to be hot on the heels of pain.

Then I had a rare stroke of luck. I met one of those exceptional people who had quietly accepted the existence of intractable pain in her life – embracing it rather than wrestling with it; not neurotically, but heroically. From her, I learned something of how to turn even this enemy into a kind of friend.

The first thing she taught me was that you must never lose hope. Even if you're not a believer in miracles, you can still remind yourself that with each new day in the progress of medical history and research, there is just a possibility that a cure may be found for your particular illness, or at least a new way of controlling its pain.

In the meantime, she told me, the only key to peace of mind is acceptance – not resignation, or a pretence that pain is a good or uplifting thing in itself but acceptance of it as something which, like every other experience in life, however difficult, can bring with it some form of benediction.

She showed me how, if you grasp the nettle firmly its sting is lessened, and helped me to see that our attitude towards pain has a very real bearing on the extent to which it makes us suffer.

I'd met an expert, and I knew it.

She told me there are certain tricks you can learn in dealing with it too. That when you've done all the obvious things, such as taking proper medical advice and treatment, the next step is to try to examine your pain objectively; become determined to think about it

calmly and try to relax under its burden. Refuse to describe it to yourself or to others in over-emotional terms. Drain it deliberately of its
dramatic quality, and make sure that you cut it down to size. Then
ride along with it, instead of fighting it every inch of the way, so that
sometimes you can reduce a rampaging giant to a manageable dwarf.

Childish tricks perhaps; but she made them work for her, and now
I'm beginning to try to learn them, I know just how much maturity
and courage they demand.

There were other things she told me, too, that have helped me. The
value of remembering, when some part of your body seems to be
irreversibly damaged by illness, that what you are as a person can
never be touched or diminished by it. Even though pain and sickness
can affect behaviour and limit function, there are still certain unassail-
able recesses in the mind and spirit into which it can't reach, and that
somewhere in every sick body, there is a whole person.

She also mentioned to me once the solace she found in the knowledge that everything passes. She had a strong religious faith and
could rest on the conviction that in time she would discard her pain,
with her body, like a chrysalis, and move freely again in another
dimension, but she felt that the atheist or agnostic could draw some
comfort, too, from the thought that nothing – not even pain, can continue unchanged for ever – and I'm sure she was right.

I noticed that when her pain wasn't too bad, she was always quick
to open her mind to reading or music or any creative activity she
could manage because she was a great believer in diverting her attention from it whenever possible.

She's gone now, but she worked on her problem of pain, right to
the end, with those simple tools of hope, acceptance and diversion,
and now she's left them to me, together with the memory of her courage. I don't use them as well as she did, but I know one thing – there
are none better.

THE SKY SIDE OF LIFE   *David Scott Blackhall*

A mysterious, conglomerate, universal psychosis known as 'human
nature' is the greatest stumbling-block in the affairs of mankind.
Because of human nature, I have a hundred different personalities for
coping with a hundred different things which can happen to me. I

have some personalities which have thin, bright faces and wings on their heels and I have others with lead in their pockets and sand in their shoes and misery in their eyes. The trouble is, I am all of the personality which is manifesting itself at any particular moment. The devil, with lead in his pockets, knows nothing of the angel with wings on his heels, so that when an unpleasant event knocks me down and jumps on me, the hero is nowhere to be found and the villain takes command. He is a travesty of myself and knows only how to be dispirited and all that is necessary for me to do is to disown him. But I can't be free to do so because this fellow has had so much practice.

In untroubled times, we know exactly what we ought to do. We ought to think what advice we would give to a friend if he were in this plight and then we ought to apply that advice to ourselves. For the rest of us, let's see how we can rid ourselves of the fetters which life has forged for us.

First of all, we can't make demands of life, we can't shout louder than life or pipe for life to dance. I can't prove it to you, but I know that it's helpful to believe that our lives are exactly right for us. The kind of life which you attract, and the kind of life which I attract, offer to you and me every opportunity we need to develop ourselves, to win something from the enemy. Unpleasant events, when they happen, we always seem to regard as extraneous, as if they didn't really belong. Everything belongs, everything is right for us, this is the life we have asked for. It makes no other kind of sense, the pain and suffering it brings. But history is full of thousands of examples of man being a hundred times better than his circumstances. It is not always within our competence but it is our birthright to cultivate the chap with wings on his heels. It is our everlasting right to be on the sky side of life. So I begin urgently, when the hounds are after me, I begin to believe that I have attracted this particular event because I am the kind of person I am. Once I have set my foot on that rung of the ladder, I can be better than any situation which life can invent. Not that I am, by a long chalk, but it is possible for me. There is such a thing as letting the event go by – this is what is meant by turning the other cheek. It is not a kind of martyrdom, it is not abject, it is a courageous thing, when we turn from asking what is wrong with life and begin to ask what is wrong with ourselves.

It is necessary to hold manoeuvres sometimes, as soldiers do, so that we are ready for battle whenever the enemy sees fit to attack. In

human affairs, we never think of being in the doldrums until we are
stuck on a sandbank. Be aware of yourself in the good times, stand
slightly apart, putting some gold in the bank while 'the evil days
come not, nor the years draw nigh when thou shalt say, I have no
pleasure in them.'

My goodness, that was written a long time ago but these things never
change.

One rung of the ladder – the sky side of life. Finding it for yourself, one minute of doing that from your own understanding, is better
than a lifetime of occupational therapy which someone else has
worked out for you. There are resources in yourself which you have
never dreamed of, and the only thing you have to abandon is the
sorrowing thought which begins with 'If only' or 'I wish'; all you
have to sacrifice is your suffering.

This talk is lesson one. It lasts for ever. The second lesson starts
when you are free.

GAMES HOUSEWIVES PLAY   *Dr Ann Faraday*

Dr Faraday is a research psychologist at London University.

As a woman who tries to be objective about her own sex, I can't help
noticing that over the centuries women have managed to establish
their own forms of dominance which may be less obvious than those
of the male, but no less real. The present day militants may well find
that their greatest opposition comes not from men but from members
of their own sex who don't want to be liberated because they're really
very comfortable, thank you, with male slaves to provide for and wait
on them. Of course, they don't admit to being kept women who enjoy
a very privileged position in society: this would never do. Instead,
they try to cover up what's really happening by means of what the
American psychiatrist, Eric Berne, calls 'game playing'.

In his famous book *Games People Play*, Dr Berne describes a game
as a 'series of moves with a snare' which is utilised by one person to
trap another into a required mode of behaviour. For example, in the
game entitled 'If it Weren't for You' it is usually the wife who blames
her husband for lost opportunities.

The version of this game played by many middle-class housewives
is, 'If it weren't for you, I should now have a career', implying that

they could have become famous singers, writers or whatever, and that the very least their husbands can do is sacrifice their 'all' to the marriage as well. We then find the men spending all their leisure hours gardening, decorating and looking after the children in order to mitigate their guilt, when the truth is, more often than not, that they've deprived the world of a mediocre shorthand-typist. In my experience, a great many women marry precisely in order to escape the slog of hard work needed to build up a successful career. No such escape is available to most men, and it seems very unfair that women should compound the inequity by trying to make their husbands into guilty slaves of the home.

Then, there's another game a wife may choose to play. It's called 'Harried' and in it she allows herself to be worn to a frazzle by taking on a multitude of conflicting and largely unnecessary tasks – mother, nurse, housemaid, cook, decorator. Then, at the end of the day when her husband returns home, she can reproach him for condemning her to the life of a slave. A little elementary organisation would enable her to cope with all the necessary work – and have time to spare. If a man were as inefficient at his job as many housewives are in theirs, he'd get the sack within a month. The trouble is, of course, that housewives don't like admitting that they're really a leisured class. As Karl Marx pointed out, a privileged class often adopts such intense defences against having its position questioned that it appears to be working even harder than its slaves.

The result of such games is that all too often the marriage ceases to be fun and becomes a chore for both partners. If the husband dares to question whether he's getting enough enjoyment out of life for the work he puts into it, his wife may well respond by playing the most insidious game of all. I call it 'You're so immature', and its object is to leave the man with a general sense of guilt for believing that he has any right to fun except perhaps as an occasional reward for a lifetime of toil. I'm amazed how easily men fall for this one, especially today when all our social prophets are saying that one of our greatest needs is to learn to cope creatively with the coming age of automation and leisure.

In fact, I'm not condemning housewives for hanging on to their relatively privileged position. I don't blame anyone for contracting out of the rat-race and the world of nine-to-five jobs if someone is generous enough to provide the opportunity for doing so. What I am condemning are the time-consuming, dishonest games housewives play in their effort to pretend that their position isn't privileged. If they'd only accept that position gratefully and use it creatively, they could well be the pioneers of the new life-style devoted to 'doing your own thing'. Of course, they'd have to come to terms with and accept their own limitations, and do something in accordance with their talents, instead of bemoaning imaginary lost opportunities. Unfortunately, it will be some time before their men can opt out of the rat-race in a similar way.

It seems to me that the basic aims of the Women's Liberation Movement are excellent, but they misfire in several respects. Of course, there should be equal opportunities and pay for men and women, but the truth is that the vast majority of jobs aren't privileges any sane person, male or female, should envy. If the Women's Liberation Movement makes housewives feel their salvation lies in breaking into the male rat-race, they're taking a most retrograde step, just at the very time in history when many of the younger generation, men and women alike, are repudiating the Puritan ethic that glorifies work, and opting out of the rat-race altogether. The truth is that we all need liberation from the tyranny of drudgery, and the housewife is in the best possible position to start this liberation.

I look forward to the time – not so far away – when the whole business of the sex war is replaced by really intimate and authentic relationships in which both men and women are able to fulfil their own unique creative potentialities.

I TAKE UP YOGA   *Eileen Williams*

I first heard of Yoga fifteen years ago when a friend lent me a book on the subject. The family had a hilarious time watching me trying to do the postures shown in the photographs. I found the breathing exercises easier, but as for standing on my head – I could never imagine myself ever being able to do it.

Some years later, I had a serious operation, and during a bout of post-operation depression, when I had no appetite and little strength, I suddenly remembered two of the breathing exercises in the Yoga book, and with an effort put them into practice. I am certain that it was due to those exercises that my recovery was so rapid and complete. I thought of my yogist friend with gratitude.

Some months afterwards, when I read in a local paper that a Yoga group was forming, I immediately applied to join, although I still felt dubious about standing on my head!

I shall never forget my first evening at the Yoga class. I was told to wear a leotard and tights, or alternatively slacks and a jumper, and to take a large towel with me. I thought that the towel was to wipe the sweat off my brow after tying myself in knots, but I discovered that it was to put on the floor to keep me clean whilst doing exercises. I didn't have the courage to wear a leotard or tights, so wore slacks and a jumper.

In Yoga, the exercises are called asanas, and they are done slowly. Then the position is held for as long as possible. The asanas are designed to exercise the internal organs as well as the muscles of the body, so gradually one acquires a completely fit body, as perfect in shape as the bone structure will allow. The Yoga teacher suggested that we measure ourselves and compare our measurements with those taken after a year's instruction.

The part of the lesson I enjoyed most was the relaxation period. After a busy day with the family chores, this was sheer bliss. I was taught how to relax completely, and I did this so well that I would have dozed off had not the instructor told the class to stretch and slowly sit up.

The class was taught how to breathe correctly. Most people breathe only from the upper part of their lungs, and consequently the lungs are never completely utilised.

I also tried to stand on my head, and with some help from the instructor eventually succeeded, but only for a minute. Things certainly looked different that way up, and I could feel the blood rushing to my head. The instructor said this would not worry me after a few weeks when I had got used to doing the asana. He said that the Headstand was called the King of the Asanas because it has so many benefits, especially to the internal organs. It should not be done, however, by anyone suffering from blood pressure.

I think everyone associates the Lotus Pose with Yoga, and it was the Buddha's favourite position for meditation. Western bodies, however, do not find this easy to do, but it can be done with practice. The instructor said it took him seven years to perfect, but of course this would vary with individuals. I found my knees and ankles far too stiff to manipulate them into the required position, but when my young daughter tried it the next day she could do it effortlessly.

I went home that first evening feeling healthily tired, and I slept better than I had done for months. I had enjoyed myself so much and couldn't wait until the next week to do some more asanas. The next day I went to the library and borrowed some books on the subject. This time I didn't find the photographs amusing, and I studied seriously. I became interested in the philosophical side of Yoga and the study of this was most rewarding.

My body was becoming fit and healthy, and my friends made remarks about the change that had come over me both physically and mentally. I felt different too. I found myself giving up habits of long standing, such as smoking, for instance, which I had not been able to do before. I didn't shout at the children any more, and they seemed to me to become better behaved. Something had come into my life for which I must have been subconsciously searching – Peace!

Yoga is something the whole family can do together. It is not a religion, but is a science which points the way to leading a good and healthy life.

The Funny Side

SILVER LINING   *Ann Suter*

'The one thing you don't want,' said the fat, prosperous-looking man, 'is money.' This startled me no end. I'd always been only too well aware that the one thing I *did* want was money. Mind you, the fat man wasn't actually talking to me. I was sitting next to him in the train, and he was talking to a friend on his other side.

'When they devalue again,' he went on, 'your money will be worth nothing,' and I thought of my small hoard of savings in the Post Office, and my blood curdled in my veins. The fat man was asking his chum if he'd ever thought of silver bricks? For my part, not only had I never thought of them, I'd never even heard of them. It seemed that they were solid lumps of silver, which you bought at the current market price per ounce, then, as far as I could make out, you just sat back and waited while the value of the silver went up and up and up, and you made your fortune. Which sounded lovely. The fat man *very* confidentially passed on to his chum the address where you could get these baubles, while I, very discreetly, listened in.

At the very next opportunity I drew all my savings from the Post Office, and rushed off to London, clutching a bundle of pound notes in my hot little hand.

Now, how this fat man had managed to give the impression that this silver shop was a sort of broken-down shack up a small side street, where you knocked three times and asked for Joe, I don't know. But somehow or other he had. Which is why the actual place was such a shock. It'll give you some idea of the size if you can imagine the Taj Mahal crossed with the Kremlin. Inside it was even worse. It was like the set for one of those Hollywood Biblical epics, with 'a cast of thousands', and it made me feel like Alice in Wonderland after she'd eaten the cake that shrunk her to six inches high. A stately gentleman in a frock coat materialised from out of the floor, bowed from the waist, and asked if he could assist me.

I opened and shut my mouth once or twice before I managed to squeak: 'D'you sell silver bricks?'

I always speak falsetto when I'm nervous, and I could hear my voice going up an octave with every word. The gentleman bowed from the waist down. I thought for a moment he was going to ask me to waltz, but he only asked me to follow him, and we went echoing in procession through marble colonnades until he threw open the door of a sort of ambassadorial reception room and said: 'Mr Digby, here is a lady who requires an investment in bullion,' which wasn't quite the way I'd have put it, but I let it pass.

It only needed one glance at Mr Digby to see that he was the sort of man who'd never heard of any figure with less than three noughts on the end. I waded knee-deep through the carpet to him. He rose and bowed from the waist (it seemed to be the custom of the country) and asked what he could do for me. I was tempted to say, 'Let me out of here,' but instead I said, 'Please, I want some silver bricks.'

By now my voice had nearly reached the pitch of those whistles that are only audible to dogs. Mr Digby asked how many, and sat with pencil poised, waiting for me to quote to the nearest hundred. So I pulled my scruffy bundle of notes from my handbag and said, 'As many as I can get for that.'

I had to hand it to him. He never blinked an eyelid. He did choke a bit, but he didn't blink. He counted the notes meticulously, then said, 'That will secure you three bars. Unpolished, of course.' Well, after a certain amount of ceremonial form signing and some impressive clanging of vault doors, my three precious bars were put in the boot of my car; Mr Digby bowed from the waist again, I suppressed an inclination to curtsy, and drove off like a shot from a gun.

It was only then that I remembered I was pledged to meet a friend for a meal and a theatre; and that the boot of the car didn't lock. So when I got to the restaurant there seemed nothing for it but to stuff the silver bricks into the pockets of my coat. And that's another thing I hadn't realised – just how much solid lumps of silver weigh. The fact that I was unevenly balanced didn't help matters much, either. With two bricks in one pocket, and one in the other, I went lurching into the restaurant like a punch-drunk boxer getting up after a count of eight.

Immediately inside, a polite waiter rushed to take my coat. I demurred; he insisted, and as he slid it off my shoulders his arms were almost wrenched from their sockets. The look of amazement on his face will be something to tell my grandchildren about. With an enormous effort he heaved it up and hung it on a hook, and as he did so it gave a sort of convulsive shudder and shook from stem to stern. The waiter gave a frightened yelp and backed away as though it were going to bite him. I could have told him exactly what was the matter.

I've always been brought up to believe that a stitch in time saves nine. I believe it. I just don't happen to practise it. What the waiter felt was the torn pocket of my coat giving way, and a couple of silver bricks descending with a rush into the bottom of the lining.

When the time came to leave, the waiter very gingerly heaved my coat from the peg and, sagging a bit at the knees, gallantly helped me on with it. Trying to behave as nonchalantly as possible I drew it round me with a careless flourish, and the weighted bottom flew out and caught the waiter the most terrific clonk across the shins. It goes without saying that I've never been back to that restaurant.

Anyway, I wasn't going to risk taking the thing off again, so all through the theatre I sat swathed in my silver-lined coat, sweltering from every pore. Afterwards I rushed home, locked the bricks in the broom cupboard and didn't sleep a wink till I'd got them safely stashed away in the bank next day.

It is probably unnecessary to add that, ever since I changed my life savings into metal, the value of silver has gone down and down and down.

SHOES *Basil Boothroyd*

Basil Boothroyd, Punch writer and biographer of Prince Philip, was among those asked by Woman's Hour *to contribute to a short series on 'The Time Has Come the Walrus said to Talk of Many Things'. Of the five immortal topics suggested by the Walrus, Basil Boothroyd chose the first.*

Shoes come in two main categories: men's and women's. And you can tell them apart by the size – well, mostly you can. I've seen women's shoes striding about my village that look like men's, but in that case the women usually look like men, too, so it doesn't really count.

If a man's cleaning his wife's shoes he soon knows the difference, because there's no way of getting a grip on the stupid things. With his own shoes he can stick a hand inside and get a bit of resistance, while he slaps the stuff on with the other. But for some reason, although the average man's hand is smaller than the average wife's foot, you can't get it into the average wife's shoe. Either you have to hold it by the heel like a gun, and the whole thing's so springy that you're firing chunks of polish off the toe on to the wallpaper, or by the toe, which means you can't clean that bit because it's what you're holding it by.

It's the smallness of women's shoes that accounts for those alarming chiropody statistics: out of every hundred ailing feet, ninety-nine are female. Well, let's make it ninety-eight, and keep the thing in pairs. I was going to say, earlier on, that shoes are inseparable from feet, only it sounded a bit hot and nasty, but the chiropodist certainly has a job to separate a woman's shoes from her feet sometimes, and when he does he'd better sit well back, because they spring out twice the size. They could knock him over. This is called the tiny-little-Chinese-foot syndrome, and it's why women at the pictures have got their shoes off even before the lights go down.

I don't know why, but it's always been all right for a woman to take her shoes off, even in a crowded train; but if a man did it the women would send for the guard. This is one of those privileges that'll have to go, once we really get sex-equality. And not only in the trains but in the home. In general, when a man takes his shoes off he throws them neatly in a cupboard. Women just leave them. That's why a husband, sent upstairs to put the electric blanket on, falls over them in the bedroom doorway and goes all his length under the dressing-table.

One of the great mysteries about shoes is how you ever get anybody to sell them. Just think of all the jobs there are that have absolutely nothing to do with total strangers' feet. It isn't only the corn and bunion parade, passing constantly before the salesman's eyes: he knows that nine times out of ten there's going to be no sale, a mound of footwear a mile high and 114 empty cardboard boxes, before the next idiot wants them all out again. Let alone pairing them off properly . . . Perhaps they don't, perhaps the reason my new shoes always feel like seven and a half on one foot and nine and a quarter on the other is that that's just what they are.

I'd rather even buy new hats than new shoes, and that's saying something. A new hat in the hat-shop mirror may turn you from a handsome, jaunty creature into a village idiot, but at least there's no physical anguish. It's just the opposite with new shoes. They look so marvellous on the foot you can't wait to walk them into the office, with all your mates enviously exclaiming – actually they wouldn't take a blind bit of notice if you turned up in gold boots with topaz buttons, but never mind. The fact is that shoes that look marvellous are going to eat clean through your big toe by teatime; and the big, broad, humping great jobs that look like Mr and Mrs Duck-Billed Platypus caress the feet like a lover.

The tragedy of shoes is that when they're old, cracked, down-at-heel and giving at the seams – looking rather like you feel, in fact – that's the time when you wouldn't part with them at any price. It's also the time, of course, when you come home from the office, dying to splay out in them, and find that your wife's given them away to a collector for the underprivileged nations. I'm sorry for the under-privileged nations, I don't say I'm not. But one privilege they've got, and that's walking around in some of the most comfortable old shoes in the world.

THE DELINQUENT WASHING MACHINE　*Fabian Acker*

As an engineer, I've always tended to regard human beings as very sophisticated machines with a complex and interrelated electro-mechanical system. Most human faults, such as turning on the radio loudly, dropping litter in my front garden, turning left after signalling a right turn, and chewing gum, could be explained in purely electro-mechanical terms. Virtues, too, such as putting the milk in before the tea, cleaning the bath after use, and closing doors quietly, could be similarly explained. After all, stubbornness, whimsy and cantankerous-ness are characteristics that machines have too. Computers have been known to send threatening notes to innocent citizens in an attempt to work off their nasty tempers, and it wasn't so long ago that a Leicester businessman was informed by a computer that he had won a competi-tion for the highest milk yield of Guernsey cows in the UK.

Yet over the last few years I've had to revise or modify my opinions. It's becoming obvious to me that humans do not exhibit mechanical faults, but that machines exhibit human faults. This has been appar-ent to my wife for many years although she has not had the benefit of an engineer's training. She knows that kicking the vacuum cleaner is only effective if its hurts both of them. My own understanding was brought about by an extended experience of two harrowing years with a psychopathic washing-machine, which unfortunately belonged to me. It had no more intention of washing clothes than the cat had, and looked at the dirty washing with as much interest. At one time, feeling its position usurped by the cat, it actually caught a mouse, and but for my intervention would have washed it. I didn't see how it was caught, but I did find a bewildered mouse staggering round the washing drum; when I let it go, the cat looked at it with the same indifference as the machine regarded laundry.

However, in my misguided mechanic's way, I blithely assumed that its sudden presence in the family meant that our laundry would be done at home in future, and accordingly loaded up with a week's dirty washing.

This was the beginning of a two-year struggle between us, which began prosaically enough with a blown fuse, but ended with both of us undergoing analysis.

One of the first indications I had of its insecurity problems was of its tendency to walk, hobble, or jump after me, particularly on the drying cycle. When it became apparent that I was about to leave it alone to get on with its job, it would begin keening, first on a fairly low note, but rapidly rising to a high pitch, something like an aeroplane about to take off. At the same time it would start to shuffle back and forth, occasionally stamping its ugly feet. Then, if I failed to take any notice, it would start hopping, and at this stage the situation became dangerous and irreversible. Humming and chattering, it would shuffle, hop and dance with rage, pulling at its water and electrical connections like a naughty child with its reins. Eventually it would pull them all loose, and with a triumphant 'whoosh' would shoot out through the door, gushes of hot sudsy water and sparks leaping from every hole, and fall down the back steps, sobbing.

Of course, cementing it down to the floor cured only one symptom, and others soon occurred. In fact as soon as the cement was dry, and I offered it a very easy light load of washing, it refused to accept any, but, looking at me with a great air of reproach, quietly vomited. It had a secret capacious stomach somewhere, which managed to hold dirty water from the washing that took place (or rather failed to take place) five weeks previously, which had been fermenting and maturing in the interval.

Soon it began to play little tricks on me that had quite a vicious flavour. Once, after one of our all-night sessions, the machine finally broke down, promised to reform, and begged for a load of the dirtiest laundry I could collect, so that it would demonstrate its repentance and willingness to work. I piled in overalls, the children's bibs, car-cleaning rags, cushions, old shoes, stuffed toys and bits of carpet. Then, pouring in a generous measure of soap powder, I retired to watch through a peephole specially constructed for secret observation.

For sheer cunning and simulation, I have never seen a performance to equal that one. To all intents and purposes each stage of the washing process was carefully and decorously carried out, in orderly sequence, with a minimum of noise and a maximum of dignity. Even the spin dry (a period, usually, of great stress) caused no problems. When I was sure it was all over, I came back in, an anticipatory beam of pleasure on my face. It's true I felt a little uneasy about the complete silence, and lack of the shudders with which I was normally greeted.

When I opened the door I understood why. A complete and thorough wash-and-dry cycle lasting over forty-five minutes using five ounces of soap powder had taken place without the benefit of one drop of water. All the items were now covered with a uniform grey lumpy slime, which looked like a compound of porridge, marmalade and gravel; I had to bury the lot.

In the end I gave it to a well-known mental institution for experimental purposes. The last I heard, it had started a fashion by washing a bra, and turning it into a pair of large, opaque sunglasses.

SLUGS AND SNAILS AND PUPPY DOGS' TAILS *Irene Thomas*

Irene Thomas held the title of 'Brain of Britain' in 1961 and 'Brain of Brains' 1962. She was a member of the George Mitchell Choir for fifteen years and also took part in Round Britain Quiz.

I've got to admit it after all these years, I am a sour-puss and there's nothing I can do about it. I've always held the firm belief that every silver lining has a bloomin' great dark cloud just behind it, but as I get older I'm beginning to see what W. C. Fields meant when he said, 'Anyone who hates children and dogs as I do can't be all bad.'

Children seem to be getting more and more repulsive every day, eighty per cent of them at least. Oh, no, not *yours* of course. Yours are absolutely delightful, I'm sure. It's other people's children I'm complaining about – especially small boys . . . you've seen 'em I know. Every supermarket has its quota of Spock-marked young mums, their necks and ears going crimson with suppressed rage, trying to reason with a howling three-year-old thug. His face is usually reduced to a rim of purple surrounding a vast square bawling mouth, and I begin to think that King Herod was not such a bad chap after all.

Small girls I don't mind. Just as kittens are very nearly complete cats even when they are very young, so small girls are really tiny women from their earliest years. The difference between the sexes can be most clearly observed by those who are foolhardy enough to take a party of Mixed Infants to the zoo. Once inside the gates, the small girls will skip off whispering and chattering to stare at the tiny, brilliant tropical birds, or the bush-baby. The small boys will go pounding and yelling in their peculiarly mindless way towards the monkey-house, where monkeys and boys will spend many happy hours jeering at each other.

Years before the 'Poppies' – and by this I mean pop-groups, pop-painters and pop-pundits of all kinds – years before they came to power I saw a small chimpanzee training future pop-stars (who are mostly male, remember). It was a wet Saturday afternoon at Bellvue Zoo, and there was this little chimp pushing an empty biscuit-tin backwards and forwards, fascinated by the monotonous noise, staring dully at his audience of – guess what – small boys.

Yes, I've got a very strong case of racial prejudice against small boys. And it all started during the time when I worked as a concert-party pianist. One of the most popular items in our shows was the Kiddies' Talent Contest, with judgement by audience applause, and small prizes for the winners. This ensured that at least one proud parent for each child would be a paying customer.

There seems to be no limit to the grotesque talents of the young. There was the fourteen-year-old who played the overture to *William Tell* on his teeth with a pencil, a peroxided ten-year-old who danced in clogs and played the spoons, and a young lady who asked me to play the 'quick bit in the Rachmaninov concerto' as an accompaniment to her acrobatic dance. When I asked which Rachmaninov Concerto she settled for 'Tiptoe through the tulips'. I finally met my Waterloo in the shape of a curly-headed tot of five or six. He was lifted on to the platform by Fred, our comedian.

'What're you going to do for us, sonny?' asked Fred. 'Sing?'

'Ess,' piped the cherub.

'What are you going to sing?'

'Ger slicky ei ger slucky eee.'

'What ?'

'Ger slicky ei ger slucky eeeeeee!'

'What's 'e say ?' said Fred in a desperate whisper.

'I dunno,' I said. 'Look dear, you go and face the people and sing, and I'll play whatever it is you sing, eh ?'

He toddled off to the front of the stage and began: 'Ger sli-icky eiii ger sluck-y eeeeeee!' I tinkled away at what I thought might be a suitable accompaniment – bits of 'Little Boy Blue' mixed with 'I Love Little Pussy'. Suddenly he stopped, and turned to look at me, and in a voice of withering scorn he said, 'You don't know it, do you . . . ?'

SENTENCED   *Ronald Davis*

There's always been speculation about which of a loving wife's announcements is most likely to confound her husband. It's been held for years that high among the contenders are the well known but slightly hackneyed, 'I gave your wardrobe a good clearout today,' and 'I've pulled out all the weeds from that new flowerbed.' These words have been known to leave a man with a permanent stammer, but they're as the music of heavenly choirs compared with what he really fears to hear. The truth is, that for sheer, throat-gripping panic, nothing, not even the tongue-numbing, 'I've scrubbed out your old pipe for you dear,' holds a candle to his coming home and finding himself greeted with, 'Do you notice anything different ?'

This playful challenge holds real menace for a man, for whatever it is, his wife has probably spent hours making it, or moving it, or choosing it, or having it done to herself; and let's face it, unless he has the great fortune to find that his favourite armchair has gone, and there's one of those wicker-dish things in its place, or a boa constrictor has been introduced as a pet, he's not going to notice anything different in a thousand years.

He is, in fact, trapped.

In this miserable situation, some very strong men, and some very weak men, have been known to say outright that (thank goodness) everything seems the same as it's always been and they bear their scars with fortitude. But the average chap takes on the enormous odds against him in much the same spirit as he does the football pools. He's cornered and he'll struggle – but he's on a loser and he knows it. For, if he's appalled at the consequences of not being able to guess, he's absolutely aghast when he thinks of the penalties of making a guess and guessing wrong.

Her hair-do first of all. Looks the same as always – brownish and fairly short with little flecks in it. Still, worth a try, might just score a bull's-eye.

'Your hair looks very nice.'

No luck this time; her eyes have taken on a steely look.

A quick look round the room. Curtains. Are they new? Sort of blue with yellowy bits, seem to remember seeing those before. Now the furniture – has that been moved around? Don't think so. Cushions? Good old red and black cushions. Red and black! That's it, the cushions are different! Wait a bit though, we got red and black covers in the spring when sister-in-law came to stay, didn't we? Crumbs – that was a close one! How about the shade on the standard lamp? No, there's the cigarette burn in it from last Christmas.

Panic begins to mount. No use asking for a clue. What did it turn out to be the last time all this happened? Earrings. She'd had her ears pierced and sleeper rings put in. Not much chance of that happening again. If only the phone would ring or a saucepan boil over – a fall of soot down the chimney would be a godsend. But there's to be no relief. He must brace up, square his shoulders, and look the firing squad in the eye, knowing that at least he tried.

Some wives have been known to relent before this stage and reveal that they've changed their lipstick colour from Party Pink to Mashed Mulberry, or that they've reshaped their ear lobes with something nauseous out of an aerosol, and then all is comparatively well.

But any woman is entitled to a little impatient foot tapping, or exercise of the well-tended eyebrows, if she's repainted the kitchen ceiling and it's gone unnoticed, and there may be tears and an indigestible supper to follow – or in some cases a clip round the head – when her husband finally accepts the inevitable and admits defeat.

So here's a word of advice to all husbands. Pretend at once that you're drunk or high on heroin or otherwise incapable. Confess even to being the compulsive cat-strangler the police are looking for. You'll be forgiven for these far more quickly than for failing to spot that she's wearing a new dress she's made up at a cost of twenty-three and nine.

THREE DEADLY VIRTUES

1   *Cyril Fletcher on Determination*

*Asked to contribute to a feature on unfavourite virtues, Cyril Fletcher,
Maureen Stevens and Michael Flanders came up with these:*

My pet upside-down-virtue is that of determination. Being a most
undetermined person myself I see this virtue in others and I hate it.
And because I have not got it I am delighted to find its negative values
far outweigh its virtues.

To start with. Had I had determination I would have passed
matriculation, as 'A' and 'O' levels were called in my day, and become
a solicitor or something of that sort. I did try three times, but lacking
the determination had to become a comedian. What a loss to the
entertainment industry if I had had that alleged virtue. Why, you
wouldn't be listening to me now. But perhaps not having the determination you have already switched off . . .

Determination is closely allied to obstinacy. And the obstinate are
self-willed and refractory. 'I am determined to finish this,' they say.
Like drinking a yard of ale, or wolfing down some enormous meal, or
papering a room before breakfast, which my wife has been known to
do. No, not the yard of ale, the papering. And then you overdo it.
People with determination are always overdoing things. Hospitals are
full of them.

Columbus was determined to discover the New World. Without
this determination the Red Indians and the bison would be having a
whale of a time and there would be no American comedians on the
telly. For that matter Mr Logie Baird was too determined. Without
telly, radio would still be in its hey-day and I love radio.

What about those determined ladies with what I call organising
feet – they always have organising feet – who arrange things like fêtes
and bazaars ? I even heard one of them say as rain was dripping off her
picture hat, 'I'm absolutely determined to have a fine day next year.'
'And someone better to open it,' I said. But she didn't hear because
she was determined to find the Vicar by then.

Then there are those very determined people who do extraordinary
things like writing out the Ten Commandments on a grain of rice,
making a handbag out of a dried marrow, that sort of thing.

Determined gardeners are very funny. You can't be determined in
a garden. Mother Nature has a way with the determined. A short

sharp holocaust here and there, hailstones the size of strawberries –
or should I say the size of crushed strawberries.

There is always that very funny dog-act from the music halls
where the dog is determined not to do what its master is telling it. I
have one of these at home, it's a beagle called Blossom – but that's
another story. When told not to run into the woodland garden she –
with determination and Betty's newest and most diaphanous underwear between her determined jaws, determined on burial – looks up
with her humorous face and seems to say, what's the difference
between bulbs and bloomers!

Determined people on camping holidays with tents are funny I
think. Especially in the rain and preferably with a high wind; and I
think those who have forgotten their sleeping bags are best.

I cannot bear comedians who are determined to be funny. Can
you ?

2 Maureen Stevens on Cheerfulness

When I was a teenager, every now and again on a Saturday night, I
used to get 'stood-up'. Then I would hang all over the house like a
big, black cloud. My mother would say, 'Cheer up, chickabiddy, one
door closes, another door opens.' Even when it did, I could still have
hit her. Because really I didn't want cheering up, not by her or by
anyone else. What I wanted, in fact, was one big, beautiful wallow.

Am I alone in finding cheerfulness so repugnant ? Am I the only
one who reacts by going to the opposite extreme – you're cheerful
and I sink into a deep Russian-type gloom. I have a friend (at least I
did up to this broadcast, I'm not sure about afterwards) whose husband
lost his seat at the last General Election. As he stumbled off the Town
Hall balcony all hurt and bewildered (I mean back into the room, not
off the edge of the balcony, he wasn't that hurt and bewildered) my
friend took his arm and whispered, 'Cheer up darling, we've still got
each other.' Her husband only told me this because he's thinking of
leaving her. Oh dear, if only she'd burst into tears, he would have
comforted her. If she'd said, 'Get yourself round to the Labour
Exchange and sign on,' he would have blessed her for the practical
advice. But just plain, unadulterated cheerfulness . . .

But are we alone, he and I, I wonder ? I don't think so. I reckon there are millions daily being driven nearer the edge by all the Cheerful Charlies of this world. Look at Christmas – if you dare. Think of all the quarrels, depressions and ugly silences that come on at Christmas, I'm sure it's only a reaction to all that good cheer. All those exhortations to 'God rest you merry' and 'Carol, carol gaily'.

And early-morning cheerfulness, just think of that. Surely any person in their right mind would agree that anyone who leaps out of bed at cock-crow, bounds across the bedroom, tosses back the curtains, flings open the window and throws out their chest, can damn well throw the rest of themselves out with it.

And so far as I'm concerned, the same goes for all those professionally cheerful people. Take heed, all you doctors and nurses; the next time I land up in the Casualty Department with a broken leg and you say, 'Cheer up, you've still got the other one,' I shall dot you in the eye. And as your eye goes black and closes up, I shall say, 'Cheer up, you've still got the other one.'

3   *Michael Flanders on Honesty*

I'm not sure that I really want to play this *Woman's Hour* game of 'Deadly Virtues'. So far as women are concerned, the obvious one has always been their 'virtue' itself and, down the ages, men have kept sniping away at that on the lines of:

> 'Had we but world enough and time,
> This coyness, Lady, were no crime;
> But at my back I always hear
> Time's winged chariot . . . whizzing along the M.1.

There's not much need for that in these permissive days. In fact if you take all the Seven Christian Virtues set up in medieval times to counter the Deadly Sins, there's little enough of them to go round. I'd say, Justice, Fortitude, Prudence, Temperance, Faith, Hope and Charity needed all the encouragement they can get.

But provided we keep the still deadly sins as our main target I suppose it's all right to take an occasional shot at some of the so-called Christian pseudo-virtues. At the 'Modesty' of people who certainly have plenty to be modest about. 'Generosity' in terms of:

> 'Whatever, Lord, we give to Thee,
> Repaid ten thousandfold we'll be;
> So *gladly*, Lord, we give to Thee!'

Or the 'Meekness' with the steely glint in its eye born of the certain knowledge that it will one day inherit the earth – and *then* see just how meek it will be!

I think my unfavourite of these is 'Honesty'. I don't mean the kind that's the best policy (though with some of the policies being issued these days you might just as well put your trust in honesty as in vinegar and brown paper or a tin umbrella). Nor honesty in financial matters. I have a friend, who shall be nameless, called Donald Swann who takes this to such lengths that if he buys a newspaper to read the review of one of our shows he enters the cost in an account book under 'Professional Expenses'. But if he just wants to read the news it goes in the column marked 'Personal Outgoings'. (I've known him lay awake all night worrying where to enter the 6d. when he'd bought the paper to read the review but the review wasn't in it). Faced with a fiscal year's worth of entries like these, the Consultant who helps Don sort out his tax affairs remarked that he'd spent a lifetime dealing with liars and swindlers but he didn't know what trouble was until he met one scrupulously honest man. I believe he gave up accountancy and went into munitions.

No, I mean the 'Honesty' in which people feel it their moral duty to tell you all the nastiest things they can think of. 'To tell you the honest truth, I have never liked you.' 'In all honesty I think that new hat makes you look years older.' 'I feel it only honest to tell you that I saw him having lunch with her in Barchester last week.'

Speaking for myself, when I ask for your honest opinion I want flattery not criticism. So please don't write in to say that to be honest you didn't care for my contribution to this programme and why didn't they have Rolf Harris ?

Because I honestly don't want to know.

A PIG, A PARTY AND A PIANO   *Norma Huxtable*

'What about this party, then ?' I asked the farmer/husband/boss for the umpteenth time. As a rule he looked forward to our christmas party, but this year at the very mention of the word 'party' he looked as though I'd made an improper suggestion. And all because I'd got it in my head to borrow a piano. Year in and year out we had the same old parties with the menfolk playing cards and whooping it up in the kitchen with a barrel of cider, whilst us womenfolk sat in the parlour, sedately sipping a glass of ruby wine and discussing how our chickens were laying.

But this year the worm was slowly turning. This year was the year of revolution. This year everybody would mingle, united in song and dance, and our corner of Exmoor would vibrate with music far into the night, whilst we poor neglected womenfolk would, for once, be the life and soul of the party.

The farmer/husband/boss said he'd never heard such rubbish in his life. He even went further and reckoned I'd be getting a bad name trying to turn our farmhouse into one of the Yo-Yo or Go-Go clubs, whatever 'tis. I told him 'twas our own friends that would be coming, not a crowd of teeny-boppers, and I didn't suppose we'd do anything more intimate than the hokey-cokey. This was sheer cunning on my part, for if there's one dance he enjoys 'tis shaking his arms and legs in the hokey-cokey.

But the farmer/husband/boss wouldn't give in without a fight. He wanted to know where the piano was coming from and what silly idiot was going to play it. I'd arranged to borrow the piano from his own sister who lived about thirty miles away, and a very respectable pianist friend of ours would be invited to the party. But I planned to keep the piano a surprise. The cheapest way to transport it would be in our pig trailer and the farmer/husband/boss could fetch it when he had time.

I half expected him to marvel at my efficiency, but instead he played his trump card. ''Taint legal!' he said with the air of a chap who knows what he's talking about. ''Taint legal to transport furniture in a farm vehicle.'

By my reckoning a piano wasn't furniture, 'twas a musical instrument, but he wouldn't be side-tracked. At that crucial point, in walked our neighbour, the pig expert, a chap who nodded wisely, considered our problem for a second, and produced a solution in less time than it took to scratch his head. 'Hexactly!' he said. 'All you got to do is to put a pig in with your piano and you'm legal.'

Realising he'd lost his argument, the farmer/husband/boss unexpectedly switched to tender concern for the pig. 'Twas nothing more than downright cruel to make a pig ride in an open trailer in winter. But the brilliant, quick-witted pig expert reckoned the pig could ride in the car, after all ''twas all part of the same conveyance. In the end the farmer/husband/boss gave in and agreed to fetch the piano on the night of the party when there would be plenty of help to unload it.

As arrangements for the party started swinging, some of my enthusiasm actually seemed to rub off on the farmer/husband/boss. My eyes popped more than a bit one day when I spotted him in the cow-shed gliding by the open door in his naily boots, arms out-stretched, then gliding back again, until it registered he was practising his hokey-cokey for the great night.

Everything went according to plan, though I must say keeping the piano secret was a bit of a strain, but I did so want to surprise everybody.

On the evening of the party, the farmer/husband/boss left in good time to collect the piano, taking with him the pig, so that everything was all legal and above-board.

By eight o'clock I had on my best lace dress with the fringe and was soon greeting our guests. The piano arrived before the pianist, but this was all to the good seeing it was to be a surprise. It took six king-size farmers to unload the piano and heave it the length of the farmhouse to the sitting-room, with frequent stops en route for liquid refreshment.

It was no sooner in place with two tastefully placed coloured candles in the candle-holders than the door opened and there stood our pianist. But what riveted my eyes was the sling round his neck holding his sagging right arm. There was a moment of stunned silence, then the farmer/husband/boss spoke, very quiet. All he said was, 'pass the cards.' The farmer chaps all followed him out to the kitchen and I fixed my gaze on the lady guests and started the con-versation. 'How – how's your chickens laying?' I asked.

FOREVER HAMLET *Arthur Marshall*

It is not easy to pass down life's crowded pathway without at some point being exposed to Shakespeare's play, *Hamlet*. I have been repeatedly exposed in the classroom and the cinema, on the television and the radio, on gramophone records and, of course, in the theatre. Nowhere is one safe. People quote from it at the drop of a hair-net. Like it or not, all must agree that those Danes really were a very bizarre lot, with Prince Hamlet winning an all-time Oscar for rum and tedious behaviour. If a more depressing collection of characters were ever gathered together in one place, I have missed them.

And heavens, how they all *talk*! I admit that it's largely in some serviceable kind of blank verse but there's so *much* of it. Hamlet's mania for burbling to himself should have been curbed in childhood. Gertrude is much to blame here. It was a mother's task and she must have heard him, for nowhere in that singularly drafty castle was there a square inch of privacy for anybody. Have you ever counted the number of lines of soliloquy that Hamlet requires to inform us that he's tired of life and isn't all that keen on Claudius? I have. It's well over two hundred, and that certainly is a terrible lot of soliloquy.

I've often wondered what the guests at Elsinore achieved in the way of grateful bread-and-butter letters. Let's imagine that an upper-crust English couple, Eleanor and Egbert, have been staying and now write to say thank you. How might it go?

Bury St Edmunds, Friday.

Dearest Queen Gertrude,

What a heavenly weekend! Egbert and I hated having to dart down to the docks before the theatricals began but, as it was, we only just caught our packet.

How to begin to thank you for all the treats? That breath-taking tour of the ramparts, the fencing display, cordials in your closet, Ophelia's impromptu cabaret, and dear old Polonius. His riddles and jokes and conundrums were a delight – such a fun person.

It's too exciting about Hamlet's unofficial engagement. What a blessing in these sadly sophisticated days he has chosen somebody as simple and unaffected as Ophelia. We adored seeing her wildflower collection and her well-stocked herbarium. I think you are right to postpone her swimming lessons until she is safely married. A snuffly cold at the altar creates an unfortunate effect on that Day of Days.

As to the armoured apparition that appeared in our room on the stroke of midnight and started jabbering nineteen to the dozen, I think you must be right. It was a nightmare caused by indigestion – no reflection, dearest Gertie, on your tasty smörgåsbord!

Greetings to Claudius – how lovely to see you both already such a team – and thank you, thank you, thank you.

Ever your devoted Eleanor.

P.S. We leave shortly for Glamis for a week's shooting with the Macbeths. He is more or less all right, but she takes offence at the merest trifle and looks absolute daggers. We always lock our bedroom door there. Things are very apt to go bump in the night.

YOU CAN'T SLEEP WITH A MAN *Anne Jones*

I've given up explaining. I used to, but I so often found myself involved in the most frightful, intricate webs of wild misunderstanding – all arising from the fact that when I said I couldn't sleep with my husband, I meant just that. Exactly that. I couldn't close my eyes and drift off, knitting up my ravelled sleave of care with my husband in the same bed, knitting up his.

Because I am a neat knitter. Elbows well in to the sides, ankles crossed, and approximately parallel to the edge of the bed. I heard, once that the normal human being changes position something like fifty times during the night, so I hope I do. But I never see any sign of it in the morning. My mother used to say that often, when she came in to wake me up, she jumped to the conclusion that I had died during the night, so still and immobile I was, and looking so peaceful too, she said.

But my husband is anything but a neat knitter-up of *his* ravelled sleave. I believe his knitting is more a form of weaving. And I mean weaving as it was before the spinning jenny. On a hand-loom with a foot-treadle. I discovered this within one week of being married to him, and this is what leads me to say, 'you can't sleep with a man.'

They have different sleeping habits from us, you see. Men seem to revert to their childhood the minute they get their eyes closed. Women don't do this. Women *use* their sleeping hours, and nothing is more calculated to keep a woman fully aware that she *is* a woman, full-grown and mature, and not a darling, drowsy little rock-a-bye-baby, than a headful of rollers encased in a slumber-net, cream all over her face, and a pair of astronaut gloves on her hands, full of hand-lotion. But men, not having any of this to go through, simply have their bath, pull on their pyjamas, and tumble off into the Land of Nod exactly as they've done since they were six years old. Not a thing changes for them.

Of course I don't mean they actually still have to have their teddy, but I find they do like to have something – for their sense of security, I daresay – and from a spot of private research I've been doing I've found that this is, very often, their handkerchief. One wife I know told me that she was woken up in the middle of the night on her honeymoon with her husband's great hand planted on her face. He was still fast asleep, but sitting bolt upright and groping wildly about, crying in a piteous voice, 'Where's me hanky? I want me hanky.'

Another husband I found out about will insist, during the summer months, on having a cold-water bottle in bed with him. Because he gets hot, he says. But his wife doesn't get hot and words cannot describe, according to her, the unspeakable horror of turning over, all warm and cosy, in your sleep, and having an ice-cold rubber monstrosity get you in the small of the back. And, of course, he only imagines he's hot. If it was so hot, his wife, with her extra layer of subcutaneous, would be hot, too, wouldn't she? And she never is, she says. She's usually just about middling–until she gets the cold-water bottle aimed at her, of course, and then she's frozen for hours.

I've discovered all sorts of things that women have to make the best of in this inquiry I've been on. Like having husbands who swear they can't possibly sleep a wink if there's a wrinkle in the under-sheet. This is clearly some sort of *The Princess and the Pea* complex, but it is sheer misery, the wife of one of these sensitive aristocrats told me, having your husband leap out of bed every few minutes to smooth out the sheet and then sidle back in again, like a limbo dancer. And when she complained, he tried smoothing out the wrinkles 'in situ' so to speak, and did so much threshing around that it was no improvement at all. Of course, this is obviously some kind of neurosis, as it is with the man I met who claimed to have only managed to stay in bed every night of his forty years of married life by employing a sort of cantilever action, bracing both feet against an ottoman which he placed at the side of the bed; he was in constant fear of being thrown out of bed by his wife, a large lady with a kick like a mule according to him. But she said this was utter nonsense; she happened to be an extremely passive sleeper when she managed to get to sleep, but her nerves were worn to shreds by all these years of lying next to a sort of human pontoon bridge, all stress and tension. And he didn't seem to breathe properly, she said. He just gulped in air, spasmodically, every now and then – with the effort of hanging on, I suppose, but it absolutely wore her out.

It's no wonder, is it, that the divorce rate goes on and on swooping upwards, with all these people sleeping together.

BRUSH WITH AUTHORITY   *Alan Melville*

I'm bitterly disappointed with the police. They are, I know, splendid chaps, dealing tactfully but firmly with demos, drunks, dangerous drivers, people who throw bottles at people who play football with a round ball, or people who chant anti-Apartheid slogans at those who prefer to play it with the oval shape. But I feel they, and in particular the Sussex Constabulary (E Division), have let me down very badly indeed. Let me explain.

I live in a part of Brighton which is just outside the parking meter zone, with the natural result that vast hordes of commuters, or visitors to the town, park their cars bumper-to-bumper along the terrace early each morning, lock them carefully, and leave them there until their day's labour, shopping or sight-seeing is completed. Around five or five-thirty they drive off, sometimes with a cheery wave to the resident ratepayers who can't find a parking space anywhere near their own homes, and in my own case on one occasion with the quite unnecessary remark that it was high time I did something about the greenfly on the roses in my front garden.

The situation has been complicated within the last few months by revised parking regulations, whereby you can park for as long as you like along one side of the terrace (one car has been there now for three months: I have a theory that it belongs to Mr Biggs, the train robber), but for a maximum of two hours only along the other side which, I need hardly say, is the side my house is on. This has had some remarkable results, by no means all of them bad. A new spirit of good-neighbourliness and camaraderie has developed along the terrace. We have formed ourselves into a sort of vigilante group. The phone rings and Mr Mair in number twelve says, 'Just thought I'd let you know there's a space coming vacant bang opposite number eighteen.' Of course, by the time you dash downstairs and find the ignition key, the space has been occupied by someone else who'd driven in from Haywards Heath to take the kids to see the dolphins – but it's the thought and the spirit of togetherness that counts. Or Mrs Lloyd in number seven rings and, lowering her voice in a conspiratorial manner, says, ' I thought I'd better tip you off. The warden's back and he's taking everybody's number, and it's that awful one who looks like Jeremy Thorpe.'

Well, now, to cut a long story not really short, but at any rate shorter, on 16 August last year I had a ticket slapped on my wind-screen. I have it in front of me. It's numbered 5236, and signed by a Mr Norris, and it accuses me of the heinous crime of parking my own car outside my own front door between the hours of 2.45 p.m. 'to/at' (what that means I wouldn't know) 5.15 p.m., on the date in question. It was stuck very firmly to the windscreen, in a position obviously carefully chosen so that when one had managed to unstick it, a good deal of the gum and gooey paper was left on the windscreen in order to make driving even more difficult than it normally is these days. And at the foot of the notice there was a neat little detachable slip saying that I enclose the sum of £2 as payment of the Fixed Penalty for the offence mentioned in Part 1 of this notice.

Now it so happens that over the past year or so I've been involved in two series on BBC television based on Sir Alan Herbert's *Misleading Cases*, so I'm in a litigious mood. £2 Fixed Penalty, my eye, I said, I'm going to fight this case and am prepared to take it, if need be, to the House of Lords, if not higher. For one thing, the car hadn't been parked in the terrace between the hours stated on the ticket. It was a gorgeous day. I'd gone down to the beach for a swim and on getting back to the terrace had found that, by some miracle comparable to the dividing of the Red Sea, the space I'd vacated was still unoccupied. For another thing, the traffic warden hadn't got the car's registration number right. He'd got it very nearly right, but not absolutely right. I sat up night after night rehearsing how I would conduct my own case when it came into Court. I almost began to feel sorry for the traffic warden when I got him in the witness-box. 'Mr Norris,' I was going to say. 'You will bear in mind that you are under oath. Are you prepared to swear that you kept this car under non-stop, ceaseless, vigilant observation between the hours of 2.45 p.m. and 5.15 on the date in question ? If that is so, Mr Norris,' I was going to say (I even practised in front of the bathroom mirror flicking the tail of my barrister's wig like they do on the films, until I realised I wasn't a barrister and wouldn't be wearing a wig). 'If that is so, Mr Norris, can you explain to the Court how you got the number wrong ?' Sensation in Court. Headlines in the *Brighton Evening Argus:* 'Local Play-wright Routs Law.' I even planned a party for all the people along the terrace who owned cars.

I was beginning to get rather despondent about the whole thing because absolutely nothing happened until 22 October, when I got a letter signed on behalf of the Chief Superintendent saying that it was still open to me to pay the £2 Fixed Penalty in respect of the offence committed on 16 October. He was only three months out, so I began rehearsing my lines again, adding a pretty devastating peroration about decent law-abiding citizens being harried by a Nazi-type alleged bureaucracy that couldn't get either their car numbers or their dates right. I saw myself being discharged without a stain on my character: I envisaged applause breaking out in the public gallery and having to be shushed. I even thought of claiming costs against the police, the traffic warden, and anyone else I could think of, for waste of time, loss of earnings and defamation of character. I then decided that the decent British thing to do would be to waive any claim for costs, take the warden out for a drink after the case, and say, 'No hard feelings, chum.'

To my horror, I got another letter dated 28 October, also signed on behalf of the Chief Superintendent: 'I have reconsidered my original decision in this matter and have decided to take no further action on this occasion.'

After all that rehearsing. After practising in front of the bathroom mirror holding my jacket lapel like Perry Mason. It isn't *fair*. Is there no justice in this country?

A FEW FOOLISH THINGS   *Ba Mason*

If wisdom comes with age I'm a very slow developer – perhaps even retarded, in which case I need special help and much sympathy. It seems to me I was born a fool and have remained one. It's forgivable to be young and foolish. Though my remembered youthful follies bring a blush to my cheek, it's an indulgent blush; my recent elderly follies steep me in hot shame.

There's no fool like an old fool. How true! I should have loved to have been a Wise Woman – not a hag in a cave casting runes and nasty aspersions at anyone who dared to cross the cave threshold – no, not like that; but a dear old lady who'd learnt from life and who never did stupid foolish things which ill befitted her age group.

Why, for instance, did I feel it necessary last week to jump about flapping my arms and opening and shutting my mouth in beak-like gestures just because someone shouted from the road while I was picking strawberries, 'What a big blackbird!'? It wasn't funny. It wasn't dignified. It was just plain folly. Then there was my wig. The longing for a wig curdled my days and nights. But it was under control because I thought wigs were so expensive as to be beyond my means. Then I discovered they had become cheaper. A wig boutique was opened in the town near where I live. 'Ah, but,' I thought, 'they will be nasty cheap wigs made of goats' hair, or coconut fibre, or crêpe paper.' Not at all. These wigs were beautiful and just within my price range. My family, who are rather coarse and insensitive where I'm concerned, couldn't understand my wanting a wig. They laughed and said, 'Oh no, not Mummy in a wig! She'll look like Danny La Rue.' My mother-in-law said quite sharply it was ridiculous to want a wig. That settled it. I was down at the boutique in a flash. Trying on the wigs was quite pleasant. A tall and beautiful girl helped me and she didn't think it was a bit strange or silly to want a wig. Obviously not – she was, after all, selling the things. She guided me away from the more extravagant ones, the long straight waterfalls of blonde hair and the cap of tight black curls. We agreed together on a modest little peruke, rather gingery, but interestingly streaked with platinum. This she settled on my head and with her magic brush she coaxed and back-combed and twisted it and, do you know, I didn't look too bad. In fact, in a quiet way, I was pretty thrilled. I left on air with my wig in a plastic bag.

I was then rather busy and had no occasion to wear my wig, which sat in its plastic bag in the cupboard for a week or two. When I came to try it on I found the magic shaping had lost its power and that my wig was a squalid nest of tight chestnut and silver ringlets. Also it seemed tighter, heavier and larger all over than it had been in the shop. It hadn't covered my ears then. It did now and also came down over my eyebrows. No amount of brushing on my part could straighten it. It was a cross between one of those curly, woolly, crocheted winter caps and a space helmet. Wearing it for more than five minutes brought on a crashing headache and partial deafness. My dogs growled when I came downstairs in it. My cat arched her back and spat. When I went out in the garden, birds flew, shrieking, into the safety of the tree tops. I knew they were shrieking from the way they flew. I couldn't hear them of course. My wig went back into the cupboard. However unsatisfactory my own hair is, it doesn't disturb the balance of nature.

Folly number two was less expensive but equally unsatisfactory. I attended a coffee morning for a good cause and among some other useless knick-knacks I bought a pair of false eyelashes. Long, dark, fringed and exotic they sat demurely in a little box along with directions for use and some sticky stuff. I read that it was recommended to apply the adhesive with a pin, but failed to notice this meant to the false eyelashes – not the human eyelid. I found that when my hand approached my eyes it developed a convulsive and uncontrollable palsy. The pin jerked dangerously near the eyeballs which watered in cataracts and refused, rightly, to stay open for a split second. The eyelashes have taken their place in the cupboard alongside the wig.

Undeterred by these failures I found myself longing for an evening trouser-suit. Why not ? Well, for many a good reason, but that didn't stop the longing. Discreet family inquiries once again brought forth nothing but jeering remarks. One of my children said doubtfully that it might be all right if I never, never went out in it; as though I'd asked him if he thought a see-through plastic bubble brassière might suit me. Being a dressmaker in a humble way I decided to make myself a trouser-suit. I was cheered to find a wide choice of patterns for these. Armed with one, I approached a singularly disinterested Indian gentleman in the fabric department of a London shop. With unconcealed disdain he ripped off five and one eighth yards of emerald green slub rayon. The next few days passed happily for me making my two-piece evening trouser-suit. The days following passed less happily in taking it to pieces again – the tunic was far too long, the trousers far too short. Reassembled, I tried it on again and saw a poor old Chinese peasant about to harvest the rice crop. All I needed was a big flat straw hat and a pole over my shoulder. The anxious wrinkled face was there already, perfectly in character, and matching the wrinkled trousers. Slub rayon, as even a fool should know, does not hang as well as pure silk shantung. Still there's a world of difference in the price. Standing with my legs stretched widely apart, like the model on the pattern, didn't help at all. I looked as if I'd got myself stuck in the mud of the paddy-fields.

Is there a ray of hope for this poor fool ? Yes. We are troubled by flocks of wood-pigeons swooping down on the vegetables. Do you think that a new scarecrow, with a chestnut wig, false eyelashes and an emerald green two-piece evening trouser-suit with wide flapping legs, would perhaps give them a nasty moment or two ?

The Practical View

HOW TO PREVENT TRAVEL SICKNESS   *Gillie Slade*

As far back as I can remember, whether I was going on holiday, or simply on an excursion, I always arrived feeling slightly nauseated and exhausted, a 'sick headache' I believe it was called.

Some years ago I was contemplating a rail journey to Scotland and I wondered whether to try travelling by night in a sleeping berth, hopefully anticipating that I'd wake the following morning with the miles behind me. I happened to mention my dilemma to an elderly friend. 'Rubbish, girl,' she said. 'A piece of brown paper, that's all you need. Put it next to your skin, over the stomach, and you will enjoy every minute of your journey.' She said she'd been told about this when she was travelling from India by sea.

I smiled and thanked her for the advice, privately wondering how this old wives' tale originated. I booked the sleeping berth, ignored the brown paper and, despite taking pills to avoid travel sickness, arrived in Scotland without sleep and feeling wretched. On the return journey we were unable to book sleeping berths and decided to travel by day. I didn't have any confidence in my elderly friend's advice, but just to say I had tried it, I carefully cut a piece of thick brown wrapping paper into an eight-inch square and put it on as advised, mentally laughing at myself for doing so. I had a marvellous journey and I was able to take an interest and enjoy the scenery. I thanked my friend for her good advice and from time to time I passed it on, only to be met with ridicule, laughter, and tolerant sympathy for my odd notions.

Last year I spent my holiday in Italy where I took coach tours without hesitation, but always wearing brown paper next to my stomach. One trip included a visit to Capri and although this is only a fifty minute journey by boat from Sorrento, the sea can be a little rough. As I sat admiring the wonderful view of Vesuvius, I was suddenly conscious of people staggering past looking ill and reaching for the rail at the side of the ship. I felt very surprised as I was enjoying the motion of the ship, and the occasional rise, dip and roll. When we docked at Capri I noticed that several of our own party were still feeling under the weather and already dreading the return journey.

When buying a souvenir of Capri I asked an assistant if I could have a sheet or two of brown wrapping paper. She looked surprised but handed them to me with her compliments. I folded the paper over and tore it into eight inch squares, then I distributed them to the suffering with the appropriate instructions. I need hardly tell you that the husbands of some of the ladies looked pityingly at me as if I had gone out of my mind, but the women would have taken anyone's advice to obtain some relief.

We boarded the boat for Sorrento and the crossing back was equally rough. They all sat very quietly and I didn't know how they were feeling. When we arrived I tentatively inquired if everyone felt well. 'Yes, we're fine,' they said. There had not been one casualty from seasickness. Some members of our party wore brown paper on the flight home. One lady said to me, 'I don't know *why* and I don't know *how*. But it works!'

THE ALL-PURPOSE DUSTER   *John White talks to Doreen Forsyth*

Following this broadcast, Woman's Hour *received a record number of letters – not only requests for the recipe but many enthusiastic testimonials to its efficacy.*

To our regret, Mr White died shortly before the broadcast was transmitted.

JOHN WHITE: The fluid for this impregnated duster is composed of equal parts of the very cheapest vinegar and any paraffin. It is better, when one starts to impregnate the duster, to have a coffee tin with a plastic lid. Into the coffee tin pour an eggcupful of vinegar first, and then an eggcupful of paraffin, replace the lid, shake as vigorously as possible, and then put in the duster. Leave it there for about twenty minutes then turn over the tin so that the duster gets thoroughly impregnated.

After taking out the duster it has rather an offensive smell, so hang it in the fresh air until it is nearly dry. This duster will be called number one. This is for general furniture cleaning, silver cleaning, window cleaning, and all the rest.

DOREEN FORSYTH: You don't only clean furniture then? You can clean other things with your impregnated duster?

WHITE: Oh yes. After I had tried it on the furniture, I then started to find out what else this duster would do, and to my absolute surprise found that all vitreous enamel surfaces, like electric cookers, refrigerators and geysers, cleaned with this duster with just one simple dusting.

FORSYTH: What about things like baths or sinks?

WHITE: It will clean the bath and all porcelain sinks. It is best to use the duster to clean the bath just after the water has run away, while it is slightly warm. Where one has very hard water it removes the scurf mark at once and leaves the bath almost as good as new. One day, I used the duster on the windows and by careful timing found that I could clean all the windows in the flat in one third of the time that it usually took, there being no water, no wash leather, no cold fingers, just a single duster. Of course one can't stay here, one has to go on and so I discovered that all mirrors, glass and china ornaments yielded to the same treatment. Then I found one day in a cupboard in the kitchen an electro-plated stand that had once been the stand for a casserole. It was completely covered with oxidisation. It was as black as could be. I didn't think it would be possible, but to my surprise this duster removed all the oxidisation and polished it.

FORSYTH: Quickly?

WHITE: Quickly, just simple polishing, so then I started on the silver ornaments and various things about the house. With furniture the important thing is that after being treated with this duster it will not, and cannot, finger mark, which is a great advantage.

FORSYTH: Tell me, do you have any worries at all about using vinegar and paraffin on precious metals such as silver. Do you think the effect could be corrosive in any way?

WHITE: I have discovered after five months of using it that I get a quick polish that lasts a very long time and has no effect upon the silver or the plated things.

FORSYTH: Have you tried it on your car?

WHITE: Oh yes. This was probably, from the man's point of view, the best of all things. Before I tried it on the car I had a very old mop. I washed this and then impregnated it with the same fluid and with this mop took off all the obvious dust and grit, and then applied duster number two which is exactly the same mixture but the duster is not permitted to dry. It's relatively moist. With the moistened cloth I then rubbed all over the bodywork. It removes the road film and all the rain spots that accumulate over our cars, cleans all the chromium at one go, and all the windows with the single exception of the windscreen. Because it leaves a slight film I always clean the windscreen with the wash leather and water. But for the rest of it, the whole car is now done with a slightly moist duster, after which I take a dry duster and just gently dust all over the surfaces, and my old car, now ten years old, shines like new. I never use any polish on it at all, of course.

FORSYTH: Apart from the windscreen is there anything else you've discovered that it won't clean ?

WHITE: The only thing it will not clean is brass. If the brass has been polished, then a rubbing with this duster will keep it polished forever, but the brass would have to be cleaned first. I can't say why. I'm not scientific enough to know this, but I also impregnated my wife's dry floor mop with surprising results, because it picks up all the dust and gives a slight shine to the woodwork around the surrounds of the carpet.

FORSYTH: Have you tried your duster on paintwork ?

WHITE: Yes, if the paintwork is a highly polished variety it will remove all stains and marks, just slight pressure on the duster removes the lot. In fact after two years of experimenting with this duster, it has not been necessary for me or my wife or anyone else in the house to buy or use any polish of any description whatever. It's a terrific time-saver and is very cheap.

FORSYTH: And do you have to impregnate your duster each time you use it ?

WHITE: Oh no. Of course it would entirely depend upon the volume of work done with the duster, but one can say that it will last on average for three to four weeks after which it is washed, and when it's dry it is impregnated again, the whole cost being about twopence.

TWO HOME-MADE FACE CREAMS, from 'Beauty Without Cruelty'.

Here are two recipes for face creams – one for a nourishing night cream, and one for a cleansing cream. You will notice that there has been no exploitation of or suffering to animals in these creams. To make these, you'll want a thermometer of the kind you use in fruit bottling.

1. The nourishing night cream:

1 oz white bees-wax	2 fl. oz water
6 fl. oz corn or maize oil	$\frac{1}{4}$ teasp. borax

In case it helps you, 1 fluid ounce is approximately equivalent to two tablespoonsful.

You heat the water and borax in a saucepan to sixty-five degrees Fahrenheit. Then in another saucepan heat the corn oil and bees-wax to the same temperature. Now mix them both together at this temperature, and stir gently until cool. Then put the mixture into a pot.

This nourishing night cream is suitable for all types of skin and it is unscented, as some people are allergic to perfume. You apply it, after thoroughly cleansing your skin, to your face and neck, and when you come to your eyes, just pat it gently round them. You can either remove it after twenty minutes with a tissue or, if you prefer, you can leave it on overnight.

As the cream does not contain a preservative, you should use it up within two or three months; and meanwhile keep it in a cool place – but not in the refrigerator.

2.   The cleansing cream:

The ingredients you need for this are the same as for the nourishing night cream, with the exception of the corn oil. In place of corn oil you use soya oil. The method of making it is exactly the same as for the nourishing night cream, and again, you should keep it in a cool place and use it up within two or three months.

You will probably get borax and white bees-wax at a chemist. Corn or maize oil at a chemist or grocer or health store. And for soya oil you will need to go to a health store.

We asked Honor Wyatt to test these recipes for us, and here are her comments:

I found these creams quite easy to make and pleasant to use. The quantities given for each make enough to fill three medium jars, containing about forty grams, or one and a half yoghourt cartons, in which I keep mine – with tinfoil over the top. Each cream costs me about sixteen new pence for the amount given.

And now the method. Oil heats quickly so I first dissolved the bees wax in the oil and left it to cool down to sixty-five degrees while heating the borax and water up to sixty-five degrees. To hasten the cooling process I put the pan into a bowl of cold water while stirring the mixture. Don't worry if it seems to be curdling at any point, it will go smooth in the stirring.

I found the ingredients quite easy to get. The thermometer I was lucky enough to have already – I understand it's known as a 'confectioner's thermometer'. They're sold by big chemists with branches all over the country.

A HOME-MADE HAND CREAM from a recipe given us by the Hand and Nail Culture Institute.

This is one of the most popular recipes we have ever broadcast, and I therefore make no apology for repeating it from an earlier *Woman's Hour Anthology*.

You will need:
4 oz lanolin
4 oz petroleum jelly
1 oz either almond or olive oil (almond keeps better)
1 oz rose water

Put the lanolin and petroleum jelly in a basin and beat well to a cream. In cold weather you may have to place the basin in an outer one containing hot water. When the lanolin and petroleum jelly are creamed, gradually add the oil, beating all the time, and lastly the rose water a little at a time. Continue beating until it is all mixed. Leave it overnight and then next day beat it up once more and put it into a pot.

HOME-MADE REFRESHER PADS *Mary Davenport*

These are the things you will need:
a small jug
a sharp pair of scissors
a small, flat plastic or tin container with a lid. I prefer plastic, but tin will do equally well, and I use one about 2½ inches in diameter by about ¾ inch deep
a roll of white absorbent lint. It must be white – on no account use the pink kind for this. This will last quite a long time you'll find.
One scant tablespoon of eau-de-cologne
One and a half tablespoons of boiling water

Lastly, an item you need only add if your skin is very fine and dry, and you wish to use the refreshers every day: one teaspoonful of pure almond oil. The use of almond oil, which is a natural substance, provides extra moisture to the skin. If you're going to use the refreshers every day, this would lessen any tendency to dry the skin.

Now my method. First make sure your container is absolutely clean and dry, next, cut the lint into circles to fit snugly inside the container. I find fourteen to sixteen is an average number. Press them neatly and firmly down, no loose edges. In the small jug place the boiling water, eau-de-cologne and almond oil, if you are using the latter. Pour the contents of the jug onto the circles of lint in the container, and gently press them down, adding more liquid until they are all completely saturated, then put on the lid.

The refreshers will still be warm from the liquid when you do this, but it doesn't matter – in twenty-four hours they will be icy cool and ready for use. They keep fresh for several months if you are not using them every day. If the weather is hot you may like to pop the container in the fridge for extra coolness. I find them wonderful after a busy session in the garden, and I always like to take some with me to the beach to use after swimming to remove the salt of the sea water. They are gently stimulating and leave your skin with a lovely soft clean feeling.

And they really do remove make-up and grime.

MARTINE LEGGE'S BEAUTY RECIPES AND TREATMENTS

Hair
As you well know, there are few dramatic cures in the beauty business. It's usually a matter of plugging away for ages before you notice any appreciable results. But I have found one which produced miraculous results for me. At least it seemed miraculous because from one day to the next it literally stopped my hair coming out in what appeared, at the time, to be handfuls! This cure is simply a rinse made with rosemary leaves.

Hair falls out for dozens of reasons and at various times in many people's lives. Alas, no one has yet found a way of making hair grow on a really bald head, especially a male one. This has something to do with hormones; but for common or garden temporary reasons such as depression, or a state of poor health, or an over-greasy scalp, I've found rosemary really works wonders.

This is how you make the rinse. Just put a couple of teaspoons of fresh or dried rosemary leaves into a large teapot and then add boiling water. When this is cool, pour the infusion over your head after shampooing. As you know, you can buy packets of dried rosemary at the grocer's, if you don't happen to grow it.

On the other hand, if your hair is in poor general condition and needs even more help, there are two further things you can do. The first is to rub into your scalp, before a shampoo, some olive oil in which rosemary has been left to stand for two weeks in a warm place. After rubbing it into your scalp wrap a hot towel round your head for ten minutes, and then wash your hair with a good liquid shampoo, finishing with the final rosemary rinse I've already mentioned.

My second treatment is particularly effective if you're suffering from the kind of condition that makes your hair look really desperate; thin, lifeless and like hay. Buy a small bottle of castor oil and pour the whole of it onto your hair – and massage it well in. Then wrap your head in a hot towel for ten minutes. After this you will probably need to give yourself an extra shampooing in order to get all the oil out because castor oil is so thick and sticky. But I have found results are really worth it. Each individual hair feels fatter and my entire head of hair looked thicker and shinier. Castor oil also stimulates growth, but if you consider it too cloying and heavy, there is an alternative which is almost as good. This is coconut oil which is cheap and obtainable from most chemists. You use it in exactly the same way.

Finally, for anyone who lives in the country, or near a rubbish dump, there is a surprisingly good hair tonic you can make for nothing. Nettles are excellent for the hair. They help to eliminate dandruff and promote growth. For a rinse you just pour boiling water onto two cupfuls of fresh young chopped nettles and then, when this is cool, pour it over your hair after a shampoo. This is really one of the best hair tonics in the world.

Face packs

As a simple pick-me-up for the skin just mix one egg yolk in a cup with a dessertspoonful of Fuller's Earth or toilet oatmeal, adding a little more of either of these if the concoction is too runny. If you haven't any Fuller's Earth or toilet oatmeal handy when you want to do this, powdered milk will do. Then smear the mixture onto your face with the back of a teaspoon or with your fingers.

Most face packs have done their work by the time they are dry, and this goes for egg packs, too. You won't look very pretty with this thick, orangey mask, all lumpy and cracked like a crazy paving, but it is worth it. When the pack is dry, soak it off gently with cotton wool or a flannel dipped in warm water; then splash with cold.

People with dry skins can add a few drops of olive oil to this mixture and those with oily skin could add a spoonful of yoghourt. The yoghourt is also helpful for anyone suffering from acne or blemishes.

Another pack I use is one which is said to have been a favourite of Catherine the Great of Russia. To make this you cut most of the flesh out of half a lemon and sit the half lemon in a small cup so that it stands up. Then fill the cavity with the yolk of an egg. Leave all night. By the following morning the yolk will have absorbed the essential lemon oils. Spread it over your face with a cosmetic brush in thin layers because it won't dry if shoved on in great dollops. Leave for ten or fifteen minutes and wash off. It is really excellent for a muddy, post-winter complexion.

With white of egg, on the other hand, you've got to be careful. It is a most powerful astringent and pulls a flabby or puffy face together like nobody's business. It also helps to eliminate fatigue wrinkles. But please only use it seldom and only when your face is at its last gasp, so to speak! Using this pack is a rather mucky affair, but it works wonders if you can bear the slimy feeling. Just brush the white onto your skin with a cosmetic brush. It will dry quickly and make your face feel very tight. As soon as it's dry, wash it off gently with a flannel dipped in warm water and then splash with cold.

Herbal skin tonics

One of the important facts drummed into anyone who discusses skin tonics with a good beautician is that the alcohol present in some commercial lotions is drying and eventually bad for the skin if used daily.

This factor, allied to the rising price of beauty preparations, is where home-made lotions come into their own. The only tiresome aspect is that you have to renew them fairly often as they don't contain preservative agents.

Being a fairly lazy person I cheat by keeping a bottle in the fridge. This way it can last for months. I also have a jar of cotton wool stacked among the other kitchen jars and every morning while the kettle comes to the boil, I slap my face with a piece of cold wet cotton wool. This habit (I was once told by a famous beautician whose job was preserving the faces of showbiz ladies, and showbiz gentlemen too!) is by far the most successful way of reducing puffiness and keeping one's face in good shape and thereby looking young for a good deal longer than nature intended.

The simplest of these lotions is a half-and-half mixture of witch hazel and rose water, both obtainable from any chemist for a shilling or two. And this one will keep fresh for months even in the warmest bedroom.

Witch hazel is a mild astringent and rose water softens the skin. It was used by Henry VIII as an after-shave lotion. If you want a slightly more astringent effect you could add a few drops of tincture of benzoin, also obtainable from the chemist.

Another alternative lotion which is particularly good to use in the summer is fennel water. This needn't cost you a penny. Fennel grows like a weed in our garden and it often grows wild in Cornwall and the South Coast. You can also buy dried fennel from many grocers and greengrocers for a shilling or so. I pick and dry my own in a slow oven and store it in glass jars.

Fennel water has many excellent properties. It is tonic and antiseptic. It softens water, allays wrinkles and soothes an itchy skin. Fennel also contains potassium which promotes the healing of tissues, which makes it particularly suitable for people with acne scars or blemishes.

Now to make this lotion: you fling a handful into about a pint and a half of water and bring it to the boil. Simmer for fifteen minutes. Then cool, strain and bottle. You must use the lotion within a week or ten days unless you keep it in the fridge.

Some cosmetic economies
Forgotten pots of foundation can easily be reconstructed when they are tired or dry by adding a few drops of rose water and whisking the mixture until the whole thing becomes creamy once again. If the stuff is positively caked, then you have to add a dash of almond oil, but go easy. You don't want a greasy mess. It's also possible to thin very thick foundations and even to lighten them by adding more rose water until you reach the consistency or colour you desire. And what about those nasty wodges of old night cream dredged up from the murky

depths of one's bedside table ? Almond oil is excellent for bringing them back to life.

I also find that gluey ends of nail varnish react very nicely to a few drops of acetone. When you've added them, shake the bottle and leave it for an hour or so and shake again. This thins the varnish and makes it almost as good as new. You'll find the more acetone you add, the paler the colour becomes, which is not a bad solution when you've bought something darker than you bargained for. But do protect your nails by first painting on a layer of varnish base because acetone is drying.

You can buy both rose water and acetone inexpensively from most chemists. Almond oil is more expensive, but a little goes a very long way.

To use up ends of lipstick

Using a knife to winkle those murky little stumps out of their cases, I then heat them slowly in a small saucepan until they melt into a satisfying pink cream. I remove them from the flame before it boils and leave the mixture for a minute or two to thicken very slightly. Meanwhile (and I've learnt this the hard way) I've propped up a cleaned and oiled lipstick case, or perhaps two or even three, in egg-cups firmly cushioned with wodges of cotton wool so that there is no danger of them falling over.

Then, very slowly and carefully I pour my mixture into the cases. A few minutes later when the stuff looks nicely congealed I lift my egg-cups and transfer them with great care to the coldest part of the fridge.

The following day I take them out and wind the lipstick up very slowly. This should be quite easy if the case has been well oiled. And there you are, a brand-new lipstick. I imagine you could do the same thing with those stick eye shadows, although I haven't tried that myself, yet. Dry sticks can always be softened in the melting process with a drop (and I mean a *drop*) of almond oil.

Another concoction, but one which requires no cooking, is a truly excellent blusher. I make this simply by breaking up the remains of a box of compressed rouge with a nail-file and mixing the resulting powder with some ordinary light face powder. In this way you can make a quite large amount of blusher out of very little rouge, adding more face powder until you get the colour you want.

A HOME TREATMENT FOR SCORCH MARKS ON LEGS
Anne MacLeod-Carey

Ingredients:
  4 oz glyccrine
  1 tbs lemon juice
  a few drops of 30-volume peroxide
  You should rub this mixture into your legs at night.

I suggest that you put just the glycerine and lemon juice into a bottle, and that each time you are going to use it, you pour out into a saucer the amount you think you will want: then add the few drops of 30-volume peroxide to what's in the saucer, otherwise children might perhaps get hold of the bottle thinking it to be lemonade.

Apart from this there are some excellent leg tints available which will hide the marks when you're not wearing stockings. Also you'll find softening creams are helpful in removing the marks – which are in fact dead cuticle.

And try to remember not to repeat the burns next winter!

KATIE BOYLE'S TREATMENT FOR HAIR ON HOLIDAY

I must be one of hundreds not to say thousands of people with dry hair, and I used to come back from holidays to groans of disapproval from my hairdresser, not to mention my own everyday frustration. Then I was given a very useful bit of advice which I'm passing on. Holiday time can be reconditioning time for your hair. I always go in search of sun, like so many of us do, and I love hiking along the sands or basking in a bikini. But before I do this, I soak my hair in oil – olive, or almond or sunflower or coconut or any good oil you can get hold of. Then I comb it through and walk bravely out into the sun. The heat will encourage the porous hair to soak in all the goodness from the oils – in fact I was amazed to find how little grease was left on my head after two or three hours of that treatment. Of course you can dive into the sea after giving the sun a chance first. Before lunch I have a good shampoo to get rid of the remaining grease and sea water. Then I towel dry and put some good conditioner onto my hair, and comb it through and put it in rollers and dry it in the sun. I always put a turban round for the rest of the day – one of those that hides rollers can be very smart, and by the evening my hair seems to look super and very shiny. I've used this method on my last few holidays and am greeted with tremendous approval and even praise from my hairdresser when I get back.

N.B. Remember, *any* kind of oil lifts the colour of bleached or tinted hair. A generous dollop of conditioning cream used with the same method works very well. Ask your chemist which ones lift the outer scale of your hair and really nourish it.

A CONVERSATION ABOUT COFFEE   *Rosl Philpot and Harold Higgins with Mollie Lee*

Rosl Philpot is the author of a book on Austrian cooking. Harold Higgins has a long-established coffee merchant's shop in Mayfair.

LEE: In coffee shops there are so many different sorts of beans. Can you very broadly tell me what the difference is between, say, Kenyan and Brazilian ?

HIGGINS: The difference is that coffees grown in East Africa, particularly those in Kenya, have a sharpness to them, an acidity, whereas the coffees that we drink coming from Brazil, mainly the Santos variety, are much smoother.

LEE: Which do you prefer, Mrs Philpot ? Is it a question of when you are going to drink it ?

PHILPOT: It's completely a question of mood. I vary my coffees constantly, deliberately. I buy sometimes three different quarters, say a quarter of Kenya peaberry and a quarter of one of the Central South American coffees, and of course also Mocha or Mysore from India, just to get the variety of it.

LEE: What about Mocha and Mysore ? What is their particular qualit...

HIGGINS: It's a very interesting mixture, Mocha coming from eith... Ethiopia or Arabia, and the Mysore from Southern India, the t... mix extremely well together. The Mocha has its slight cheesiness – this is the only way one can really describe the flavour; it has a cheesy taste – and the Mysore, which is a very thick, rich, smooth coffee. The two blend extremely well together.

LEE: Now not everybody, of course, has the facilities to be able to go into a shop and choose their beans. But if they have, how much should they buy at once ?

I bet you're not the only one to play with fire on these cold winter evenings! Don't worry, here's a mask which should put things right after you've used it a few times. Mix the juice of half a lemon and the white of an egg into a paste with light carbonate of magnesium, then spread it over the scorch marks. If your skin has become wafery thin and ...m put on a film of moisture before the mask. Let the ...harden, then soak it off with ...ater.

HIGGINS: If they are going to buy beans and grind it themselves they can take at least a fortnight's supply of coffee, although it's best really to buy as little as one needs at a time. If you are buying the beans and grinding it yourself it will stay more fresh than if you are going to buy ground coffee.

LEE: How much should they take already ground?

HIGGINS: About enough to last them a week. Because one begins to notice the staleness after the period of a week.

LEE: And how should you store it?

HIGGINS: A glass screw-topped jar is one of the best ways of storing coffee, either earthenware or glass. Plastic is quite good. The most important thing is that it should be airtight.

LEE: What do you store yours in, Mrs Philpot, or do you never store it?

PHILPOT: I store as little as possible. I have various sorts of little schemes. I buy coffee together with friends, so that we get small quantities, or occasionally when a member of my family passes the coffee shop I ask them to buy me a little coffee.

LEE: Do you grind your own?

PHILPOT: Yes, I do.

LEE: With an electric grinder?

PHILPOT: No, with a very old-fashioned hand grinder. This is sentimental, because it's made in Austria.

LEE: Now to the question of making. What do you think is the chief fault of English coffee-makers, Mrs Philpot?

PHILPOT: I think probably the chief fault is that people don't make it clear from the start for what method of making coffee they buy their coffee. I think probably they don't use the right grind of coffee for the method of making coffee.

LEE: What method do you use, Mr Higgins? What is your favourite method of making coffee?

HIGGINS: I like the method that uses the filter paper.

LEE: This is a rather big earthenware jug, is it not? With a filter paper in the top.

HIGGINS: The filter that I use will fit on almost any jug. So you can have a large jug if you are making for a lot of people, or a much smaller one if it's only for two. Then you put the filter paper in the top and use very finely-ground (not pulverised) coffee and pour on the boiling water, and the coffee simply infuses and filters through into the jug.

LEE: And it doesn't get cold, while it's doing it?

HIGGINS: I don't find it's cold for the first cup of coffee. If I am going to have several cups I then put my jug on the gas-stove on a very, very low heat.

LEE: Mrs Philpot, do you also use this method with filter paper?

PHILPOT: Yes, I do.

LEE: And for that you need to buy fine-ground coffee, is that right? What's the proportion of that coffee to water? I have a feeling that we in England possibly don't put in enough coffee.

HIGGINS: I put in about a dessertspoonful per person – at least that. But I like it rather strong. The makers of this particular way advertise much less than that, because the coffee can be ground so finely. But I use at least a dessertspoonful.

LEE: But how much per half pint?

HIGGINS: I would say about an ounce.

LEE: An ounce to half a pint.

HIGGINS: Two ounces to a pint.

LEE: Now do either of you ever use the method that I think quite a lot of people use, of simply warming a pot – as you do with tea – putting your coffee in, and pouring on your boiling water?

HIGGINS: Yes, I do. I'm most terrible at remembering to take coffee home. After working with it all day I forget it and get into trouble with my wife. So sometimes I'm searching around in the cupboard and I find some medium-ground coffee and then I have to make it in either the saucepan method or the jug method.

LEE: In the saucepan method you put it on the top of boiling water. Is that right?

PHILPOT: Actually I don't put it into boiling water. I take freshly-drawn water, put the coffee on the cold water and just bring this to the boil. As soon as it comes to the boil I turn it very low and let it simmer just for a little. Then I draw a spoon over the top, pour in about a spoonful of cold water and put the lid on and let it settle. This is a very old-fashioned method of making coffee, but I've used this for years.

LEE: I wonder whether you two experts agree with the glass-container method?

HIGGINS: The vacuum method.

LEE: Do you approve of that?

PHILPOT: I think it's a good method if you will follow the instructions and take the time. It's a sort of social game. You wheel it in on a trolley and you take your luck on how long it's going to take. But it is good coffee.

LEE: But only, I would have thought, for quite a large amount.

PHILPOT: Oh yes, three-quarters full or nearly full is the right amount.

HIGGINS: I agree. I think it's a very good method of making coffee. So important with it to have the right grind.

LEE: What is the grind for that one?

HIGGINS: The grind is a little coarser than medium. One of the difficult things about grind is that everybody has got their own idea of what a grind should be, and what medium grind is. I always think of medium grind as being something like granulated sugar, and the grind for the vacuum method should be slightly coarser than that.

LEE: And what about all these plug-in electric coffee-makers? Do you approve of those, Mrs Philpot?

PHILPOT: I'm inclined to think they are white elephants, like so many other things one often gets as wedding presents. Perhaps one should treat them as such and pass them on in the next jumble sale.

LEE: You wouldn't use them?

HIGGINS: I'm not fond of them. They are very easy in that they make the coffee for you. But I always think that the best coffee is where you take some trouble and do it yourself.

LEE: You're a romantic. It needs love, does it?

HIGGINS: I think it does, yes.

LEE: Do you have any feeling about using a different sort of coffee for the morning and for the evening?

PHILPOT: Yes, I do have quite a strong feeling. I think quite a lot of people like a good so-called Continental coffee for breakfast, it's like having good strong Indian tea, it's a good waker-up. And for after dinner I think it depends on the dinner. If you've had a rich and heavy dinner, a slightly acid after-dinner coffee has a sort of sharpness.

LEE: What do they mean when they say Continental coffee?

PHILPOT: Nothing, except a very high roast – meaning a coffee which looks black.

LEE: And the sharp one in the evening, which one would that be?

HIGGINS: Quite often a Kenya or a Tanzania. There are some very good Tanzania coffees, very nice in the evening. Or a Costa Rica, which has a particularly delicate flavour.

LEE: Do you ever experiment with blending? I mean two ounces of one sort and two ounces of another?

HIGGINS: I think it unwise to buy coffees that are already blended unless you know exactly what goes into the blend. The word 'blend' opens the door to more than one coffee being used. By all means experiment with different coffees, and here it is important to ask your local coffee man his advice about what to use.

LEE: But I suppose for people who haven't got the facilities to go and choose what they want, the vacuum-packed coffee is very good, isn't it?

HIGGINS: Yes. There are companies that put some very good makes on the market.

LEE: But the smaller the tin the better, I imagine.

PHILPOT: The smaller the tin or the pack the better. It's like everything you buy. If you buy it and you like it then you'll probably go and buy it again.

LEE: What about the question of milk, Mrs Philpot? Hot or cold?

PHILPOT: If you take a very little milk I prefer cold milk. Nice fresh cold milk. But if you are inclined to like a milky coffee then you simply have to warm your milk. But please, please, don't boil it.

HIGGINS: I think timing is important with the milk. If you're making coffee don't have the milk ready and then waiting and waiting on the heat until the coffee is ready. Time it.

PHILPOT: Yes. Milk is the last thing you prepare, when you make white coffee.

LEE: And do either of you object absolutely to warming-up coffee you've got left over?

PHILPOT: I object thoroughly.

HIGGINS: Not altogether, no. With the filter method I think that one can warm it up without having that horrible bitter flavour. I always prefer freshly made coffee, but I don't throw up my hands in horror.

LEE: What about water? There are all these legends about water, with coffee as with tea. Do you think the water makes any difference?

PHILPOT: It must make some difference, but I'm inclined to treat this legend as a legend. London water is quite good enough for me.

HIGGINS: London water is quite good for coffee. We do notice a difference up and down the country. I think tea is more affected by difference in water than coffee. We usually say that hard water is better than soft for coffee; some coffees don't go at all well in very soft water. The mild soft coffees such as the Jamaican and the Brazilian Santos are very difficult to use in soft water.

LEE: Is it a fact that at one time firms used to offer to analyse water?

HIGGINS: Oh it was, yes. Before the war you could send samples up from the country to a firm and they would analyse the water and recommend different blends. It was all part of the service.

LEE: One last question to the two of you who are both coffee drinkers, how do you sleep?

PHILPOT: Very well, because I probably drink more tea than coffee.

HIGGINS: Like a top.

SOME CONVERSATIONS ABOUT GARDENING BETWEEN MARJORIE ANDERSON AND FIVE WOMAN'S HOUR BROADCASTERS:

1 *Ba Mason on silver-leaved plants*

BA MASON: Silver-leaved plants are marvellous in a mixed border as a foil to hot and bright colours, and they're very useful for cutting, and they're very good ground cover. But I love them chiefly because of the leaves. There's an enormous variety of silver leaves, and you can have round ones and long ones and spiky ones and feathery ones, all covered with this lovely sort of white fur.

MARJORIE ANDERSON: Where do they like growing most?

MASON: They love sun. They must have good drainage. Water's really their chief enemy, they hate standing in pools of water, and they hate shade, because the little white hairs that give the silvery look to the leaves are the protection against the sun.

ANDERSON: Do you grow them only for the look of their leaves?

MASON: Well, most of these silver plants that I've got have rather boring little yellow flowers like buttons, and I just pinch them off, because that makes a nice bush plant with a lot more leaf, which is what I really want.

ANDERSON: And what do you grow with them? You must have some colour, I imagine, with them?

MASON: Yes, because a thoroughly grey border would be very demure and dim. My border is against a red tile-hung wall, and I've got Iris at the back, because I think their leaves are rather silvery and complement the silver plants. And for colour I grow ordinary Salvia, not the silver one, and Aquilegias, which have beautiful flowers as well as rather silvery leaves, and Auricula along the front.

ANDERSON: Are they cheap to grow?

MASON: Oh yes, some of them are. For instance, Catmint, Nepeta, which is a beautiful silvery plant, is very easy and cheap and there's Sage, and a marvellous one is Stachys Lanata, or lamb's ears, as I call it. This is gorgeous, because it will grow between a crack in paving stones, make a lovely great flat silver sort of pad. And then there's Verbascum, if you've got room, because that's a huge plant. I've got two silver Achillea, Argenta and Moonshine, and Senecio, that's a marvellous plant, which grows into a big bush.

ANDERSON: Are they all perennials?

MASON: Most of them are perennials. I sent for a collection at a place in Colchester about two years ago, which cost about twenty five shillings, and now that I've got these established in my border, I'm going to try for some rarer ones.

ANDERSON: Are they good for taking cuttings from?

MASON: Yes, in early autumn these silver plants make a kind of woody stem, almost like a little tree, and once that's really tough and ready for the winter, you can take the little cuttings off the side and prop them up in sand.

ANDERSON: Would you say they really are good-tempered? I mean, we don't get much sun here, do we?

MASON: Oh, they're pretty good-tempered, as long as you give them as much sun as you possibly can, and drainage. The thing that really kills them off is a soggy bed, in which frost pockets will gather, and then they're just no good at all.

2   *Cyril Fletcher on roses*

CYRIL FLETCHER: I like shrub roses the best. The old shrub roses like cabbage roses, moss roses, musks and damasks. There is one disadvantage. They do really only flower once properly. You get a second lot in September, but they usually flower best in June. I think it's very silly to have any rose that hasn't got any scent. To me a rose is scent principally, all these old ones I've mentioned, they all smell, and I want to take to task these wonderful rose breeders who produce the most marvellous looking blooms specially for colour or specially for shape, or because they're weather resistant and that sort of thing. They don't concentrate on roses that smell. I do. My roses have got to smell. I'll give you a list of roses that do smell. The best of the modern ones, I think, is a rose called Papa Meilland; it's a very dark rose, almost black as you look into it – a velvet rose and it smells wonderfully.

MARJORIE ANDERSON: And another ?

FLETCHER: Fragrant Cloud is a very good modern rose that smells beautifully, as of course it must do with a name like that. The colour is Geranium Lake, or that's what the rose breeders call it. A crimson scarlet rose that smells beautifully is Ena Harkness, and Super Star is a very famous prize winning rose – very fragrant, but it is, to my mind, a nasty sharp shade of vermilion. I don't like these sort of vermilion, fluorescent reds. A rose to me is an old-fashioned romantic thing, and it shouldn't have a nasty sharp colour like a bus.

ANDERSON: Any more ?

FLETCHER: Iceberg is a very good pure white one. That's a floribunda so it flowers lots of times during the year and is also pretty good for weather resistance. It doesn't smell very much but it smells enough. And I might say that it's not a bad idea, if you've got a tiny garden, to have as many climbing roses as you can, because you're not using space, you can have them all round the house. Two points to remember – you want to get the roots as far away from the house as you dare, so that they don't get too dry. And you want to put plenty of fertiliser, preferably farm animal manure, peat and that sort of thing, round them.

3 Isobel Barnett on hostas

LADY BARNETT: Hostas are hardy with the emphasis on the hardy. Put them in and forget about them – they last for years. They are, I think, mainly attractive because of their leaves. There are various varieties but each variety does have the most beautiful leaves which make a contrast for other plants and are, of course, very useful for flower arranging.

MARJORIE ANDERSON: They're not evergreen are they ?

LADY BARNETT: No, they are in leaf from about the beginning of April until the frosts come at the end of October or November, but they do vanish totally during the winter.

ANDERSON: And when do they flower ?

LADY BARNETT: Depending on variety, they flower from about the beginning of June until the first or second week in September. The flowers are various shades of lilac and violet and lavender and some of them have white flowers. The flowers are pretty and very long lasting in water; they look rather like hanging bells of Solomon's seal.

ANDERSON: Do they mind where you plant them?

LADY BARNETT: Not really, they will grow in a herbaceous border in full sun, though you must make certain they don't dry out – they do like moisture, but where they're particularly useful is somewhere where almost nothing else will grow – in shade, or in a north-facing border. I've got a whole north-facing border that's nothing but Hostas partly because I love them, but secondly because I'm a terribly lazy gardener. And once the leaves are out not a weed can grow, so that April until October I don't have to do anything about that border at all.

ANDERSON: What about pests – do they like them?

LADY BARNETT: Yes, they do. The slugs adore the lovely luscious new young shoots so you've got to put down a bit of slug bait in the spring and perhaps renew it again once during the year.

ANDERSON: When do you plant them in fact?

LADY BARNETT: Well, any time during the herbaceous planting season, from October until about March. I usually plant mine in the autumn and give them winter to establish.

ANDERSON: Can you take cuttings from them?

LADY BARNETT: I've never, myself, tried that; I've just tried dividing them.

ANDERSON: Would you like to suggest some of your favourite varieties?

LADY BARNETT: Well, there are so many, I've chosen three which are the least costly. Firstly, Hosta Fortunei Aurea. This one has gold leaves, a very nice shape and nice long stems for putting in a vase. Then an even prettier one is Fortunei Albo-Picta. This one has very pale yellow leaves which are splashed with lime green and a darker green brilliantly coloured in the spring – a little less so as the summer advances. And then one called Hosta Sieboldiana. This one makes an enormous plant with great big leaves which are the bluest of blue-greens and the leaves have a beautiful surface bloom on them rather like velvet. They're furrowed and puckered and look as though they had been sewn with a sewing machine. Again wonderful for flower arranging. Those are the less expensive ones. For rare varieties one can go up to fifteen shillings a plant.

ANDERSON: And they are varied in height?

LADY BARNETT: Yes, the flower spikes vary from about eighteen inches up to four feet which is a bit much for the average garden, but it does mean one can do a border with the flowers at varying heights.

ANDERSON: And they don't need much attention?

LADY BARNETT: Well, I must admit mine have been in for ten years now and they've had absolutely no attention from me at all.

4 Elisabeth Beresford on wallflowers

MARJORIE ANDERSON: Why wallflowers, Elisabeth?

ELISABETH BERESFORD: By accident, to be honest. I saw some going cheap on a barrow in a London market, and I couldn't resist a gardening bargain. I bought them, put them in and to my astonishment they came up with no trouble at all. Also because the colours are beautiful, these lovely rich velvety colours, and thirdly because of the magnificent smell. Wallflowers make you think of summer and of hot days and of bees, and . . .

ANDERSON: . . . and walled gardens.

BERESFORD: And of walled gardens, yes. It's a good old-fashioned flower, but I think very lovely. I found in my London garden which is, after all, surrounded by houses, streets and factories, that last summer I had no end of bees, and dozens of those wonderful tortoise-shell butterflies. It really made a London garden like an old-fashioned country garden.

ANDERSON: What about the blooming period?

BERESFORD: Well, you plant them in October, they will go through the winter, and then they will start to come out in about March. They bloom through March, April and May and there is one which goes right on and will bloom to the end of June. That's the Siberian.

ANDERSON: And the soil, what about that?

BERESFORD: That's another bonus for anybody who happens to live in a town, because they really don't like rich soil, in fact they hate things like manure and with London soil you do tend to get it rather dry and thinnish, and wallflowers love this – rather like nasturtiums. This is what they really take to. They don't like damp and they don't like shade. They want it very sunny. You've got to plant them in clumps. You can't have them like, say, tulips, separately. With wallflowers you've got to have them in a great mass and then you will get a lot of colour.

ANDERSON: What about the snags ? Are there any ?

BERESFORD: Well, they do tend to go very woody if you don't look out, you know, more leaves than flower and things like this and of course you can't really keep them more than two years, because they do start to deteriorate.

ANDERSON: That means a lot of work, presumably.

BERESFORD: It does, but then gardening is always a fair amount of work and wallflowers are so tough that you don't have to be very careful with them, as you do with a lot of other plants.

ANDERSON: What about the best places to grow them ?

BERESFORD: I grow mine facing south. Also, I've got one of these low walls with a trough in the top, and I planted them in there last October and they're all coming out. And I've also planted them round the base of the rose trees which I've got in tubs.

ANDERSON: When do you sow them ?

BERESFORD: You put the cuttings in in October. But if you're doing it from seed, and I have done this quite successfully, you put the seed in in April or May, and then they'll start to come up in June. Now, this is when you prick them out, because you know that when you sow seeds, they come up in a great mass, all thick and close together, so when they're about two to three inches high, you've got to take out the strongest little seedlings and plant them separately, so that they've got room to expand. Now, I was given a tip by a very expert nursery gardener, who told me that when autumn comes, if you really want to have good wallflowers next spring, you must make the wallflower panic. Now this sounds very odd, but you pick your plant which is very nearly six inches high, and you quite literally cut the roots. The wallflower roots are very fibrous and you just cut along the bottom – cut quite a bit off them, and this will make the wallflower panic. It will think that it has got to produce more roots quickly to save its life so that when it comes up in the spring, it will also of course produce more shoots to compensate for more roots. He also tells me that when I plant them out in October to put them in a mixture of one of lime to one of earth, mixed up to a nice sloppy paste in water. Dig your hole, put in this mixture, put in a wallflower, good and hard, and then press the earth down very firmly all the way around it. It seemed to me a very strong mixture, because lime does burn, but it does seem to work.

ANDERSON: What are your favourites?

BERESFORD: I think Siberian, because it's such a late flowering one; Blood-Red because of its magnificent colour; and also there is a very good one for rock gardens which is called Harper Crewe. This is a very bushy plant and you can keep it going for quite a long time and it's a wonderful colour.

5 Molly Weir on japonica and broom grown from seed

MOLLY WEIR: I tried unsuccessfully to grow Japonica from cuttings, then I saw a lovely one in my friend's garden and I asked her if I could pick two of the ripe fruit, which she allowed me to do. So I gave them a little rattle, just the way one does an apple, to see that it is ripe, opened them up and picked out the seeds. They're rather large brown seeds. I planted each one in a little individual pot, in a mixture of peat and good garden soil, and put them in the greenhouse – a cool house incidentally, there's no heat. I kept them watered until they were about three or four inches high, when I transplanted them into bigger pots until they were about six inches high and then put them in the open garden.

MARJORIE ANDERSON: What sort of conditions do they like?

WEIR: They like the shelter of a wall. I've two against the wall of the house and I have one against the greenhouse.

ANDERSON: How long before they bloom?

WEIR: They make leaf at once but they didn't make any flower until about the third year. Last year they were absolutely covered in blossom.

ANDERSON: Any tips about pruning or looking after them?

WEIR: Well you simply prune them if you want to keep back the growth. You actually regard them as apples when you start pruning them. Keep them shaped to your taste.

ANDERSON: Now what about your other success story, Broom?

WEIR: Oh, the Broom is a great success. I didn't actually get this for nothing, but it was next to nothing, because I bought a pack of twenty one Broom seeds which cost one and nine. These were fairly large seeds, too. Instead of putting those into little pots I brought them on in a seed box and that was almost the same mixture – peat and good soil plus a little coarse sand. I kept them in the cool green-house until they were about an inch high; then when they were able to be handled I put them into little individual pots. They grew about four or five inches high, and then it was out into the garden with them.

ANDERSON: Any snags?

WEIR: Yes. Brooms only grow for about seven years and you must watch for wind rock because they're like roses, if there is wet weather, or very windy weather, you'll get a little space at the bottom which you must heel in, for this causes them to rot.

ANDERSON: Molly, when can we plant the seeds?

WEIR: Leave it until the autumn.

And when you've grown your flowers, cut them, and taken them into the house for arranging, take note of this warning from Graeme Hall.

I've survived yet another orgy – a competition *they* call it. I have my flower arranging friends back again.

I've done my social duty with what I hope looked like enthusiasm without being too much of a hypocrite and I've made all the right noises such as – Haa! Clever! Interesting! M'mm! and Imaginative! and, with luck, it won't be necessary for me to repeat the performance again this year.

Competitions are over, cups are won. Now I'm left to wonder what possesses my friends – nice, ordinary, sensible women with growing families; what incites these stalwart citizens doing worthwhile things like meals-on-wheels and garden parties for the RSPCA to run amok with flowers.

Throughout the summer, these women suddenly neglect home and hearth, abandon their husbands' ulcers and their children's A-levels to work in frenzied concentration throughout the night producing the most fantastic, outlandish, flamboyant arrangements of flowers – by the cart-load!

Mind you, it's all very skilful stuff that needs endless practice and concentration. It is, I'm told, tremendously rewarding. It must be for the florists. But don't any of these normally intelligent women stand back, look at their creations with a hard eye and see, as I do, a con-trived, self-conscious abnormality?

I believe we should look more often at one single bloom. By that I

don't mean Ikebana. I shall survive if I never again see a single lily
reclining against a piece of driftwood that is thrusting up out of a
large slab of stone. Even if it does symbolise Light Out of Darkness!
Nor do I need moth-infested stuffed birds, back drapes of cheap
rayon taffeta or toy aeroplanes to make me appreciate flowers. Nor
can I class curls of rusty old barbed wire or lumps of some grotesque
loofah-like material, hung about with aubergines or cacti, as suitable
accompaniments to my lovely flowers.

I can see and well understand the necessity of knowing how to put
flowers in a vase – sorry, container! – so that they don't look like
mine. But surely such an art should stop short of torturing flowers
into shapes that only deformed plants could produce ?

Take the Hogarth arrangement, for instance. In case you, too, are
not a disciple, that means S-shaped, leaning over backwards. Bulged
or stretched, according to the inclinations of the particular arranger,
or, it would seem, according to her own natural shape. Little fat
flower-arranging ladies make little fat flower arrangements while tall,
gaunt ones make long attenuated cones spotted about with artichokes,
teasels and other prickly things.

But back to the Hogarth – I've seen blooms tied up in circles or bent
and weighted to distort their natural upstanding form. They are
snipped at and moulded until they conform to a completely unnatural pattern dictated by the undisciplined flights of the arranger's
imagination. Large headed flowers are decapitated, depriving them of
their leafy stems so that they become graceless 'glumps' of colour. If
they are too big, petals are stripped away. If not big enough, other
blooms are slaughtered to bulk up the best ones with additional
petals expertly wired on to make them larger – much, much larger –
than life.

And at the end of all this frenzied activity, all this snipping and
tweaking and crimping – what ? A work of art, maybe, to the flower
arrangers. But to me it is a distorted, unnatural gob of home décor,
often in doubtful taste, that just happens to have been constructed
from real, beautiful, natural flowers. Why not use plastic, paper,
plasticine or some other malleable material ? Why destroy living
flowers ?

It's the art bit that really gets me – this arrangement has *feeling*, that
pedestal is *evocative*, *she's* only a copyist but *her* work is full of
emotion. All flower arrangers talk in italics, and they have a language

of their own. The crescent has exquisite balance. Just look at that for transition. She's so clever with her contrast.

Immediately the last competition is over, these frenzied competitors revert to nice, cheerful, kind women, devoted to their homes and families. Devoted even to the friends in whose bosoms they would gladly have buried their floral stub wires short hours before.

But for how long will it last I wonder? Someone is sure to think it essential, very soon, to do something absolutely dastardly about Christmas – to depict, in flowers, Season's Greetings or Scenes of the Nativity or – how about this for a novel suggestion – Silent Night!

And I hope they get stuck on their own holly prickles!

This Blessed House

WHAT MAKES A HOME?
1   *Michael Green*

I suppose home means something different to me from what it means to most people. Firstly, because I am a bachelor, and not many bachelors are installed alone in houses of their own; and secondly, and more importantly, because I work at home. It's this working at home which conditions my whole relationship with the place. The theory is delightful. Downstairs I have one large room for dining, entertaining and relaxing. Upstairs are a bathroom and two bedrooms, one of which has been converted into my study. Here I intended to work undisturbed, returning after a certain number of hours to the domestic part of the house, where no trace of work would be allowed to sully my leisure time. But in practice it doesn't work like that at all. My work spreads throughout the house like damp in the wallpaper. It follows me into every nook and cranny like a demanding child. I am not safe even in the lavatory, indeed I am probably more vulnerable there than anywhere else. The trouble is that I'm one of those writers who is always making notes. At any moment, even in the middle of a meal, I'm liable to seize a scrap of paper and scribble 'Should his trousers come down at the end of Chapter One?' Like so many writers I think best in peculiar places, not my study. I can waste hours at my desk and find inspiration in the middle of Ealing Broadway station. No wonder, then, that I sometimes leap from my bath like Archimedes, and scribble madly on the toilet roll with an eyebrow pencil left by some long forgotten girl friend, before sinking gratefully back into the warm water. The result is that the house becomes covered with scraps of paper and even pathetic messages scribbled on walls.

Guests being entertained to dinner are likely to find scrawled on the tablecloth things like, 'She should not have her illegitimate child until Chapter Three. But is Jack the father query exclamation mark blot.' When you add to this personal exhortations such as 'Cut the padding and concentrate on the funny stuff' it will be seen how difficult I find it to get away from work. The sheer volume of paper involved in a writer's life is another reason for my overflow into the living-area. By the time I reach the end of a book there is only one place to deal with the paperwork – on the floor, and for three weeks in the living-room, which is the only one with the necessary floor space, every inch of the carpet is covered in first, second and third versions of the book, together with insertions, second thoughts, corrections and the like. Since even the dining table is equally covered, during this period I have to eat every meal outside. But if work intrudes all over the home, the home intrudes all over work. I defy anyone to write with the plumber moving around the roofspace above, or with the continual drip of a tap from the bathroom. The nervous strain of waiting for the gasman to call is enough to wreck concentration for a whole morning. The result is that I lead a sort of topsy-turvey existence. My home throbs with life during the day but by evening I've had enough. I want a change. So at the hour when most people settle down to a good evening at home I am on my way – out. I don't suppose I spend one evening a week indoors. This doesn't mean I don't appreciate my little home. I do. But by a ludicrous paradox of a writer's life, I just have to leave home every evening – to escape from my work.

2   Mary Stott

Mary Stott is Woman's Editor of the Guardian.

'Home is where your heart is.' I think that simple saying is as near to a true definition as we can get. We all know that strange tug to some place where we have been very happy. We call it 'nostalgia' – an ache for home. And when we go back, whether it's to some village in Suffolk, an island of Greece or a street in Streatham or Stockton where we have stayed with dear friends, we say when we return at last, 'It's like coming home.'

What we mean is that we felt we 'belonged' in that happy place. What matters most about home is 'belonging'. Very few of us can cope with our daily life unless we feel we belong somewhere, belong to – or rather, 'with' – someone. It might be much more efficient if we pooled our resources and lived communally, sharing common services to provide us with meals, cleaning, laundry, a nursery. Only it probably wouldn't be 'home'. We shouldn't feel we had a special place that we belonged to and belonged to us.

And there's the second clue about the meaning of home. It's a place of our own. I understand very well why students and other young people set up in flats together. We, their parents, may think anxiously, or angrily, that it's because they want to throw off all restrictions, have all-night parties, live it up. Perhaps. But I remember when I had my first flat, not as a student but as a quite young unmarried woman, that the best moment of the day, of every day, was when I put my key in the lock, opened the door, and shut it behind me. It was *my* place, *my* castle. Human beings, like animals, have a very strong sense of territory. I should think that everyone who goes out to work, man or woman, wage-earning father or grant-aided student, knows this feeling. And the woman who stays in the home, caring for it and its inhabitants, has this feeling in a rather different way, but just as strongly. She may not be paying for it in hard cash but she has made it what it is. She has swept and dusted and polished it. The furniture, the decorations are her choice, an expression, almost an extension, of her personality. It belongs to her and she to it.

Can 'home' mean quite the same to growing-up children? Perhaps you say, 'Why ever not? They belong there, don't they?' Yes, of course; but it's the only place they have ever known, not the special place they have *made* their own. Perhaps that is why, though they wouldn't be able to put it into words, so many teenagers contribute rather grudgingly, in money and services, to the upkeep of the home. Emotionally, deep down, they are on the way towards finding their own bit of territory, their own castle.

DOORS *Kaye Wilson*

I opened the front door on a bitterly cold morning to let in the workmen who were going to put central heating in our home. I hastened them inside and closed the door against the cutting wind. Over a cup of tea they gave their names as Fred and Joe. They went out to the back. I closed the back door. They walked round and knocked at the front door. Would I open the garage door, as they wanted to put their equipment in there. I closed the front door and let them in to the garage. They opened the back door, and Fred went out through the front door to the lorry. The wind blew through the house. I closed the back door and the kitchen door. Fred came back through the front door, and I went and closed it.

My two chihuahuas began barking at the intruders. I put them in the dining-room and closed the door. The men finished unloading, so we closed both the outside doors and had another cup of tea. After which, Joe wanted to survey the job. Could he go over the house ? 'Certainly,' I said. Joe went through the kitchen door, Fred set off through the back door. I closed the doors. I heard Joe open the front door and call to Fred to get something off the lorry. I went into the hall and closed the front door. Fred opened the back door. 'Missus, I think your dogs are out.' I looked at the dining-room door, it was open. I flew to the open front door and saw the dogs disappearing down the road. I grabbed a coat, changed my shoes, thanked Fred and closed the back door. I took my key, and closed the front door. By the time I returned both doors were wide open and a howling gale was blowing through the house. I took the dogs and their basket into the front bedroom and closed the door. On my way down I closed the open front door. Joe came in through the open back door. He said they couldn't open the french window, was it locked ? I opened the french window, and closed the back door. I closed the kitchen door and made some more tea. I called the men in and closed the doors. There was still a bitterly cold draught from somewhere. 'If you've finished carrying things in,' I said, 'I'll close the french window.' Joe promptly volunteered to do it for me. I tried to imagine I was feeling warmer as we drank our tea.

Joe had to go out to the lorry again and went through the front door. The french window which he hadn't closed properly blew wide open as the wind once more swept through the house. I closed the french window and locked it. I heard Joe return, so I closed the front door. Fred was bringing in tools through the wide-open back door. I went upstairs and put on an extra woolly and another pair of tights. The dogs were scratching at the bedroom door and making the sort of noises they use to indicate their need to go outside. I let them out through the back door closing the front door on my way through the hall. The dogs set off down the garden. I closed the back door and went to answer the knocking on the front door. It was the milkman. As I paid him he expressed his envy at the comfort of central heating. My smile was a little forced as I bade him good morning and closed the front door. As I passed to put the milk in the fridge I automatically closed the back door. The dogs returned and barked to come in. I opened the back door, let the dogs in, and closed the door.

I carried them upstairs past the wide-open front door. Fred was taking out the debris from the fireplace we had removed, through the wide-open front door. Joe was carrying in buckets of cement through the wide-open back door. I retreated to the bathroom. I filled a hot-water bottle, and the dogs and I sat huddled together under an inadequate bathroom heater. With one hand I splashed hot water around in the washbasin making as much wet noise as possible. If they thought I was having a bath they surely couldn't possibly contemplate opening this door? I'm glad to say they didn't.

INTERIOR DECORATING   *Anne Jones*

I never met anyone yet who moved into a house and actually liked the previous people's wallpaper. 'Of course we'll alter all this,' they tell you. 'It'll be a different place entirely when we've done it up.' I know – I've said it myself. But it came as quite a shock to me when we were selling one of our houses to come upon a couple of prospective purchasers in one of the bedrooms, giggling and making faces at the wallpaper. 'We'll have this lot off, for a start,' said the man. I was terribly offended.

But what he was, I now realise, and what I have been, up to now, is a victim of euphemism.

You see how it works. You or I might go to have a look at a house. And upon entering – *recoil*. Simply *recoil* – from the shock of the revolting pea-green walls. And *we'd* giggle. And make faces. And wonder why the vendor wasn't making haste to explain, saying how very sorry he was that we should see it like this. A discrepancy in the shade card, he might say, or a friend in the trade, able to obtain quantities of paint, below cost price, but *only in this colour*, and we'd understand perfectly, and forgive him. But he doesn't say a thing. He stands there, smiling. He might even go so far as to act proud of his walls, referring to them fondly as the Green Room.

And the reason is, you see – he being a victim of euphemism – to him, they are not pea-green at all. They are *Willow-wand Green*. Or *Translucent Jade*.

Like the man who didn't like my William Morris-type wallpaper because he didn't know it was an exquisitely executed design, evocative of a bygone, more leisurely age. It was just a load of old fruit and veg. to him, and 'We'll have it off,' he said.

It depends entirely, you see, on what you read and how responsive you are to the finely-turned phrase. Just now the posher magazines and Sunday supplements are great on Art Nouveau, lots of pictures on the walls, and the impact of vibrant, singing colours. A little further down the scale, those magazines that go in for more do-it-yourselfery are still going on about uncluttered effects, and plain white walls. I was an uncluttered, all-white woman myself . . . until I came across a posh magazine at the dentist's, and found that white has absolutely no impact, and, furthermore, is clinical.

Well, I was clean off white, in a flash – I went home and painted the bathroom royal blue (every bit royal blue . . . ceiling and all). And I now have a cosy, intimate bathroom with so much impact that people come reeling out breathing heavily and crying, 'What *possessed* you ? It's *terrible* in there.'

Just as they entirely missed the point of my cushions on the floor period. Well, not just *cushions* – chunky shapes of resilient foam, close-covered in fun-coloured hessian, they were *really*, and you were supposed to sit on them and be casual and relaxed and talk about modern poetry and all that. But nobody did. They just kept on picking them up and handing them to me. And I kept on hurling them back on the floor again, getting madder and madder. The whole thing was a complete farce, really. And of course, it was round the family in a flash. 'They've got no chairs! Don't go *there*. They make you sit on the floor all night.'

So I'm glad, now, that I didn't go in for the television well I was so keen on last year. A television well is a bit like a paddling-pool, in the middle of your sitting-room; and you sit in it, to watch television. Not *excessively* like a paddling-pool, and it would have been carpeted, of course, wall to wall. But my husband said it would just look like a carpeted paddling-pool and rejected it on these grounds. So we didn't have it. And as I say, I'm glad now, because the magazines are full of perfectly level floors again. Wood-blocks or – better still – tongue and groove. And *there*, you see, you have a perfect example of my principle – the lovely euphemism – tongue and groove, sanded, sealed and deep-polished, revealing the beauty of the natural wood-grain. (With the odd Mongolian goatskin scattered around.) But you see, if I hadn't read all about that and hadn't said it out loud to myself, rolling the words around – tongue and groove – sanded – sealed – deep-polished – well, they'd just be rotten old floorboards to me, you know. Varnished floorboards with mats on. Which goes to prove . . . I think . . . the truth of the Jones Principle. It ain't what it is . . . it's the way what you say it is . . .

BEDS AND FEATHERS *Pamela Vandyke Price*

Pamela Vandyke Price – writer and journalist – is perhaps best known as an authority on wine.

I don't know when the eiderdown appears historically, but the feather bed has been with us as a luxury at least since medieval times. Remember that girl who left her goosefeather bed and went off with the gipsy to the 'cold open field'? I used to sleep on a feather bed when I was a child and visited my grandmother and it was wonderful to sink into – but you had to be conscientious about shaking it out and plumping it up when you made the bed, and a great lollopy thing it was to handle. Mattress-wise I progressed from school horsehair to interior springs, and my eiderdown was merely a rather agreeable but characterless source of extra warmth. Until recently. The feather bed has come back to me – but it's on top instead of underneath.

I'd seen a variety of the things when I went abroad. Of course there's no sheet. The cover of the feather thing is invariably dazzling white. In Copenhagen there was one divided into several rectangles. This was particularly light in weight to me, because I was used to fairly heavy bedclothes, and as the central heating was turned up high, and the bottom sheet was unusually slippery, I alternated between sliding about the bed clutching at the topping, and sticking out my arms and legs in an attempt to air them while asleep.

Quite the reverse occurred in Switzerland, where I encountered a bed on which the mattress was in three parts, which were *not* joined together, and the top coverlet also was in sections. Perhaps the mattress and the topping were interchangeable? Anyway, sleeping in that bed required real strategy. You had to position yourself so that neither your hips nor your shoulders got into the mattress cracks – if they did, a draught of cold air came up from somewhere underneath and, if you moved to avoid this, the two sections of the mattress gave you a soft but definite pinch. At the same time, you had to manage the three top sections so that they covered you up, which I found absolutely impossible, especially as the joins of their sections coincided with the joins of the mattress and you got icy blasts striking you from above as well as below. Eventually I curved myself into a pre-natal position, and utilised only two bits of mattress; the plumeau, duvet or whatever the Swiss called the Thing was on top of me in a kind of overlapping rosette, with two sections shoring me up at the sides and the third like a bit of garnishing on top. I don't see how anyone could have slept in that bed unless they had adopted the posture of someone in a tomb – and kept like it.

My most memorable experience with a feather bed took place in Germany. I was staying at an otherwise charming country inn and everything was very comfortable and up-to-date. But on the bed there was a very, very large feather-filled case – no dividing up of it at all. It was so very large that none of me stuck out at all, even to start with – usually you have to get accustomed to keeping yourself in a feather-topped bed sandwich and this can take a night or two.

It was a cold night and the feather bed was deliciously, soothingly warm. In the middle of the night, the moon shone starkly into my bedroom and woke me. I turned over, about to go to sleep again – and was struck, terrified, just like a person on a tomb, or the Thurber man, cowering in bed with a horrid ghostlike Thing looming at me.

A white mound, pointing upwards, absolutely towered above me. It trembled. I clutched at what, in a normal bed, would have been the sheets – and it began to collapse. *It* was the feather bed Thing, which, with the heat of my peaceful sleep, had swollen like a roll of cotton wool in front of the fire and puffed up to twice its daytime size. I pronged it down with a finger – but it had given me a turn.

And then, recently, I sent my eiderdown to the cleaners. Immediately, of course, the English summer-winter set in, and I thought I'd buy a cheap eiderdown while mine was being picked over, refurbished, mulched, or whatever they do to eiderdowns. And I came across a whole range of feathery Things, which, I was told, would revolutionise my sleeping. They are divided into sections, joined up – so that they can't loom above you or get into lumps, and you can sleep under them without blankets and even without sheets. They have pretty covers, mostly drip-dry. I admit, though, that I do use a sheet, as one of my indulgences is linen next to me while I sleep. I took the Thing home – it was much meeker and lighter than those of past experience – and almost waited for bedtime to get under it and see what it would do. Well, it dominates the bedroom and my sleeping ways just as solid fuel cookers are said to dominate people's kitchens: the poor old eiderdown, fresh and clean, languishes in the linen cupboard. You do have to adjust yourself to it, however, because it's so light that you risk hoicking it right up in the air, as you turn round clutching at what would have been heavyish bedclothes in former times. It then comes down lightly on top of your head. You sleep with an enormous sensation of spaciousness in the bed – it's warm and light all over, because the Thing gently curls itself up against you as you move – you don't have to think, as it were, where you're going when you shift around.

I'm not frightened of *this* Thing at all. I'm devoted to it. But of course it *is* a feather bed and it *has* got on top of me in its way – can those old geese be getting their own back at last ?

The Backward Glance

MY FIRST WEEK AT WORK   *George Abbott*

I was just twelve years old and I had been looking forward to this day for a long time. I was to work from six a.m. until twelve thirty mid-day. That morning hadn't come quick enough and I had hardly slept all night.

I had been awakened by a grating sound on the bedroom window, and a loud voice shouting: 'Come on, George, it's five o'clock and very foggy.' It was the Knocker-up as they called him. He used a long pole with thick wires on the end, and with this he tapped on the bedroom windows – it was very effective.

George, my dad, with whom I shared the room, shouted back, 'OK Bob,' and immediately got out of bed. I was going to do the same when dad said, 'You can have another quarter of an hour, laddie.'

That quarter of an hour seemed an eternity, but when I eventually went downstairs into the gas-lit kitchen, dad had already got a big coal fire going; it was a welcome sight. I sat down and polished off three rounds of home-made bread with a covering of jam.

After a few minutes in front of the fire, I put on my clogs and an old overcoat, and a tartan scarf. The scarf had been my birthday present. I had about fifteen minutes' walk to the mill and after bidding my mother 'Good Morning', I opened the door and disappeared into the fog.

To find the mill, I had to stick to the walls of the buildings along the way. Then I walked through the gate and was met by a kind old gentleman. He remarked, 'So you are the new boy.' My heart was beating quite rapidly now, I was so excited. He led me up some stairs and into a very hot room. This I was to find out later was called the Jenny Gate, named after the Spinning Jenny. I was handed over to another man who was to be my boss – they called him 'The Minder', and he was in charge of this particular section of machinery.

I can remember him patting me on the head and remarking, 'You'll be all right son.' He had to bend down to touch my head, I was so small. I took off my clogs and socks and donned a pair of cotton overalls. The reason for the bare feet was to get a grip on the floor, as it was fairly oily and slippery. I was then shown my duties. Our work in this part of the mill was reducing raw cotton that came in bales to the cops – a cop is like an overgrown cotton reel. After this process the cotton was then ready to be made into cloth and finally garments. My particular job was called 'little piecing'. I had to follow the machinery backwards and forwards, piecing the broken strands that were coming off the bobbins on to the cops.

After two hours' work, at 8 o'clock, the machinery started to slow down and finally stopped. It was breakfast time, but as I had already had mine, I settled for a mug of tea. At 8.30 the machinery started up again, and went merrily along until 12.30.

I felt quite proud walking out through the gate to make my way home – I hoped I had satisfied the boss. My mother had a big bowl of soup waiting for me, and of course she wanted to know all about my work. After dinner and a wash I discarded my scarf for a white collar – well, I could hardly go to school in a scarf – you see it was work in the morning and school in the afternoon.

Each day went by pretty well the same, but Friday was a special day – I was to be paid my first week's wages. At 11.30 that morning I was called over by my boss who placed six and fourpence into my hand – my reward for about thirty hours' work. This was going to help my mother, who had had a very hard life. The weekly rent of our house was only five and eightpence so it would pay that. I couldn't get home quick enough to hand it over. She asked me how much I wanted back – 'odd money' they called it – and we settled I should have the odd fourpence. After all, one could get four ounces of sweets for a penny and the other coppers could be saved for a day at the seaside.

It had been a great week; and I was so pleased to be called a 'little Piecer' and to be a member of the labour force. Since then I've worked for fifty-three years but I know the comradeship and help I got during that first week at work made it one of the happiest and most exciting ones of my life.

GRANDMOTHER RAMSDEN   *Dick Gregson*

I don't think my grandmother believed in the equality of the sexes. At any rate, she didn't practise it. She was the undisputed boss of her family, and she ruled them all with a rod of iron – or rather a coach-man's long whip.

And that whip wasn't just a symbol. It was a weapon which she used impartially and effectively on both the goats which strayed from the nearby livery stables and our quarrelsome teenage uncles and aunts. Our weekly visits to this callous old matriarch were as much a trial to mother as to us. They began with one unvarying nauseating ceremony.

Ushered in by mother – 'pushed in' would be nearer the mark – we would see the indomitable old dame seated on her hard wooden chair between the slopstone-sink and the long table under the window. And on the table, close to hand, making our hearts sink and our stomachs heave, would be an earthenware jar of brimstone-and-treacle and a too-large spoon.

Her eagle eye raking us fore and aft, the old lady would bark, 'Let's be havin' thee! . . . Nearer!' The wooden spoon would be dipped into the jar, brought out brimming over with the sickening, gooey con-coction, and twirled expertly so that not a drop was wasted.

'Oppen thi gob!' she would bark. 'Wider nor that!' And the spoon was in one's mouth. 'Nah lick it clean! Clean, I said!' Satisfied at last, she would retrieve the spoon, and the ordeal was over for another week. She certainly taught us to 'take our medicine' – in more senses than one.

It was a red-letter day if we arrived to find the house empty, the ogre having been called away unexpectedly to attend a confinement or to wash and 'lay-out' someone who'd just died. As I once heard her say, 'I see 'em in, an' I see 'em out!'

But I never remember her anywhere really – except on that wooden chair, her face as clean as a new pin, her thin white hair scraped back from her pointed nose and sloping forehead into a tight, skimpy bun. She was everlastingly busy, as it seemed – darning an endless pile of corn-sacks. It was fascinating to watch the expert movements of that long, curved needle which she called her bodkin.

There was really no need for grandmother to work so hard and so continuously at that darning, for besides her odd jobs as midwife and 'layer-out', she also acted both as a bookie and a money-lender on a small scale, charging a halfpenny a week interest on every shilling she loaned.

And on top of everything she had the wages of those single, nearly grown-up uncles and aunts to collect. And she saw to it that they all brought their pay-packets home intact each pay-day – which was when the horsewhip came in handy.

We youngsters felt no love for the old dame – I don't think she expected it. Respect was good enough for her, and she got it from me, especially when I learned that, but for her resource, mother might have been drowned when two years old and I might never have had the chance of being born.

In those days mother's parents were bargees, living with their very young family on board. Grandfather was a big, bluff, easy-going man with a fondness for drink, and that night, as the boat lay in the canal basin at Brighouse, he came back from the pub more than a little the worse for wear. He found his tiny . . . did I tell you she was one of the smallest women I ever knew ? . . . he found his tiny wife nearly distracted by my two-year-old mother's incessant wailing.

Nothing would satisfy him but that he should try to quieten the child. Walking up and down the deck, whilst grandmother went on with the supper down below, he tried to sing the child to sleep. All in vain. She only wailed the louder until, suddenly, the outraged night was suddenly silenced as he went overboard.

Grandmother heard the splash, dashed up on deck, found a boat-hook, and somehow managed to haul the pair on board, her husband still clutching the quietened child. She wasted no time on the baby except to take it from him and lay it on deck and then, using the boat-hook, gave a man nearly twice her size the thrashing of his life.

Well, she worked, bossed and scraped to the last day of her life, and, as was only fitting, the family gave her a grand funeral, the hearse and no less than six coaches each drawn by a pair of shiny black, long-tailed 'Belgian' horses. My sister and I rode in the second coach, clad in stiff new black out of the insurance money. And when this grand affair was over, the family repaired to the old house for the 'sharing out', for not only was the hoard of savings to be divided, but the furniture and furnishings. It was all carried out on a strict 'one-for-thee, one-for-me' basis and, to us youngsters, was a dreary, long drawn-out process.

But it was over at last and there was a general move to leave, when our youngest uncle caught sight of the old dame's whip. Making it crack viciously, as it had so often round his own shoulders, he laughed, 'Hey! Onnybody want a whip?' Then, not without some difficulty, he broke it in two across his knee.

The heavens didn't fall!

MEMORIES OF THE WASH-HOUSE *Molly Weir*

I was going home rather late one evening, through quiet streets, on what was almost the last bus. As we stopped to let passengers on, my eye was caught by a lighted window, and inside were at least twenty people, some were reading, some chatting to one another, others moving around to pick up a basket or a package. Of course! It was a modern launderette, open right round the clock to suit the whims or odd hours of its customers. It was a bit like a club, whose members were enjoying each other's company rather than sitting alone in bed-sitter land watching telly. And, as a sort of bonus, getting their washing done at the same time. The whole thing looked so social and chummy, and yet so different from the women in our tenement who, for various reasons, preferred to do their washing in the evenings. My mother tut-tutted over this, for she felt washings ought properly to be done during the day when there was a possibility of the clothes being hung out in the fresh air and the wind to dry. And granny shook her head and pursed her lips at the thought of pulleys in the kitchen at night, laden with wet steaming clothes, flapping in the faces of the unwary as kettles were wanted from the range, or coal needed for the grate.

My mother would say, 'Aye, Mrs So-and-So must be awful glad to get away from her man and her weans when she'd put up with the damp cold of that wash-house instead of sitting at her own fireside.' And then she'd soften when granny would say, 'Och well, maybe she's better off at that, for her man's a surly blackguard and gey poor company.'

Some of the night washers were younger women, daughters of those too old to do their washing in the day-time. There was never the same fierce competition for the right to use the wash-house at night as there was in the day-time. There were twelve families to a tenement, and as nobody wanted to wash clothes at the weekends, each person's turn came round every twelve days. A strict rota system operated for all the days of the week. With the meagre wardrobes we all possessed it must have been an almost impossible task for mothers to keep their children in clean and dried clothes for the twelve days between washing days.

Come to that, where would any of us have found storage space for twelve days' soiled linen in a room and kitchen? Far from sharing my mother's condemnation of the night washers, I used fervently to hope that she could be induced to become one of them. There was something about the whole scene which made a great appeal to me. The ordinary grey stone wash-house of the daylight was transformed. Guttering candles were stuck into the necks of bottles and ranged along the window sill, and provided the only light in what seemed a vast cavern. When the lid of the huge brick boiler was raised from time to time, to see how the 'white things' were progressing, the white things being our name for all the household linen, swirling steam filled the wash-house, and the candles spat and flickered through the clouds, and the whole scene became fearsome as pictures of hell.

Like animals attracted by the light, other women would drift from their tenements into the back court, and pause at the wash-house door. 'Are you nearly done, Jessie?' was the usual greeting. The patient figure at the tubs, or 'bines' as we called them, would pause from her vigorous rubbing of the soiled clothes against the wash-board, charmed to be the centre of attraction for once, and say cheerfully, 'Just aboot half-way through. I've just the dungarees to do, and then the white things will be ready for sighnin' oot.' I don't know where the word 'sighnin' came from, but we always used it when we meant rinsing.

At the mention of the word 'dungarees' the women would groan sympathetically. Washing dungarees was a job they all hated, and as ours was a railway district, and most husbands or brothers or sons worked there, and returned home with grease-laden dungarees, it was a task they all had to face. They all had raw fingers, our tenement women, from using the slimy black soap and soda which was the only way they knew for ridding the filthy overalls of their accumulated grease and workshop dirt.

The women's eyes would lazily follow the washer's movements as she scrubbed and rinsed, and put clothes through the wringer ready for the pulleys.

Then came the scene I liked best of all. The white things were judged to be ready. The heavy boiler lid was lifted right off and leaned carefully against the back wall of the wash-house. Clouds of steam rushed everywhere. Up the chimney, out of the open door, into every corner. The washer picked up a long pole, bent over the seething bubbling mass in the boiler, fished out a load, then ran with the precious linen, and slipped them quickly and neatly into a tub of clean water. Back and forth, back and forth she went, her figure ghost-like in the swirling steam, until the boiler was empty. I longed to be allowed to help in this exciting operation, but was met with scandalised refusal. 'Do you want to scald yourself to the bone? You'll have this job to do soon enough, hen, and then you'll no' be so pleased. Run away hame to yer bed, or I'll tell yer granny on you.' They were more amused than angry, for they were quite diverted at my interest in their activities, and they made sure I went nowhere near the steam.

The watching women, lingering at the doors, couldn't resist a bit of advice, especially if the washer was a younger unmarried woman. They would say, 'Take oot the plug Jessie and let the clean water run through the claes. You'll get rid of all the soap far quicker that way.' Another would warn, 'Jessie, you're just squeezing the soap into them again – you'll have to give them another water. You're wringing them too soon.'

They were all experts, and the washer woman would listen to them all, glad of their company, and glad of their advice, for it was a great source of pride to have someone say, 'Aye, she hangs out a lovely washing.' And the most disparaging thing a tenement woman could say of another's washing were the damning words, 'She's hanging out her grey things!'

Surely the night washing women were wise in preferring the cameraderie which came with the candle-lit wash-house, rather than face this drudgery at their solitary kitchen sink. And I marvelled at the astuteness of the present-day launderette owner for realising too that any necessary dull task becomes more palatable if it is shared, and done in circumstances different from the normal.

GETTING AWAY FROM GRANDMA *Olga Franklin*

My Manchester aunties all got themselves liberated, and that was during the first world war. My Aunt Hettie shocked everyone by going, so to speak, commercial.

Aunt Hettie's the only one left now. She's eighty and lives just off Lord Street, Southport. Lancashire girls in those days all dreamed of ending their days in Southport – that is, if they didn't get married. Marriage in that time of shortage of men was often just a hopeless dream. To get married, you needed good chances, and they weren't on every tree. For one thing, you had to meet men and there were so terribly few about.

So Aunt Hettie, very daring, became Britain's first woman commercial traveller. Anyway, there weren't many of those about then, and there aren't many of them now. I don't mean high-ranking lady representatives who nowadays get whisked elegantly to Italy to select the latest range in hats. Or even the brisk ladies who talk business over the coffee-cups for the Egg Marketing Board or the Potato Council.

I mean the real thing. Aunt Hettie had a suitcase with samples like any real commercial traveller. And she went out every day, on foot of course, trudging round the little retailers and big wholesalers from Preston to Oldham, and Stockport to Manchester. This was her area and all the stores and chemists knew her and used to chaff her about her most unusual job. Aunt Hettie travelled in a somewhat intimate or personal type of goods, so it often led to that kind of conversation. I remember when I grew up and learned about it – it was rather hush-hush in our family – I was very surprised. Because Aunt Hettie, like her sisters Aunt Sophie and Aunt Mirrie, was quite excessively shy and modest. And Grandma suspected this was why they didn't get married. Grandma was always on about her daughters not getting enough chances to meet men. Chance is a fine thing, Aunt Sophie, who worked in a mill, always used to say.

My mother, the eldest girl, was the first to find liberation. She left home secretly one day, creeping out of home in Higher Broughton, Salford, to join up. She became a nurse at the Manchester Jewish Hospital and came home in a rather elegant navy costume with high navy bonnet which was so becoming that it almost took the edge off Grandma's hysterics when it was revealed what her eldest daughter had done. Grandma thought her unmarried daughters had quite enough to do nursing her. She'd gone on having babies right up to her fifty-fifth birthday, so there was plenty of nursing to do, naturally. Also nursing was considered terribly fast, because you saw men naked. So Grandma took to her bed again and wailed blue murder for about a month.

Next Aunt Ray went missing, and was found secretly married to Flying Officer Joe Kennedy, and hardly had Grandma got over that one, when Aunt Mirrie startled everyone by getting her chance. Aunt Mirrie, the youngest, was even gentler and shyer than Aunt Hettie and she was the only one of 'our lot', as mother called it, to stay at home and look after Grandma. Then, suddenly, there was Aunt Mirrie, engaged, with a whopping great ring on her finger and out to lunch and dinner every Saturday with a man whom Grandma had never met. But things took a most unexpected turn. Because Aunt Mirrie and Uncle Cliff stayed officially engaged and courting for the next thirty years and though the wedding was often discussed, it never actually happened. I suppose the present-day Liberationists might have understood it, but we never did. They were a most devoted couple, which even Grandma, who outlived them, had to admit. For one day Uncle Cliff suddenly died, leaving all his considerable fortune to Aunt Mirrie, who thereupon died soon afterwards, rather as though she felt she'd had her chance and now it was all over.

To make matters worse, there was Aunt Hettie plodding around from one customer to another, with her little bag of samples, and even mother thought it would just about ruin her chances of an honourable and suitable marriage. I remember the day that Aunt Hettie called on us too, in a business way. Father was something in hair-oil at the time. Mother gave an evening in Birmingham for people to come and see Aunt Hettie. She was a sort of freak. A woman in a man's world. The ladies giggled and said they all knew what commercials got up to when they were away from home. Aunt Hettie blushed and hung her head. She said her buyers weren't like that. They gave her tea and a nice, cosy chat. 'It's good money,' Aunt Hettie said, 'so Sophie and me can live in Southport one day.' Not today's idea of liberation but at least Aunt Hettie and Aunt Sophie thought of it first.

OH THOSE POOR NUNS! *Joan Rice*

I heard a programme recently. It was by a doctor describing how he was lecturing to school children about venereal disease. It made me realise as never before how times have changed since my schooldays. Now I know it was a long time ago – more than thirty years. And it was a convent. Not exactly the sort of school you expect to find out in front there with all the new ideas. But if any of those poor nuns have survived to see what is going on in schools today, how can they believe it's the same century – let alone the same planet ?

If anyone had suggested telling even the older girls – the seventeen year olds – about VD, or pregnancy, or even the most elementary facts of life, those nuns would never have got over the shock. But then there was no such thing as sex instruction in that convent for anyone, ever. They simply ignored the whole distasteful subject. It was difficult sometimes of course. Not being told what you were in for didn't stop the seniors from starting their periods. But even when this happened you weren't told why. Only given a solemn warning that this was something you must never, never talk about.

Going to the lavatory – or admitting that you needed to – was almost equally taboo. Something men must never know about. It took me years to overcome this particular inhibition. And I can look back to many an evening ruined in my youth because I couldn't bring myself to admit to my escort that I wanted – oh so badly – to leave him just for a minute.

As for another of today's trendy ideas, the one that says parents mustn't lock their bathroom doors or their children will grow up a mass of inhibitions, what would our nuns have thought about that ? At my convent – and I was eight when I first became a boarder – we weren't allowed to see ourselves naked. We had baths with a long clammy cloth spread over us from neck to knee. And we washed what was underneath as best we could without peeking.

Getting undressed also had to be done under wraps. First we retired to our cubicles and drew the curtains. Then it was all right to take off our dresses. But that was all. Before going further we had to put on our nightdresses over our remaining clothes. This made a sort of modesty-protecting tent beneath which we wriggled out of our underwear.

When I was about ten a chicken-pox epidemic tore through the school, and I woke up one morning with spots on my stomach. Now I did have a problem, because I had to call Sister to come and identify them. But I couldn't do anything as immodest as pulling up my nightie to show her. So before she came through the cubicle curtain I had to struggle with a towel to cover up everything except a two inch sample strip. And you can imagine the scandal, the shock, the outrage when a seven year old in an over-excited moment raced down the dormitory naked.

As for school meals today, how many children are really forced to eat what they hate, the way we were ? If you left anything at all on your plate – gristle, fat, cabbage stalks, or that dark grey lumpy porridge – back it came again at the next meal. And the meal after that if necessary until even the most rebellious spirits forced it down. It wasn't that the nuns meant to be cruel, but they knew – just as they knew that day followed night – that it was wrong for children to be fussy over food.

I suppose religious instruction is where the gulf is widest between then and now. No one asked us whether we wanted to go to church. All of us boarders, including the seven year olds, got up at five-thirty on Sundays to sit through an interminable service in Latin. And don't think we had breakfast first. And what really would have shaken our nuns was a headline I read recently in my daily paper, 'Schools Religious Syllabus Bars Brainwashing'. Because what were they on earth for but to convert the heathen ?

At this they were very successful. Though I doubt if today's educational authorities would have approved of their methods. At my convent any child who became a Catholic got a new name and a splendid tea party to which all the boarders were invited. All, that is, except for the few remaining non-Catholic outcasts. I was one of these and spent my school holidays vainly begging my parents to allow me to be saved. I wasn't wild about the new name part. Evelyns and Dorothys and Pamelas became Anne Mary or Mary Anne with monotonous regularity. But I longed for my hour of glory and some of that cake with the frosted icing.

But so far as I'm concerned, the really ironical thing about it all is what's happened to the generation gap. It was there all right when I was at school, every bit as rigid as it is today. But the other way round. Then it was the adults, the older generation, who had the power and the freedom, who knew everything, who were always right. They were the ones we envied. But one day it would be my turn. I should be one of them. Well, so I am. But I don't need to tell you, in today's youth-orientated world, just what good that has done me.

THE SNOWDROP MINSTRELS *Norman L. Goodland*

Norman Goodland is a male nurse in a Southampton hospital. He is a Hampshire man born and bred, and the reader should imagine this piece being spoken in a warm, rich Hampshire accent.

The snowdrops will soon be out, in Hampshire they are out for weeks already. But do you know the best time to see them? After dark, under a full moon.

You must look where they are, and wait. Then they seem to appear – but of course it's your eyes getting used to the dark. You see crisscross shadows from the gnarled old apple-tree, all across the leaf-fall from last year. You see the moonlight reflected from the leaves of the laurel hedge, running down behind. And then you see them; quiet, chaste clusters, sheltering between curled couch-cushions all dead and bleached by the frost on the top; and what you thought were frost patches just beginning, or pools of moonlight, you suddenly realise are crowds, and companies, and family groups of snowdrops.

I am always reminded, when they appear, of a story told to me a long time ago by my foster-mother. As I may have said before, I was fortunate enough as a lad to be brought up by a Hampshire thatcher and his wife. The story goes a long way back, to the January of 1901. It happened in the North Hampshire village of Baughurst, near Basingstoke. Basingstoke was a quaint little country market town in those far-off days.

A well-known 'musical family', the Goodenoughs were young and in their heyday in the village at this time. They were Cecil, Fred, and a sister whom I believe was called Elizabeth – but here I may be wrong. Old Schoolmaster Smith presided down at the schoolhouse.

They were the days when people made their own fun, and it was decided to form a team of the old-time minstrels. So, early in January, those likely to be interested were invited to the school room. I've tidied the story up a bit, but not too much, and we enter in upon it as my foster-mother was dressing for the occasion.

She called down the stairs to her husband, 'Come on, Frank! I'm not going across on my own!'

My foster-father was not too sure that he wanted to become one of 'they minstrels'. But still, he was very curious to see how they would get on. Nonetheless, he was fearful of making a 'hexibition' of himself, and in this mood of indecision, he burst out, 'I bain't going, mother! Me with black on my face and singing up there in front of everybody – I wouldn't do that if you was to give me a thousand gold sovereigns!'

My mother was irritated. She snapped down the stairs, 'You can at least come and watch!'

But as she peered into the mirror by candlelight, she suddenly imagined her face covered all over with blackening cork. She went off into a peal of laughter, joining father's guffaws down the stairs. They both laughed and laughed, but it did them good; for they were both very nervous over the prospect. But they decided they would go, whether they made asses of themselves or not.

And there were the snowdrops, just as I have described them. Mother picked a small bunch, and father pinned them to the collar of her coat. Then, in high expectant spirits, they passed through the orchard gate, round the end of the playground, and into the school-room lit by the yellow light of the paraffin lamps.

They were greeted in high humour by strange, black-faced beings. Men were seated on the school desks in their shirtsleeves, while Elizabeth Goodenough and the schoolmaster's wife were busy applying make-up. Mrs Taylor from across the road was there; so were the Saunders from Causeway Farm, all most embarrassed beneath their layers of burned cork, with no idea of how their embarrassment heightened the comedy of their appearance.

Cecil Goodenough was in charge of musical arrangements. His brother Frederick arranged the drama and stage settings, with the help of the black-faced, ponderous old schoolmaster. Elizabeth Goode-nough was mistress of the wardrobe. Banjos, tambourines, concertinas, mandolins made their miraculous appearance. There were other strange wind and string instruments, home-fashioned by other would-be performers.

It was a confused, gay evening. Even on this first night Cecil managed to wield this truly rag-time orchestra into energetic form. The high old schoolroom rang to such songs as, 'Oh dem golden slippers!' 'Way down upon de Swanny Ribber!' and many other tops of the pops of the day.

As confidence increased, one or two solos were put in. The most notable, in view of Cecil Goodenough and his young lady Florence now 'going strong', was a rendering by Flo of a song called, 'I won't be a Nun'.

The meeting was reaching its end when it was suddenly realised that the new Minstrel Team had no official title. It was then that Frederick Goodenough had his inspiration. Like mother, most of the ladies wore snowdrops on their collars, and his suggestion was that they should call themselves 'The Snowdrop Minstrels' and it was received with enthusiasm and delight.

So the 'Snowdrop Minstrels' were born, and joined with the August Hill Drum and Fife Band, and the Tadley Temperance Band in a round of hilarious engagements. They were well received at Baughurst and in the neighbouring villages.

And there was that never-to-be-forgotten occasion when, after a late Saturday night engagement, some of the performers, who were also members of the Church Choir, omitted to clean the inside rims of their bowler hats. Next morning they walked sedately up the nave to their places in the Choir Stalls, with grave and solemn faces, and about their foreheads a halo of burnt cork!

TWENTIETH-CENTURY INFLUENCES
1   *Hugh Cudlipp on Lord Northcliffe*

This was the title of a series for which Woman's Hour *invited a number of people to talk about those whom they considered to be major influences on their life and time. Here is Hugh Cudlipp's memoir of Lord Northcliffe.*

Stop anybody in the High Street of your town tomorrow morning and ask, 'Who was Lord Northcliffe?' He would probably shrug his shoulders and say, 'Don't know.' After all, the man died forty-eight years ago.

If you strolled down Fleet Street in London, the area in which most of our national newspapers are produced, and put the same question, everybody would know the answer. Lord Northcliffe was the saviour of the *London Evening News* and the founder of the *Daily Mail* and of the *Daily Mirror*.

The last years of his life, and his end, were uncompromisingly grim.

He was calling himself the Ogre of Printing House Square, where *The Times* was produced. He had become the chief proprietor of that newspaper, much to the discomfiture, fear, and chagrin of its staff.

He was exulting in the title of the Napoleon of Fleet Street, trying on the Emperor's hat during a visit to Fontainebleau and finding it too small for him.

He was signing communications to his executives with the preposterous pseudonym, 'Lord Vigour and Venom'. He was by now a megalomaniac, suffering from the final stages of general paralysis of the insane.

He imagined the Germans were pursuing him. They weren't: he was demented. It was all a very sad and very silly end to a most important life.

Alfred Harmsworth, later Lord Northcliffe, is the man I choose to be named among the major influences of the twentieth century. He was the creator of popular journalism as we still know it today. Lord Beaverbrook said that he was the greatest figure who ever strode down Fleet Street. And Max Beaverbrook was right.

I was nine years old, editing a typewritten, one-page paper in our street in Cardiff, insensitive enough to inflict it on neighbours at a penny a time, when Northcliffe died in 1922. But he influenced, and possibly dominated, the lives of journalists – including mine – who lived long after him.

The picture of Northcliffe as the heavily-jowled, Napoleonic press tycoon who had used his power irresponsibly to bully our statesmen is a true picture, but applies only to his declining years.

He is the only journalist and publisher in my time or before my time to whom the accolade of genius can be indisputably applied. A genius must be creative, and Northcliffe was all of that. His effect upon the lives of ordinary people in this country, including yours, was tremendous.

Curiously, only a handful of books have been written about him.

I enjoyed the privilege of working with his nephew, Cecil Harmsworth King, for many years. Stories about Northcliffe, his attitudes and his achievements, therefore became part of my blood-stream and journalistic education.

He had no assets apart from his good looks, his abounding creative energy, and his wits. He was the eldest of a penniless family of fourteen children, three of whom died in infancy. His father was a charming barrister who failed in his career and died young because he met too many chums over too many bottles in too many bars and clubs. Fortunately, his mother was a most powerful and dauntless woman.

Alfred's work as a journalist was really accomplished by 1914, before he was fifty years old.

By that time he had created two best-selling national daily papers, the *Mail* and the *Mirror*, and rescued and rebuilt *The Times*. All this, as well as starting scores of magazines. Before he began the great journalistic revolution, only one person in six read a daily newspaper regularly. Today only one person in six does not. Readers of a new paper must feel that they belong to a community who share their interests and feeling, in fact almost belong to a club.

Before Northcliffe's time, the ordinary people of Britain had no such solace. Right up to 1896, the daily papers were made for their betters, the leisured minority who had time and patience to wade through columns of Parliamentary reports. Alfred Harmsworth had learned his journalistic craft on magazines, particularly on the one he created called *Answers*.

In 1894 he and Harold, the brother who afterwards became the first Lord Rothermere, bought the *London Evening News* and within a few days converted a weekly loss of a hundred pounds into a profit of five pounds.

Harold was the financial brain. Alfred, the editorial genius, had no experience of newspaper journalism but he boldly changed the type overnight, got rid of the flatulent politics, printed three short leaders instead of one long one – and introduced a woman's column.

Yet all this was merely a rehearsal for the creation of the *Daily Mail*. What he did seems pretty obvious now. But it was not obvious then. He made all the items in the *Mail* briefer and simpler than in rival newspapers. He imagined his readers to share his tastes. He lacked formal education, and so did they. They wanted to know about travel, new inventions, new ways of living. They wanted in fact a daily encyclopaedia.

The snobs jibed at Harmsworth's *Mail*. Salisbury snootily called it a paper written by office boys for office boys. It was not. It was written for men like Harmsworth himself, men of push and go, the enterprising lower middle classes, and – don't forget – for their wives.

What kind of man was Alfred Harmsworth? He had some of his father's charm as well as his mother's courage. He loved pure English and read widely.

He knew exactly and by instinct what popular journalism must be. 'Every day,' he said, 'there must be a new surprise, something to make people talk, something unusual.' He insisted that reporters must ask Who ? Why ? When ? How ? Where ? and get the answers right.

One of his rare failures was the paper for which I have worked most of my journalistic life, the *Daily Mirror*. Harmsworth launched it in 1903 as a daily paper for gentlewomen, written and edited by women with the help of half a dozen or so male professionals.

It started well and then flopped dismally. He lost £100,000 within a few months and only a romantic would have clung on.

He fired the women – it was like drowning kittens, the Editor said – and was rescued by one of his minor editors who had found a way of printing half tone photographic blocks on a fast rotary press. So the *Mirror* was reborn as an illustrated paper and achieved remarkable success even before World War One.

But the *Mail* was the first daily to reach a million sale and that, in those days, was fabulous.

Of course popular newspapers are always controversial. They are accused of frivolity and certainly they have their frivolous side. They are much more a reflection of the kind of mood society is going through, than they are the creators of that mood. The permissive society of today presents these newspapers with problems. Nobody can say any longer what are the limits of propriety or good taste.

The popular papers, remarkably, have been more cautious than the so-called 'quality' papers in printing four letter words. Alfred Harmsworth would have pursed his lips at the bosoms and buttocks which swing and sway through the pages of most of the popular news-papers today.

Yet, side by side with the frivolous and the ephemeral, of course, are always items of serious purpose. All the cleverness of popular journalism is used to attract people towards their democratic responsi-bilities. But, thank God – and Northcliffe – these popular papers do have their frivolous side.

2 *Mary Stott on Hitler*

I wouldn't talk about Hitler being the greatest influence on the twentieth century unless I thought it the only honest thing for me to do. But there it is; the way I see it, Hitler didn't only disrupt the lives of more people than any other individual in this century except perhaps Stalin, he didn't only destroy our homes and many of our families and friends, he destroyed something in us – I can only call it our innocence.

Perhaps I can begin to explain what I mean by saying that though I grew up next door to a synagogue, it simply never occurred to me until the rise of the Nazis, when I was in my very early twenties, that being a Jew was any different from being a Celt or a Scandinavian – or indeed from a Rotarian or a Rechabite. People had different backgrounds, attended different places of worship, belonged to different associations. It was interesting to find out about, but there was no pushing individuals into labelled pigeonholes, no automatic reaction to the word 'Jew', any more than to 'Scot' or 'cockney'. There is now, isn't there, in every single one of us? Hitler did that to me, and the fact that many of the characteristics I have learned to pigeonhole as Jewish give me great joy doesn't comfort me. It was far, far better to be able to take people as they came, like them or not like them, just for their own sake.

My age group grew up under the influence of Shaw, of Wells, of the Webbs, all the Fabians, and we believed in the power of reason and in the perfectibility of man. We thought that it was their intolerable environment that made people into thieves, murderers, prostitutes, sadists, perverts. The notion of original sin was anathema to us.

Hitler destroyed that innocent view of life. We had, of course, admitted to ourselves that under the stress of war kind and decent men did many horrible things, which was basically why many of us were pacifists. But it was a shock from which I personally have never really recovered to realise that Hitler could recruit men and women, presumably decent husbands, wives and parents, to herd millions of innocent Jews into cattle truck trains, ship them across the country and almost literally shovel them into gas chambers. This vast operation was carried out in cold blood, with perfect precision and efficiency. It was devastating to me to discover that stark evil clearly existed in apparently quite normal people, ready to be unleashed by the passion in the voice of a maniacal demagogue.

The voice of a demagogue – was there any other man in our day and age like this apparently ridiculous Austrian house-painter, pasty, flabby, with his Charlie Chaplin moustache, and his sloppy raincoat, who could deprive an audience of thousands of the power of rational thought? I can hear now that senseless, almost animal roar, 'Sieg heil, sieg heil'. Man a rational animal? Hitler showed us the naivety of that simple faith, too.

So Hitler knocked most of our props from under our feet and left us floundering. And I doubt if this is only our tragedy. You could put it that Hitler quenched the torch that was handed to us; the torch that we ought to have been able to hand onto the next generation. Once we had beliefs that offered ready-made answers. Now we can only say, 'I don't know. I don't know what causes violence and cruelty. I don't know how they can be controlled, much less sublimated. I don't know how people can be persuaded to co-operate unselfishly for the common good. I don't know. I don't know.' Is it any wonder the young spend so much energy on being 'anti' when we have so little to offer them that they can be 'pro'?

There is just one thing we can offer, just one area where the impact of Fascism has not weakened, much less destroyed, our convictions. We who lived through the dark night of the Nazis know that once you start putting disparaging labels on people, as it might be on black, brown or yellow people and their black, brown and yellow babies, you start on the slippery slope towards Auschwitz; towards regarding them as second class citizens, as not quite human, as subhuman, and finally as a sort of vermin whom it is positively desirable to exterminate.

Perhaps by the time I am really old I shall be able to put Hitler and the Nazis into their historical perspective and see that rebuilding faith and hope takes longer than rebuilding bombed cities and that in this bewildering, alarming ferment we are living through as a result of that shattering destruction, something new is being born.

These Islands Now

Gwyn Thomas, Monica Sheridan and Alan Dent were invited to broadcast for Woman's Hour *on St George's Day.*

England, to the outsider, is a land of powerful self-assurance that can border at times on an almost idiotic complacency. For all the battering to pride and pocket she has taken in the course of this wickedly destructive century, she is still sure of herself, aware of an integrity that gives her a single, stable spine in an increasingly broken-boned world. Quite unlike the Celtic communities where accidents of history and geography have shattered what once might have been a national identity into fragments that no amount of genius or effort will ever again weld into a working unity.

A pub conversation in Wales will, at some point in the evening or another, become stormy with theory and dispute. By contrast a conversation of the pub type in England will be placid. A murmuring commentary on work, hobbies and a simple unanalytical recital of political shibboleths. No rage, no enthusiasm, no mystical wrangling about the nature of man and his universe. This I find very refreshing. I can still recall my delight, in a Midlands pub, after long Welsh years of having my beer flattened by major philosophic propositions about the nature of guilt, sin and Lloyd George, sitting next to a man who, in two hours, said nothing except, after each sip, 'Ah, it's good ale is that, is that.' I suppose he would have regarded the repetition of 'is that' as an exotic conversational flourish. I cherish, too, the memory of a man in a pub set on the banks of a superb lake in Cumberland. All he said, from one end of the evening to the other, was, 'We'll be all right when we get top-side o' them revolutionaries.' No hint of what subversives his prophecy was directed against. Kosygin, Mao Tse Tung, student rebels, striking dustmen. I don't think he cared. Nor did I. I am sure that if I had asked him to broaden his assertion with a few more details he would have regarded me as one of the revolutionaries it was necessary to get top-side of. I liked that. The essential England is full of silences we could do with a lot more of.

And I would say the same of those golden townships of the Cotswolds, built of the loveliest stone under the sun, charged with a will to endure, dedicated to a simple cult of crops and ale, food and geniality. Quite unlike the mining valley communities and steel towns that look as if an army on a wild, blind march had flung its barracks down to stay for just a week and stuck it out for a century.

2 *Monica Sheridan*

I'll tell you the thing that absolutely fascinates me about England and particularly London, and that's the food shops. When I look into the vegetable shops there and see them, with all the apples pyramided up and polished, and the oranges all looking so delicious, I wonder if you have an idea what luxury vegetables you have here that are within the scope of your price. They cost twice as much in Ireland. And, of course, the fish shops. Did you ever look into a fish shop and think of the artistry that they put into it ? Another thing that I like very much is English food. You know, the English always tend to think that only the French can cook. I think that the war perhaps has given people a sort of inferiority complex about their food. But I think the English should be enormously proud of what is traditional English fare. Heavens, look at the roast beef of old England. They're eating it all over the world now and there's nothing to compare with it, you know. There's another thing that I love about England. And that's English men. When I go out to lunch with an Englishman he sits there and he listens to you and he makes you feel as if you're the most amusing person he ever took out, and he laughs at you and he laughs with you. Back in Ireland it's the men who perform and the women must sit and be nice and quiet and behave themselves, and they're lucky if they get a word in now and again. But an Englishman, good gracious no, he's sweet. I went into a porcelain shop, an absolutely specialised place up in Bond Street. Now I know as much about porcelain as I know about nuclear fission. But there he took me into the shop, this most exquisite place, and took me round every one of the display cabinets and explained to me every piece of English porcelain – the Chelsea and the Bow – and it's not even as though I look terribly rich or anything, because really I'm a rather tatty-looking middle-aged woman, you know. For him to do this for me with such exquisite manners and kindness, and the interest that he took. Where would you get this, for heaven's sake, anywhere else in the world but in England?

3   *Alan Dent*

Well, I like everything about England beginning with its literature. I
think Scottish literature, beginning with Robert Burns, is distinctly
over-praised – especially by the Scots. But English literature has
William Shakespeare at its head and William Shakespeare (not the
mysterious St George who was a young man born in Palestine with no
English connections whatever) ought, in my opinion, to be the patron
saint of England. The greatest dramatic literature in the world is
English, and some of the finest poetry in the world is purely English.
I'd say the best of the poetry in the world is English. That, for many
reasons, is why I love England above all countries – although I love
any country that isn't too conceited. The Scots are far too conceited
by the way. The English people, in my opinion, are the most un-
conceited people on the earth.

I've written in a book on Robert Burns this sentence: 'The funda-
mental difference between the Scots and the English is that the Scots-
man loudly and incessantly talks of himself as being the cock of the
walk, and the lord of creation; whereas the Englishman quietly and
unostentatiously knows that *he* is.' I've written this in a book on
Robert Burns and the book wasn't very highly praised in Scotland,
though it seems to have been quite a lot read everywhere else. That's
what I like so much about the English. A kind of modesty, even if it's
assumed, is better than the loud, conceited Scots way of talking
about themselves and nothing else.

The English, too, in their poetry have a strong tendency to be
lyrical. I need only mention Shelley, Keats and Byron to name no
others. The English are good at lyrical poetry, because they have the
lyric in their heart. They have a poetical nature. Just as the Welsh
have a musical nature. And the Scottish have, shall I say, a thrasonical
nature, a boasting of their prowess in sport as well as in war. And the
Irish have a lyrical nature as the English have. Maybe less so.

And there again, going back to the saints, the English have the
ideal date for a patron saint. 23 April. Not only is it St George's Day,
but it's also the birthday of Shakespeare. And almost invariably for
some reason or other – mainly connected with my work – I find my-

self at Stratford-on-Avon on that day. And to be in the heart of War-
wickshire on 23 April is as near heaven as I want to go.

WHAT I LIKE ABOUT TODAY   1 *Ann Jellicoe*

*The natural inclinations of those engaged in the communications industry
often seem to be towards unrelieved gloom. So, occasionally, when the
cries of woe and doom become too deafening,* Woman's Hour *invites contributors to say what they actually like about living in Britain today.
Here are five positive responses.*

Among Ann Jellicoe's better known works are the plays Sport Of My
Mad Mother, *and* The Knack.

What I like about this extraordinary decade is not space travel nor
any of the fantastic technological advances. For these demand that
the individual totally suppress his individuality in order to achieve a
common dehumanised aim.

What I like has come about very much as a protest against this
denial of individuality – it is an assertion, at a very basic level, of the
dignity and usefulness of individuals.

For instance, I'm glad I'm living at a time when such bodies as the
National Childbirth Trust have given mothers real insight into what
happens when their child is born, and a technique of coping with the
various stages, so you can actually help your child at birth, and not be
treated as an ignorant, hysterical moron. I like the attitude of the
doctor, who, at my own confinement, said: 'Now when the baby is
born we won't say what it is – we'll let you see the sex for yourself.'
It's an expression of a whole new attitude – an absence of authoritarianism, of paternalism, of 'We know what's best for you so do what
you're told and don't ask silly questions.'

This new attitude to people means you don't just tell them what's
good for them, you try and help them to see what's best – and you
don't assume what's best for you is best for them. This absence of
authoritarianism seems to me a most significant development. Many
of us need to be bolstered up by power, it helps cover up our weaknesses. We make ourselves seem cleverer and stronger by showing
others how stupid and inefficient they are; like the teacher who
shoves information into his pupils instead of leading them to make
discoveries for themselves. But in a curious way it's much more

satisfying to stand back – to try and help people to grow and develop by making them solve their own problems; instead of giving answers ready made, to try and provide tools so a man can find the answers himself, and then even to begin to formulate his own questions.

This development seems to me healthy, and most welcome, and it leads directly to the question of student unrest. Student unrest is above all a direct questioning of authority and paternalism, in universities, and finally in society. To many of us this challenge to settled values is deeply disturbing, and we are right to be disturbed. This questioning of authority could mean immense changes, and few of us like change. But the great thing about the students, to my mind, is that they are rejecting ready made answers, they reject communism as readily as they reject capitalism. They are young enough to think they can try and discover the nature of truth and then guide their lives by it. This seems to me a noble aim. I think this is what I like about our time: the passionate eagerness of numbers of people to try and see things as they really are, and to act accordingly.

2   Nicholas Tomalin

Compose a list of conventional British bogies: the weather, the crowds, the roaring machinery on the burgeoning motorways, the plasticated progress that obliterates both the peace of the countryside and the taste of its produce, the decline of our world power, and the incredible mix-up of old-fashioned snobberies, and newfangled technological intolerance. These very things, if looked at intelligently and honestly, are all the most wonderful bonuses. For all of them give us choice, freedom, comfort, gentleness and consequently tolerance.

Our weather. Much libelled but, in fact, the kindest, most varied climate in the world. And nowadays beatable by central heating.

Our crowds. Crowds, if you come to think of it, breed choice; freedom for even the most eccentric to discover exactly what he needs. Yesterday – in our most crowded place, London, I ate an Indian meal, bought a French lemon squeezer, a Yugoslav poster reproduction, and a pair of American roller skates. And all it requires to escape the crowds is not money or power, but simple ingenuity.

And as for the plasticated progress. You don't have to buy frozen peas and fish fingers. But they are there, if you are short of time and energy. I don't think anyone sufficiently acknowledges that a form, at least, of the really luxurious good life is now available to three-quarters of the population instead of just one twentieth. Nowadays our job is not so much to attack technological progress as to make sure it helps the final quarter.

Finally, and this I think is the most important thing of all, we are supremely lucky to live at a time when Britain – without an Empire – need no longer sacrifice happiness to duty. And at a time when the tyranny of the old social class structure has broken down, and the new tyranny of technology has not imposed itself. Just at this moment in Britain, it is possible for almost everybody to feel superior to every-one else.

The old aristocracy can feel that, even though they may be poor and stupid and powerless and old, they are, at least, still Dukes. The new aristocracy can feel that, although they are young and low-born and brash, they are at least clever and powerful, and the future is theirs. And between them are a multitude of ordinary people – ice-skating champions, top dahlia growers, beauty queens, university lecturers, lead guitars with the Bee Gees, matchstick model makers: all of whom – in their eccentric ways – are able to feel the finest. We are nearer to genuine equality in British society today than we've ever been, or ever will be.

It is this odd mix-up which, to my mind, provokes the kindness, the willingness to accommodate, the tolerance, which is the dis-tinguishing mark of today. The old fanaticisms are dead, the new not properly born. That's why I'm glad to be alive now.

3   *Amabel Williams-Ellis*

If I'd been born at any earlier period, if I'd been alive at all, I'd have been a bent old crone – deaf, mumbling, almost house-bound, half blind and living on slops. I get cross with people when they grumble – all that nonsense about the *golden past* and how we're on *the road to ruin*, and how the young don't respect us, and how all the *graciousness* has gone out of living . . .

You see I can remember quite a lot of that *golden past*, but besides that, I'm just finishing writing the text for an illustrated *History of Life in England* – so I've been spending a lot of time trying to find out about the past nine centuries of living in England. Now the work's nearly done and I bless my stars that I was born when I was – especially since I happened to be born a woman. (By the way, when I was little I bitterly regretted being a girl, but my grand-daughters don't seem to regret it a bit – in fact they seem to think being girls is rather interesting.)

Skip medieval days – come to Oliver Cromwell's times. Girls then must have been very much like girls today. Take Lucy Hutchinson: she says how she managed to get an education by listening while tutors taught her brothers – how she was, she says, not just a scholar but 'a hoyting girl', a 'hoyden', a girl who loved riding and being out of doors – and politics. *But* . . . she was a *girl*, so . . . ! No one heeded women. Even the dresses made an active life impossible. Have you ever thought about wearing a floor length dress, very full, and later, hoops and crinolines, not just for evening, but whatever you were doing ? And a tight-laced bodice into the bargain ? And how there was *no dry cleaning* and none of the lovely stuffs would wash ? Well, for hundreds of years that was the way of it, from medieval days right up to the Edwardian times, that I can well remember. Small things, but . . . !

Of course plenty of things about the past concern men just as much as women. People complain nowadays about the ways in which a lot of people amuse themselves in England – bingo, watching football, watching the sillier or more violent programmes on tv. But compare! In the 'good old days' – for centuries in fact – it was bull baiting, bear baiting and sometimes horse baiting and worse – public executions, men and women being hanged, burnt alive, or hanged, drawn and quartered. Mothers took their children – the crowds laughed, drank beer, ate pies and oranges.

There are complaints about modern politics, the Services and the Church. But we don't any longer take it for granted that a Minister of the Crown has been bribed, or that half the MPs have simply bought their seats, that Church livings and Deaneries and Bishoprics or the Command of Regiments are sold, or else given out to the fools of the great families. Heaven knows politics and the Church and the Services aren't perfect today in England – but it's *not* plain graft, bribes and jobbery – and we know it isn't.

So many things in the good old days would give us – and rightly – fits if they happened today. Drake starting off the slave trade, the

Chinese opium wars (we forced opium on China), the state of English prisons in Howard's day; the way Clive behaved in India, the little colonial wars, the things we did and didn't do in Africa.

But come back to us women, to our feelings – our deepest feelings. Poor silly Queen Anne bore sixteen children, and not one of them lived to grow up. This wasn't particularly uncommon. A woman did commonly face year after year of painful pregnancies and dangerous births, only to see half her children die in infancy. Did mothers feel the loss of a baby or a young child as we do ? I think so . . . I fear so. 'Rachel mourning for her children and will not be comforted . . . ' That or celibacy. Would you want either for your daughters ?

No! Give me the times we live in – with its dangers but also opportunities for us all.

4   *Christopher Jarman*

What I mostly like about living today is the fact that I am older than I was yesterday. This may not appeal to some people, but I am still young enough to be astonished daily by the fact that I seem to have grown up. I love the corny truth that policemen actually are younger than I am. And that the schoolgirls I see walking about pushing prams are mothers, not elder sisters, is a constant delight.

Most of the other things that give me pleasure are the very ordinary modernities like being able to take colour snaps and the high quality of the paper in glossy magazines, quite exciting to feel and smell, even modern paper bags are luxurious. When I was a boy in wartime all paper was a kind of hard thin pterodactyl skin, and colour photos in periodicals and books were virtually unknown. I love all the colour there is today. I especially like the tremendous variety of plastics in place of that funny brown bakelite stuff we used to have (everybody used to say it was made from milk: I don't know why, perhaps it was). Another good thing now is all the electric plugs being the same thirteen amp three pin (if you're lucky anyway). I've probably lost more years of my past life in hopping frustration trying to coax small two-pin bakelite plugs into large horny three-pin sockets . . .

But look what else we have today which is really a benefit – margarine that spreads straight from the fridge, and fibre tip pens, marvellous for putting false moustaches on children or making handkerchiefs into flags.

One of the best things about living today for us is our doctor. We have a family pew in his surgery for the winter months, and the children use his waiting room books as a kind of lending library. They know they'll be back the following week to return the latest volume. The National Health Service may be tottering in London, but it's the centre of social life in our village. And while I'm on the subject of pillars of the community; surely life is much better today now we know that parsons are real people and can be allowed to admit to a few human weaknesses without losing face.

And, as a college lecturer, I have some professional pleasures which are unique to today. One of these is the contemporary frankness and outspoken attitude of my students. After a lecture the other morning, I was walking away and one came up to me, took my arm in a very charming way and said, 'I did enjoy that, it was most helpful, thank you very much indeed.' Well, what more could a teacher ask! The next week they were all on strike, but you know, what a refreshing change from the dull grey cloisters of before!

Well, what else is there? Chicken to eat each week now instead of only once a year, and fresh frozen vegetables and fruit all the year round, if you can afford it. It makes me think of the old saying, 'When the revolution comes we'll all have strawberries and cream.' It's come so far as food's concerned.

Most of all though, I suppose I enjoy the unconscious humour of the mass media today. The newspapers, the radio and television programmes. They have all become so stuffy and serious and in consequence have become funnier and funnier. I mean, when an announcer tells me for the thousandth time that our trade gap is the difference between our imports and our exports I laugh out loud. And when the newspapers have another 'probe' I skip with joy, or I read another description in perfect journalese . . . 'Grey-haired bespectacled mother of eight, ex-bomber pilot (53) said today at her soon-to-be-demolished home,' etc., etc. Well, it just makes my day.

Yes, the fun of living today is that it *is* today, and if your senses are kept sharp and you notice the immense variety of activities going on around you, it's OK.

5 *Jane Gregor*

I've just been sitting in a modern café, the winter sun warming me
through the plate-glass windows.

I watched as pretty a scene as you could wish for; old houses on a
grassy slope, bare willows trailing over a pond and a fountain where
ducks and gulls gathered round bronze statues. Nearer at hand were
the square outlines of new buildings and a busy shopping area.

As I sat, I ate fresh sandwiches and drank pretty good coffee for a
shilling a cup.

I certainly wasn't in Rome or Venice or Pango-Pango or any other
exotic-sounding spot in that magical 'abroad' which so many Britons
persist in sighing for.

I was, in fact, sitting in the café of a popular multiple store in one of
Britain's much criticised 'new' towns. All right; so it wasn't exactly
the Ritz. But the point is that, arriving in England after a spell in the
tropics, filled with apprehension about the current fate of my poor,
battered old homeland, I was having to give myself a mental shake and
to reassess all I'd been reading and hearing of her 'pitiful' state.

Yet here was colour, warmth, bright chatter and, downstairs, a shop
bursting with things at, viewed globally, remarkably low prices. Furniture, pots and pans, children's clothes, cosmetics, food . . . it didn't
matter what I looked at . . . compared with other places I know, the
quality was astonishingly high, the variety bewildering and the prices
. . . yes, honestly, low.

After the stringy meat, monotonous fruit and vegetables, sky-
high-priced butter, occasional cheese and sometimes tea, sugar or
coffee-less lands I've visited and lived in over the past five years,
British food shops are like Aladdin's caves. I decided that even if you
bought the very cheapest grade of every food on display in any supermarket, you'd still eat a good deal better than millions of other folk on
this earth.

Yet all I keep hearing is, 'Oh, this country's going to the dogs,' and
'If I'd half the chance, I'd get out,' and 'You wouldn't catch them
putting up with this on the Continent . . . ' or 'In America,' or 'In
those foreign places,' according to where the speaker's fancy places
his Utopian dream-land.

Please . . . please . . . stop it!

So, life's not perfect. Is it ever ?

Certainly not in those 'magic lands' of perpetual sun which Britons seem doomed to envy. I know. I've lived in too many of them.

Blazing sun in a featureless sky gets dreadfully boring. And, unless it's to be a desert, a tropical land must have equally intense rain; try *that*, sometime!

Why, you don't really know what weather is, in these islands. No tornadoes, no line-squalls, no dust-storms, no year-long droughts. But infinite variety, gentleness, a sky to make poets reach for their pens, a landscape of continual subtlety. People who are, essentially, gentle and kindly. A good measure of justice, free speech . . . forgive me; at this point I could awfully easily become pompous.

But you've so much . . . honestly you have. Even going in to a public library I'm filled with envy; all those just-out, still stiff-in-the-cover new books, and a reference system capable of finding almost any book on earth . . . free. The quality of your newspapers, radio, television . . . that indefinable 'something' which comes merely from being an 'old' civilisation and full of delicious eccentricities. These are riches.

Mind you, there *are* snags.

I'd give a lot to see, next time I'm home, for instance, a system of pavement traffic lights . . . I mean, how else can the luckless pedestrian, already harried off the roads, escape injury from all those trolleys, baskets, shoppers, bags, strollers or whatever you call them, on wheels, which two thirds of the female population of the southern counties, at any rate, clash and manoeuvre along their High Streets?

Ruination to stockings, entanglers of dogs, small children and the absent-minded, I can see them leading to the war of the women unless someone steers their predatory prows away from the legs of the shopping public.

I'm only joking, of course. At least, about our pavement traffic. For the rest, I've never been more convinced. This is a wonderful country . . . still.

WHAT'S GOOD ABOUT BRITAIN

Yehudi Menuhin, Riccardo Aragno, Jo Park

In 1969 a book was published called What's Good About Britain.* *It consisted of a collection of articles – first published in the* Guardian *– by people from overseas who know Britain well. Three of the contributors – violinist Yehudi Menuhin, Italian writer Riccardo Aragno, and writer Jo Park who is a South African married to an Englishman – came together in the* Woman's Hour *studio to discuss the quality of life in Britain.*

MENUHIN: There will come a time when the values for which people live, or will live in Britain, values that are being formulated now, will take the place of cars and speedboats, because the future of the world is not being predicted by the statistics of production. I think every prediction today that is assessed by the experts is bound to be wrong and the only thing we can be hopeful for is the capacity to meet the unexpected, which is certain to happen, and which this country is going to meet better than any other.

ARAGNO: Do you think this country is meeting the challenge of modern civilisation better than others? My whole point is that there are extremely good philosophical reasons for coming to settle in Britain and that the economic reasons are superficial, just as the statistics about the standard of living are. I think, philosophically speaking, this is the best country in the world nowadays. It's the one that faces modern civilisation better than any other. It's the one that preserves freedom, it's the one that preserves the dignity of the individual. I think it's the one that points the way to the young.

MENUHIN: I'd be most interested in your explanation. Why is this country able to face the future in the positive way it does?

ARAGNO: Well, partly because of its training, partly because of its structure, and partly because of the educational system, which happens to be the best in the world. There is hardly any other society, at the moment, that shows such utter resistance to the weaknesses of the so-called new civilisation. The idea that a gadget civilisation is necessarily a better civilisation than a civilisation of people who can sit under a tree and have a picnic, is completely wrong.

PARK: Yes, I quite agree.

MENUHIN: Yes, it's a pity sometimes that the British aren't true enough

*What's Good About Britain. George Allen & Unwin, 1969. 62½p.

to themselves to have their picnics a few yards beyond the road; sometimes they will settle right at the roadside and it seems to me that there are so many lovely meadows that lie beyond.

ARAGNO: Isn't that part of the fight that the poor British are fighting in a way, let's say conserving, preserving, their own way of life, which is essentially a highly civilised country life.

MENUHIN: They know what trees are like, how long it takes for a plant to grow. They know what animals are like.

PARK: And their knowledge of bird-life is fantastic.

MENUHIN: Fantastic. All the other approaches to life that are trying to divorce human beings from the organic elements of existence are all going to fail. They're all going to collapse. And I think the role of the alien in Britain is to awaken the British as much as possible to the basically British values, that we appreciate and that are going to save the world and save the British people eventually.

ARAGNO: Absolutely. This is our function, this is one of the reasons why we'd better stay here and tell them. I mean for ten years they have been in competition with each other at who was best at criticising Britain. I was delighted a few days ago that a Minister of the Crown finally made a speech in which he said some of the things that I wrote a couple of years ago; and that is, simply, that this country is considered by young people, and I would say from experience, particularly those in Europe, as the leader country, in the sense that this is the way things are going. The laws about abortion, all these sort of things, these are the civilised things of today.

MENUHIN: Unfortunately there is a school of thought today that assumes that everything that is made tomorrow is going to be automatically better, that everything new is automatically better and people are not able to reconcile this with the basic fact that something which has evolved, survived and matured, is better than anything new. Now you have two fields of thought – one is the living human being, and the other is the machine. Obviously the machine made tomorrow is going to be a little better than the machine made yesterday; but the human society evolved over 800 years is going to be much, much better than any society evolved in a shorter time.

ARAGNO: So what is the yardstick really, in your opinion?

MENUHIN: Man is the yardstick and flexibility, tolerance and the suppression of such feelings as envy or greed, or hate, are the yardsticks of the heights of human civilisation.

ARAGNO: Rather egotistically we said man but it's also woman.

PARK: This is one of the things which I welcome about Britain – the fact that although I am a woman I'm allowed to function as a human being far more in this country than I am in my own. Emancipation, as far as it exists anywhere, exists in this country, whereas I don't think it can work in South Africa. For instance, one cannot just simply go out of an evening by oneself, purely because of fear, so of course, one's emancipation is stifled in all these ways.

ARAGNO: There's a state of siege.

PARK: Ah, yes, true – it's a state of siege. A freedom from fear is what Britain gives one. It's for me a very personal freedom.

MENUHIN: And the same thing is happening unfortunately in the United States ?

PARK: May I just bring in one point here. The police – I find the bobby a friendly person, an extremely friendly person. I would go up to him, ask him the time of day, this sort of thing and this is what one would like to teach one's children, to regard the police as friends.

MENUHIN: Exactly, but how long has that taken to evolve ? That's why it's so precious, it's so precious.

ARAGNO: I must say that the bobby is a lovable creature and almost a great character in the history of modern Britain, but it really is the relationship between the individual and the whole state. It includes the judges, it includes the neighbours, it includes the teachers. The relationship with the teachers, which is one of the essential secrets of a civilisation – it's all different from other countries. I mean in my own country, we have about sixty million tiny ridiculous dictators in the family, in the office, in the car, wherever you like. And, of course, we all like ourselves very much, but nobody else. I remember in 1952 when they opened the Festival Hall there was a marvellous exhibition and one of the opening statements as you walked in was that the Romans came here and stayed four hundred years and gave Britain a social sense. Well, it just so happens that since then, the social sense has gone out of us and certainly has settled here, as we have done.

MENUHIN: Britain has always absorbed the best of foreign influence.

ARAGNO: While maintaining a very, very strong feeling of its own uniqueness. And this sense of uniqueness must be preserved. England will be first as long as she remains England.

ARAGNO: On the other hand, the danger for Britain has been that during the last twenty years she has tended to isolate herself a little too much. This applies not only to the export drive, but also to the cross-fertilisation of modern, rational influences. Now that the young are going out after criticising Britain so bitterly, they are discovering how marvellous it is to assert the qualities of British life.

MENUHIN: Yes, even the climate isn't holding them back. For my part I think that it's the best climate in the world, because it's a walking climate, a temperate climate, one in which you can always go outside and one in which the house doesn't become unbearable. The room can usually be aired. In fact air and water are perhaps the secrets of Britain, draughts included, and when it doesn't rain you're communicating with nature. There's nothing more lovely than England in spring or summer.

PARK: And then the English make such a festival of summer. They make a real festival of all the seasons.

ARAGNO: I'll tell you something about Norman Douglas, who after writing *South Wind* settled in Capri, and he said, 'I wouldn't go back to England for anything – it's like living inside a lettuce.' The funny thing is that when he said it he was sitting on a very hot rock. I mean it's all very well to talk about marvellous weather in foreign countries but who wants to spend a lifetime on a hot rock!

MEHUHIN: At the moment Britain is enjoying a marvellous early summer, not so much in the quality of its own internal art, I would suggest, but in its popularity around the world. British art today is carrying the message of British life around the world and people are fascinated by it.

ARAGNO: I would suggest that even in this field of the arts, the exceptional position of Britain today is due to the fact that it's the only country which is inspired by an amplification of personal freedom.

PARK: I certainly think it's a country to write in, don't you?

ARAGNO: That's why I'm here.

MENUHIN: It's a country to play Chamber music in and to work with one's colleagues too, better than anywhere else.

ARAGNO: And friendship.

MENUHIN: Friendship.

PARK: Ah, yes, magnificent, magnificent. They talk about the English being cold. But people talk to you. In the shops, in the streets, they really are friendly.

MENUHIN: More courteously than in any other place.

PARK: Far more courteously, yes. And I think that although it takes much longer perhaps to make firm friends in this country, they really are firm friends, when one has made them.

ARAGNO: And my God, they fight for all this, because as soon as somebody suggests something racial, or somebody puts five demonstrators in jail for some stupid reason or other, thank God this is a country that immediately reacts.

DARKNESS AT NOON

E. R. D. Goldsmith and Professor Ivan Morris with Mollie Lee

Mr Goldsmith is the Editor of The Ecologist; *Professor Ivan Morris of Columbia University is an authority on Japan.*

MOLLIE LEE: Mr Goldsmith, I think this is a very wide question, but I wonder whether you can answer it quite shortly. What are the main causes of the pollution that we're all worried about? What are the main basic causes? Is it too many people?

E. R. D. GOLDSMITH: People undoubtedly. Of course, the impact that people make on their environment is proportionate to their standards of living or more precisely their consumption of energy and their mobility, which of course are closely related.

LEE: Any other main causes? Not enough social thought?

GOLDSMITH: Well, theoretically one should be able to eliminate a good deal of pollution by technological means. Lots of waste products can be recycled and reused by industry. Unfortunately very little has been done although there's been a great deal of talk. Most pollution control so far has taken the form of shifting pollution from one place to another. You've got highish chimney stacks which move pollution up into the air. You've got smokeless fuel which reduces smoke in the cities, but it doesn't mean you're not going to get pollution where the smokeless fuel is made. In fact in the Welsh valley where the smokeless fuel is made it's apparently almost impossible to breathe. The countries with the worst pollution problems are those which are the most highly industrialised and the most highly populated.

LEE: Yes, well, while we're on that point, Professor Morris, you know a lot about Japan and I believe this is an object lesson in many ways

on what pollution can do. Can you tell us something about your
impressions of Japan from this point of view ?

PROF. IVAN MORRIS: Yes, I was in Japan a few months ago. I'd heard
that it was becoming one of the most – if not the most – polluted
country in the world, but one never really believes things like that
until one sees them. I arrived in Tokyo on a polar flight. The plane
arrived in the afternoon but because of the change in time zones and
so on one gets completely confused about whether it's morning or
night, and when I arrived it seemed almost pitch-black in Tokyo, a
sort of a yellowish-black and I thought I'd made a mistake, that the
plane in fact had arrived in the middle of the night and I went on this
assumption for quite a long time. The people who had met me at the
airport drove me into Tokyo. I said it's remarkably light for the
middle of the night, because one could see, and they thought this was
an example of western humour because in fact it was half past three in
the afternoon. In fact the city was covered with a thick yellow pall of
filth which made it virtually night, which also made it virtually impossible to breathe. I was coughing very soon. Many people in Japan go
around with masks around their mouths – people who have weak
lungs because of this pollution. It happened that this was a particularly bad day. There are pollution meters all over Tokyo showing the
degree of pollution. But even on a fairly good day it's gone far further
than anywhere else I've seen, certainly than anywhere in England.
Japan sets the pace now in so many ways that I rather think it's an
example of what's going to happen here fairly soon.

LEE: What about rivers ? And bronchial-type diseases ? Is there a lot
of that ?

MORRIS: Yes, well the rivers for one thing used to be very, very beautiful. Even twelve years ago when I lived in Japan for some time, there
were water festivals and people went swimming in the rivers and they
were very pleasant, we had fireworks and boats going out on the river
to watch the fireworks. They have now become cesspools. Not only
can one not go into them, but even being anywhere near the river one
is overcome by this appalling stench; and the people whose houses
are near the river, who used to be considered very lucky, have now
had to leave because it's extremely dangerous to live there, the
noxious filth that comes out.

LEE: Would you say, Mr Goldsmith, there was any danger of London
becoming like this ?

GOLDSMITH: The situation here is unlikely to improve because the problem is now becoming a global one. It's not only a question of keeping pollution out of a few cities. Pollution is spreading out over the whole world. You've got dust accumulating in the atmosphere world-wide. Eventually the amount of sunlight coming into the world is going to be reduced, as it already is in certain cities. I read the other day that the sunlight in Washington had been reduced by seventeen per cent.

MORRIS: You mean that even if one country had managed to solve its pollution difficulties, it still wouldn't be safe because the filth would be coming over the borders?

GOLDSMITH: I don't think it's any more a problem that can be dealt with on a national level. We all share the same oceans, don't we? It's a global problem and one of the most important American scientific organisations issued a report the other day to say that the world wouldn't be able to contain the heat produced by burning all the fuel that we'll probably be burning in the next thirty years. What's important is that energy consumption is increasing world-wide, about four per cent per annum, which means that it will have trebled by the end of the century. We're consuming energy every time we use electric light, every time we use a motor-car, the whole time we're consuming more and more energy.

LEE: But is there no scientific answer to this? Is there no way of reversing it? Are they doing anything, for instance, Professor, in Japan?

MORRIS: All they're doing as far as I know is to take measures to protect the population. For instance, just when I arrived in Japan I was horrified to read that there are large parts of Tokyo where the policemen are only allowed to stay on the street for half an hour at a time after which an oxygen van comes along and they get into the oxygen van and sit there breathing for a quarter of an hour and then they get out again and have another half an hour on the street. The people who live in those parts of Tokyo, of course, haven't got oxygen vans coming along so they have to stay indoors as much as they can. At schools in such areas, and this is not only in Tokyo, the children are all given warnings not to go out and play at certain times of the day and so on. They are aware of these dangers very much, the Japanese Government, but they are not attacking them at the source. They're trying to limit the harm that the symptoms do.

LEE: It seems to me that presumably there is some relationship in Japan between the rate of productivity and this pollution, is there not, and as every government in the world appears to be encouraging high productivity, does this mean that pollution inevitably accompanies the industrial process, and if so what is the answer?

GOLDSMITH: Obviously a very difficult question because of course our whole society is geared to an expanding industry, and by expanding we're going to create more pollution and if we take the necessary measures to get rid of the pollution our costs are going to go up enormously. Take the following case. In England we're producing, I believe, something like seven million tons of sulphur dioxide. It pours out of our chimneys and some of it is going over to Sweden. The Swedes are complaining bitterly that their forests are not growing properly because of the pollution from British factories, and sulphur dioxide is also very harmful in other ways. In America it costs American farmers something like 500 million dollars a year just in its effect on plant growth. Sulphur dioxide may also be a mutagenic and give rise to deformed children. It has all sorts of terrible effects and this stuff is being produced in ever greater quantities. Now we could reduce the amount produced because sulphur could be recycled. A company has recently invented a device for getting this sulphur out of the smoke and reusing it but it would have to be sold at £30 a ton, while the present rate is only £15 a ton. So here's a problem we could solve, simply by doubling the price of sulphur. I should have thought it would be certainly worthwhile doing. It's better to pay a little bit more for sulphur and avoid all the abominable side-effects which I have just mentioned. But this is just one example. If you want to take all the necessary measures to avoid pollution we would have to spend an enormous amount of money. We'd probably have to spend so much, that our manufacturing prices would go up very substantially and our industry would no longer be competitive unless all other countries were doing the same thing.

LEE: So that really it needs an international body to control this.

GOLDSMITH: But even then, even if we took all these necessary measures, if we recycled all our sulphur dioxide, if we got rid of the carbon monoxide in the exhaust of cars and if we did everything possible to control pollution we still wouldn't solve all the problems. No pollution device can get rid of more than say 95% of the pollution. All we have to do is increase productivity by twenty times, which at the rate we are going will not take very long, for us to get back where we started. As I mentioned earlier, whatever we do, whenever we're using power we're producing heat. There's no way out of it and you cannot go on producing more and more heat because it would eventually change the climate, and if you change it sufficiently you would melt the polar ice caps and you'll flood the major cities of the world. This is likely to happen in the next hundred years at the rate we're going but technology has got a lot of answers to provide, as long as we're ready to accept the increased prices. It can't solve the problem by itself.

LEE: Anything ordinary people can do ?

GOLDSMITH: I think there are lots of things that ordinary people can do. For instance, youth can join organisations such as the Conservation Corps which is involved in cleaning things up and they're really trying to do everything possible to make the environment more agreeable. People can boycott products which are obviously harmful to the environment. There was a very good precedent in Toronto the other day where housewives successfully boycotted detergents with a high phosphate content which are of course particularly harmful to rivers. So much so that the sales of the high phosphate detergents have gone down dramatically.

LEE: Where does density of population come into the question? I imagine in Japan the population is as dense as here, Professor Morris ?

MORRIS: Oh, very much more in all Japan except the northern island. I should have thought there was a direct relation between the degree of pollution in any area and the density of population.

GOLDSMITH: The damage done is proportional to the degree of industrialisation, not only to the density of population. There are extremely densely populated areas in India, and yet the average Indian does infinitely less harm to his environment than does an average American, with his unbelievably high material standard of living.

MORRIS: Yes, I should have said density of industrialised population.

LEE: But it does point a bit, doesn't it, towards another way of helping, which is population control I assume.

GOLDSMITH: Population control, of course, is very, very difficult to achieve. It's by no means certain that family planning can be successful. So far family planning has had very little effect. It affects mainly the middle classes rather than the masses and it's not going to solve the world population problem.

MORRIS: Japan, you know, has reversed the rate of increase of population owing to its family control.

GOLDSMITH: Mainly by legalising abortion, I believe?

MORRIS: Abortion and prevention. I think it's the only big country that has done it and it's rather depressing to think that the country which has succeeded so remarkably in beginning to bring its population under control is probably the most polluted country of all.

LEE: Mr Goldsmith, have you anything hopeful to say at all?

GOLDSMITH: Yes, I think we need a new set of values, a completely new set of values. At the moment we're entirely geared to producing more manufactured goods and to increasing our so-called standard of living, measured in terms of the consumption of often quite useless consumer products, like electric tooth-brushes and God knows what else. Well, one simply has to realise that we can live without electric tooth-brushes, but we cannot live without pure water to drink, and clean air to breathe and the sort of environment to which we have been adapted by millions of years of evolution. Man cannot live in the ghastly shoddy monotonous urban waste-lands that he's being called upon to inhabit more and more, and this we've got to realise. The only solution is to create new values and new aims in life. Among other things we must spend more money on string quartets, less on electric tooth-brushes.